26 Complete Programs For Children's Church

Traveling With Bible People

By Carolyn Lehman

Illustrated by Olga Packard

Cover art by John Ham

STANDARD PUBLISHING
Cincinnati, Ohio   3324

Library of Congress Cataloging-in-Publication Data

Lehman, Carolyn.
  26 complete programs for children's church.

  1. Worship (Religious education) 2. Bible stories, English. I. Title. II. Title: Twenty-six complete programs for
children's church. III. Title: Traveling with Bible people.
BV1522.L44 1986   268'.432   86-5728
ISBN 0-87403-060-9

Contents

Introduction

Using this book, you can take your boys and girls on a journey TRAVELING WITH BIBLE PEOPLE. Let them "take a look" at the customs and historical and geographical settings of some Old and New Testament times and learn meaningful lessons from twenty-six Bible characters. With memory tickets in their hands (and Bible verses in their hearts) and the Guidebook to direct their course, the students will receive guidelines for their life's journey with Christ. The correlating craft souvenirs will help to reinforce the spiritual applications.

This book is divided into five units of from four to eight undated lessons each. This arrangement is designed to give the students a change of pace in learning experiences and to vary the teacher's leadership if desired.

More material is provided than you will need for a one-hour session. This enables leaders to be selective. Some leaders will want to use both the activity book and the craft souvenir; others will use only one.

In addition to children's church, TRAVELING WITH BIBLE PEOPLE can be used for Sunday-evening or midweek study groups, Saturday or after-school Bible clubs, camps, etc.

Learning Centers

Three rotating learning centers are suggested: Preview, Memory Ticket Office, and Guidebook. To get the most benefit from these centers, plan to have the students visit all of them. This can be accomplished by dividing the assembly into three groups and assigning a teacher to each center. (Each teacher conducts the same center three times.) At the sound of a bell or some other signal (at about five-or six-minute intervals), all groups move to the next center. If there isn't enough time to cover all the material, choose that which will be most beneficial for your students.

PREVIEW. Pictures, objects, word cards, and maps are used to introduce students to the Bible material to be studied and to provide background information.

GUIDEBOOK. At the Guidebook Center, children learn about our Guidebook, the Bible. Simple Bible drill games are suggested for many of the lessons. As an alternative, the Scripture verses may be used as Bible studies without drills.

MEMORY TICKET OFFICE. Students come to this center to memorize the key verse correlating with the day's lesson. (You may want to set this center up to resemble a ticket office.) Each unit has suggestions for making this short period interesting and full of learning experiences.

Prepare "memory tickets" from 1½ by 4 inch cards. Punch a hole in the end of each card and write the day's Bible reference. When a student can quote the verse satisfactorily, his name and the teacher's initials are put on the ticket. A student's tickets may be hung on a sturdy straight pin that has been pushed on a slant into a cork or corrugated cardboard bulletin board.

If the student is not able to quote his verse in the amount of time, give him a "stand-by" ticket. This will give him more time to memorize the verse. Even though some may not memorize the verses, the teaching moments will have lasting spiritual value.

Award those who have learned all the verses for each unit. A small treat, a party, or a game will encourage students to continue the program. Specific suggestions are given for Units 4 and 5.

Front View Adventure

Front View Adventure is simply a term used for a variety of learning activities. When children travel, where do most of them want to sit? In the front seat, of course. They like to have that first front view. The "front view" experiences are introductions to the Bible stories, object lessons, and other activities. The skits require three "people" puppets—two boys and a girl. A puppet stage can be made from a refrigerator carton. Or use a Dutch door or a large table placed on its side.

Worshiping Our Guide

Even though this is a brief section in the book, give emphasis and time to it, for after all, worship is the chief purpose of children's church. A suggested outline is provided for each worship time. Adapt it to your own needs. Some of the songs are included on the back pages of this book. Others can be found in most church hymnals. A theme chorus is suggested for each unit. Words are sung to a familiar melody, or a familiar chorus is used. The page numbers are given for the songs included in this book. Those without numbers can be found in most church hymnals or are very familiar and often-used choruses.

Bible Story

Each Bible story is a short character study. The Bible Story Application helps apply the Bible story to the lives of your students.

Activity Book

Two activity books are available for use with this course—*Traveling With Bible People, Activity Book 1* for use with Units 1, 2, and 3 and *Traveling With Bible People, Activity Book 2* for use with Units 4 and 5. The books provide opportunities for students to learn Bible facts and truths through reading and writing activities—puzzles, quizzes, games, etc.

Craft Souvenir

A correlated craft is suggested for each lesson. Patterns for some of the crafts are found in the back of this book. The crafts reinforce Bible teaching and carry it into the home.

PREPARATION FOR EACH UNIT

Unit 1: God Shows His Power Through Bible Travelers.

The **goal** for this unit is that the student will have greater appreciation for the power of God and its effect on his own life.

The **memory verses** for this unit are taught with the use of symbols and puzzles. Cut the shapes (see each lesson) from construction paper. Print on them the portions of the verses as shown in the illustrations. Spray with adhesive spray, or "rough-up" the backs with a knife, or glue on flannel or suede-backed paper so the shapes will adhere to the flannelboard. The students may take turns removing the shapes as they work at memorizing the verses.

The rules for the **Guidebook** learning center's Bible drills are as follows:

1. Hold the Bible in one hand. Listen for the reference and teacher's signal "Search."

2. The first student to find the correct verse reads it aloud after the others have found it.

3. Read the verse carefully and ask for comments on the meaning before continuing the Bible drill game.

A suggested **theme chorus** for this unit is "God of Great Power." The following words are sung to the melody of the chorus of "Jesus Loves Even Me."

> God of great power, omnipotent, He;
> I am so glad that He loves me.
> God of great power, omnipotent He,
> Yet He loves even me.

Looking ahead: Collect and paint small flat rocks for craft souvenirs. Make a sample. (Lesson 2)

Unit 2: God Honors Bible Travelers' Faith

This unit of five lessons is planned to help strengthen the students' faith in God. They will learn from men who believed God and were rewarded for their faith.

The chalkboard is the suggested method for teaching the **memory verse**. Print the verses on the board and let the students take turns erasing one word or the reference. After each word is eliminated, the group tries to quote the passage. Continue this game until the entire verse has been erased.

The suggested **theme chorus** for this unit is "Believe and Obey" sung to the melody of the chorus of "Only Believe."

> Believe and obey;
> Believe and obey.
> All things are possible.
> Believe and obey.

Looking ahead: Collect small, empty match boxes for Lesson 5. Collect small Styrofoam meat trays for Lesson 1 of Unit 3.

Unit 3: God Teaches Bible Travelers to Obey

The lessons in this unit are on obedience. We want our students to obey now, and we want them to grow up to be obedient citizens. But most important, we want them to be obedient Christians, living in harmony with God's Word and will. Consistently stress the rewards for obedience and the results of disobedience—always taught in love and with the Bible as the final source for the answers.

The **memory verses** for this unit are taught with the use of the pocket chart. Here are directions for making the chart.

Materials:

One large piece of stiff, heavy paper about 26 by 30 inches

One large piece of heavy cardboard

Scissors, pencil, ruler, staples, stapler, and tape

Procedure:

Four inches from the top, measure and mark a dot on either edge of the longest sides of the paper. Mark the dots "A."

One inch below these, make dots on either side and mark them "B." Continue this procedure (marking off four inches and then one inch) to the bottom of the paper.

Beginning at the top, bring "B" up one inch and fold on "A." Staple the ends of the folds. Continue folding on the dots until five pockets have been made. Cut the cardboard to fit behind the completed chart. Tape along all four edges to hold the finished chart to the cardboard backing.

Print the memory verses on strips of paper and place them in the pockets. Students can place the strips in the pockets in the correct order.

The **theme song** for this unit is the chorus of the song "Trust and Obey"(church hymnal).

Looking ahead: Collect white 6 by 9 inch Styrofoam meat trays and small frozen-juice cans. Collect and paint large metal unwanted buttons.

Unit 4: God Teaches Bible Travelers to Serve.

Someone has said that the youth of today are the future of tomorrow. Boys and girls must be more than good listeners. They need to grow spiritually. They need to know there is joy in serving Jesus. Therefore, we need to stimulate their desire to be the Lord's helpers and give them opportunities to serve. This unit has been planned with serving as the emphasis.

To keep **memory work** enthusiasm from lagging, try this:

Those who have earned the five tickets for this unit may be awarded "passports" entitling them to take an imaginary trip to a foreign country. This trip could be to Israel or to one of the church-supported mission fields.

Consider giving them a "Going Away" party at the close of this unit and the "trip" at the close of Unit 5. (For Unit 5, "visa" can be stamped on the "passport.") At the "Going Away" party, play games of that particular country and ask the children to make posters and banners and draw the national flag. These can be posted in the assembly room to arouse continued interest in memorization for Unit 5. For the devotional time, tell a missionary story, using a strong application on serving.

Theme chorus for this unit: Sing the following words to the tune "Row, Row, Row Your Boat."

Serve, serve, serve the Lord.
Serve Him every day.
Surely, surely, surely, surely
He will lead the way.

Serve, serve, serve the Lord.
Serve Him faithfully.
Surely, surely, surely, surely,
Joy for you 'twill be.

Looking ahead: For craft time, collect unwanted pin-on buttons and small Styrofoam trays. Plan the praise and thanksgiving program for Front View Adventure, Lesson 14.

Unit 5: God Gives Guidelines for Young Travelers.

We must teach our students practical Bible truths in such a way that they are challenged and changed by what they are taught. We must pray as we present practical materials that will help them solve their problems. Colossians 2:6, 7 sums it up: "As ye have therefore received Christ Jesus the Lord, so walk ye in him: Rooted and built up in him, and stablished in the faith, as ye have been taught, abounding therein with thanksgiving."

Those who earned "passports" for **memorization** may work for a "visa" for an imaginary trip to Israel or a mission station. (See Unit 4.) Use a stamp and pad to apply the "visa" to the "passport." Mark them "Tourist Visa to Israel" (or whatever country,) and the date.

Have a special party which is an imaginary trip to Israel (or a mission station). Decorate the room with pictures and objects reminding the children of that country. Teachers may want to dress in costumes. Play "native" games. Serve refreshments of some of the foods of that land. You may want to have the children meet at the church building and begin their trip by driving in the church bus or cars to a home or an outdoor spot for the destination.

Theme chorus for this unit: "Young Travelers." Sing the following words to the tune of "On Top of Old Smokey."

I'm just a young traveler,
With Christ as my guide.
I fear not the future
With Him by my side.
Though problems be many,
And Satan is sly,
The Lord will defend me;
His help not deny.

Looking ahead: Collect the following for craft time: six-inch plastic lids; one sample wallpaper book; small tuna-fish cans; cardboard tubes (wax paper, plastic wrap, and others).

PROGRAM: Consider having a Children's Church program as a part of the Sunday evening service. Do group singing, using worship-time songs, and repeat a special musical number. Quote a few memory verses. Retell one each of a preview story, a Bible character study, and a short illustrated story. If a mission station was "visited," include a report. You may want to conduct a Bible drill and include congregational participation.

Use tables to display pictures and curios of Israel (and/or the mission field) and samples of the craft souvenirs. Display some of the completed activity books. If feasible, display the students' tickets and "passports."

A Steady Boat Builder

Genesis 6—8

Goals: That the student (1) will know that God has power over nature and (2) will trust God as Noah did.

Student Responses: As a result of this lesson, the student should be able to

• Answer questions about the story of Noah.

• Tell of at least three other events of Bible times in which God showed His power. (See "Front View Adventure.")

• Thank God for His great power.

• Say the memory verse.

Learning Centers

Preview

A Look at the Ark

MATERIALS:
Pictures of Noah's ark and Mt. Ararat
Card with "God is omnipotent" printed on one side, and the definition "all-powerful" printed on the other.

No one knows exactly where Noah lived when God told him to build the ark. But the Bible tells us that the ark was 450 feet long, 75 feet wide, and 45 feet high. *(Compare the length with a familiar street.)* The height would be equal to a three-story house. The ark had one door on the side and one window near the top. The ark was made of gopher wood, which is light and strong, and coated with a sticky pitch similar to our asphalt.

When the flood waters went down, the ark settled on a very high mountain, Mt. Ararat, in the land of Turkey. *(Show picture if you were able to find one.)*

Our Bible story will remind us of God's wonderful power. God has all power. Bringing the great flood upon the earth is an example of God's power.

Memory Ticket Office

"Thou, Lord, in the beginning hast laid the foundation of the earth; and the heavens are the works of thine hands." Hebrews 1:10

THINK

1. Who did not have a beginning?

2. What two things does the verse tell us God created?

LEARNING GAME

Print portions of the verse on the following symbols. (See "Preparation for Each Unit," page 5.)

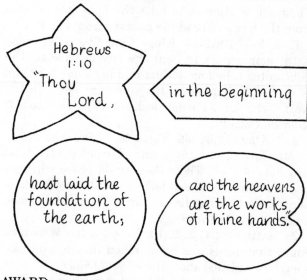

AWARD

Initial the tickets of those who learned the verse. *(See Introduction.)*

Guidebook

"God's Power" Bible Drill

This interest center will help students find verses

that tell of the power of God. (See Bible drill rules on page 5, "Preparation for Each Unit.")

1. Psalm 62:11 – Power belongs to God.
2. Jeremiah 10:12 – God made the earth by His power.
3. Exodus 15:6 – God's power is glorious.
4. Psalm 93:1 – The Lord is clothed in strength.
5. Luke 9:43 – The disciples were amazed at God's power.
6. Matthew 28:18 – All power is given to Christ.

Front View Adventure

Bible Views of God's Power

MATERIALS:
Cardboard box with "Great power" printed on the side.
Paper sun, moon, and star; jar of water; a small leafy branch and a similar branch with withered leaves; a plastic fish (placed inside box)
Filing cards with the Bible references below printed on them.

PROCEDURE:
Give the cards to the students. Briefly tell each story. Let the students help if they know the story. Then ask a student to take the appropriate item from the box and read the passage from the Bible.

1. Joshua 10:12-13. Kings from five cities came with their armies to fight the city of Gibeon. The Gibeonites called on Joshua and his army for help. They fought hard until the sun went down in the west. Who knows what Joshua asked God to do? *(Sun and moon)*

2. 1 Kings 18:38, 39. Elijah told King Ahab to go to Mt. Carmel with the people of Israel and the false prophets of Baal. There they would prove who was the true God. Who can tell us about the results of that contest? What liquid burned? What happened to the stones? *(Water)*

3. Matthew 2:1, 2, 9, 10. How did the Wise-men know that Jesus was born? When they left Jerusalem, how did God show His power? *(Star)*

4. Matthew 21:18, 19. When Jesus was walking in the country with His disciples, they came to a fig tree *(leafy branch)*. He decided to teach a lesson on prayer and faith. He said, "Let no fruit grow on this tree forever." What miracle did the disciples see? *(Withered branch)*

5. John 21:10, 11. The disciples had fished all night and caught nothing. In the morning Jesus stood on the shore and said they should cast the net on the other side of the boat. How was God's power shown here? *(Fish)*

Worshiping Our Guide

Quiet music: "Holy! Holy! Holy!"
Song: "My God Is a Great God" (page 117)
Theme chorus: "God of Great Power" (see page 5)
Song: "He's Got the Whole World in His Hands"
Bible reading: Psalm 95:1-6
Prayer
Offering and announcements
Special music: "Holy! Holy! Holy!"
Song: "God Is So Good"

Bible Story

A Steady Boat Builder

Can you imagine what it was like in the world when only Adam and Eve were living here? The only voices they heard were God's and each other's. They had good thoughts and they obeyed God perfectly. Even after Adam and Eve had disobeyed God and were put out of the Garden of Eden, God still loved them, and they loved Him.

God gave children to Adam and Eve. When the children were grown, they had families of their own. As the years went by, more and more people lived on the earth. People forgot all about God. They did not love Him. They lied and cheated and killed. They thought of new evil ideas to spread throughout the world. The wickedness grew until almost every person was sinful. The Bible says, "God saw that the wickedness of man was great in the earth" (Genesis 6:5).

One man had not forgotten God. That man's name was Noah. Noah faithfully worshiped God. He was good to his sons, and taught them to worship the Lord and respect their parents. He was honest and fair in his business. Even though all the people around Noah had wicked ideas, Noah kept on loving God.

"Noah, stop and listen!" God commanded. Then God told Noah that He was going to destroy every living thing on the earth. He explained to this good man how to build a floating vessel. He told him the exact size and shape, the materials to use, and to put in one door and one window.

Noah believed God. He believed that the people would be destroyed if they didn't turn from evil. He set to work, and his sons, Ham, Shem, and Japheth, helped him. They made grooves in the ends of boards so they would fit perfectly. They carved pegs to hold the boards together. Finally, when the flat bottom lay on the ground, the boards, one by one, were added to the sides and ends.

"Whatever is this strange thing sitting on the sand?" people asked as they passed by.

"It's an ark," Noah said, "God is going to destroy the world with water. Only those who turn from their evil ways and come into this ark will be saved from drowning."

The people laughed. "Who ever heard of destroying the world with water?" they said. "The rivers and seas have always stayed in their places since we have been here. How could this clumsy vessel float on water?"

Noah kept right on building and preaching God's warning year after year. "Where's the water to sail your ark?" the people mocked. "You have been building this thing for years, and we have seen no sign of changes in the rivers or seas."

At last every board was in place and the boat was covered with pitch. Noah and his wife and their sons gathered food for themselves and for the animals and birds, and stored the food in bins. They filled storage rooms with grass, grain, and other foods. Noah did everything just as God had commanded.

At last the day came when the door of the ark was let down and, two by two, the animals, great and small, were guided up the gang plank. What a parade it was! And how marvelous to see the birds come to the door and fly inside! Besides the animals that came in two by two, Noah took in seven of each kind of clean animal, just as God had told him to do. Last of all, the family entered the ark. Then God shut the door and sealed it.

Soon clouds covered the sky, and a terrible rain came tumbling down in torrents! No one ever before or since has seen it rain like that! The Bible says, "The same day were all the fountains of the great deep broken up, and the windows of heaven were opened" (Genesis 7:11). Torrents of rain and the waters in the rivers and seas and from below the surface of the earth pushed up and began to cover the ground everywhere!

"The ark is floating!" shouted Shem in excitement. "I can feel it! We are rocking on the water!" And it was so. The water had picked up the ark and it was sailing.

Folk on the outside ran for cover, but soon left their homes for higher ground. Many hurried to the hills for safety. Animals climbed to the mountain peaks. But trying to escape was useless, because the water rose twenty feet above the tallest dry place. At last the earth was a great, blue sea. Only Noah and his family were safe and dry.

The waters came up for forty days and forty nights. After the rain had stopped, the earth was covered for 150 days. Noah looked out the window and saw nothing but water. But he knew the power of God that had brought the water would also take it away.

One day Noah and his family felt a thud, and they knew that the ark was no longer sailing. It had settled on a mountain.

After forty days, Noah opened the window and sent out a raven. A week later he sent out a little dove. The raven never came back. The dove returned because it could not find dry land. Noah sent the dove out a second time, and it returned with an olive leaf in its bill. When the dove did not return the third time, Noah knew it had found a dry place to build a nest. Soon they could safely leave the ark.

One day Noah removed the covering from the ark and looked out. The ground was dry.

God said to Noah, "Come out of the ark and bring your family with you. Bring out all of the animals and birds so they can live on the earth and have families."

So Noah and his family and the animals and birds came out of the ark. Noah built an altar and thanked God for His power and His care. God sent a beautiful rainbow as His promise that never again would the world and its people be destroyed by a flood.

Bible Story Application

In the beginning God created the heavens and the earth by His power. He has complete control over what He made. The power of man is very limited, but with God all things are possible.

Only those who believed God's warning and went into the ark were saved from the terrible flood. Only those who believe in Jesus and obey Him will be saved to live with Him forever.

No matter how much people laughed at Noah, he kept on trusting God. Because he believed God, his name is on the list of famous people in the Bible in Hebrews 11. When we read it, we can think about this steady, faithful boat builder who trusted God. We can be like Noah by trusting in God and His wonderful power.

Let's bow our heads now and each of us silently talk to God, thanking Him for His great power.

Activity Book

Distribute copies of the activity book *Traveling With Bible People, Activity Book One* and pencils. Show pupils how to do the crossword puzzle. At the bottom of the page, pupils can look up the Scripture references and fill in the blanks.

Provide help as needed as pupils do the True or False Quiz and the Noah Acrostic. Pupils look up the verses in the ovals and fill in the blanks.

(Answer to Noah Acrostic: Never; Obeyed; Always; He; Obey.)

Craft Souvenir

Noah's Ark

MATERIALS:
Blue, brown, and light gray construction paper
Felt pens, crayons, scissors, glue
One paper fastener for each child
Stickers (and/or tiny pictures of animals, birds and insects)
Bible character seal or tiny picture cut from a Sunday-school paper (for Noah)
Pattern from pattern pages in the back of this book

PROCEDURE:
Trace the ark on brown paper and the wheel on gray paper. Cut the door of the ark on three sides so it will open down. Push the point of scissors through the dots on the ark and wheel. Place the wheel behind the ark, and adjust the paper fastener.

Cut one 9 by 12 inch sheet of blue paper in half lengthwise. Squeeze a thin line of glue along the edges of the two sides and bottom. Lay the paper on the lower half of the sheet of gray. Use crayons to color a rainbow.

Squeeze glue on a few places on the underside of the ark, being careful not to get glue on the wheel. Arrange the wheel on the blue water near the bottom of the page.

Stick the variety of stickers on the wheel through the door, turning just enough to clear the space from the previous sticker.

A Courageous Boy

1 Samuel 17

Goals: That the student (1) will know that God has power over enemies and (2) will trust Him to help him win victories.

Student Responses: As a result of this lesson, the student should be able to

- Tell the story of David and Goliath.
- Say the memory verse and explain what it means to him.
- List times when he needs God's help in winning victories.

Learning Centers

Preview

A Soldier's Arms and Armor

MATERIALS:
Six large cards
Small pictures of arms and armor
Bible dictionary

PROCEDURE:

Paste the pictures to the cards and print the names of the offensive and defensive weapons on them. If pictures are not available, make simple sketches. (Refer to a Bible dictionary.) Flip the cards over and print the definitions on the other side.

1. Sword—A short weapon having a blade with a cutting edge, usually carried in a sheath.
2. Spear—A long weapon with a sharp blade.
3. Javelin—A small, light spear to be thrown.
4. Breastplate—A plate of metal covering the breast.
5. Helmet—A metal hat or headpiece of armor to protect the head.
6. Shield—A broad piece of metal carried in the hand to protect the body.

Memory Ticket Office

"Put on the whole armour of God, that ye may be able to stand against the wiles of the devil."

Ephesians 6:11

THINK
1. Who is the enemy?
2. How much of the armor are we to put on?
3. What are "wiles"? (Tricks or schemes)

LEARNING GAME

Prepare the symbols below following the instructions on page 5. Cut the shield apart as shown.

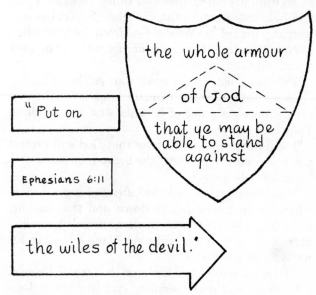

AWARD

Initial the tickets for those who learned the verse.

Guidebook

David's Thoughts About Enemies

Sometimes we have enemies—people who try to

hurt us, or say mean things to us or about us. Our greatest enemy is Satan. David had an enemy who tried very hard to kill him. Let's see what David thought about his enemies.

(Follow the rules for Bible drill listed in "Preparation for Each Unit," page 5.)

1. Psalm 18:3. David prayed to God to save him from his enemies.
2. Psalm 4:8. David knew the Lord would keep him safely through the night.
3. Psalm 27:11. He asked the Lord to teach him and lead him because of his enemies.
4. Psalm 60:12. He knew the Lord would help him be brave.
5. Psalm 37:28. He knew the Lord would not forsake him when enemies were around.
6. Psalm 141:9. He asked the Lord to keep him from being tricked by his enemies.

Front View Adventure

The Bookseller and the Bandit

"New Bibles! New Bibles! Does anyone want to buy a Bible?" asked the cheerful bookseller of people who stood in the marketplace. Then he climbed down from his horse, took two Bibles from his pack, and held them before the villagers. Several people bought copies of the Word of God from the bookseller.

"Now it is late. I must go on my way to the next town," said the man.

"But you must not go now," warned the villagers. "It is not safe to cross the mountain pass in the evening. There's a gang of bandits who live in dens. They will kill you."

"I will hurry and I will pray that God will protect me, and protect His Word," the brave man answered. Then he rode away.

"Halt! Stop where you are," shouted a gruff voice when the sun was nearly down and the shadows were long. When the bookseller turned, he saw a man dressed in black, riding a black horse. In his hand he held a pistol.

"You were selling bad books in that town," he said. "You are a bad man, peddling bad literature. I demand that you remove every book from your pack. Then gather sticks and build a fire."

The bookseller laid his Bibles on the ground, gathered the wood, and built a fire. The robber dismounted, and they sat together.

Picking up a Bible, the bookseller read the story of Christ's birth. As he read, he prayed silently for the Lord's help.

"That's not a bad book," yelled the robber. "I want you to read one of the bad ones."

From the next two Bibles, the bookseller read the miracles of the healing of the blind man and the feeding of the five thousand people.

"Neither of those is bad. Read more," demanded the robber.

One by one, the man read a little from each Bible until the story of Christ's death on the cross, His resurrection from the grave, and His return to Heaven had been told.

"Keep your books," said the bandit. "I will not kill you, but I will take your money and your horse." While the bandit was preparing to lead both horses away, the bookseller noticed that the black horse was lame. He asked the robber to wait while he looked at its leg. By the light of the fire, he examined the wound and from it he pulled a long, piercing thorn. Then he poured on healing oil from a bottle he always carried with him.

"You are not a bad man; you are a good man," said the bandit quietly. "I have decided not to take your horse or your money."

Before they parted, he was given a Bible to take to his robbers' den. As he rode away, he must have thought of what was read to him from the good Books. The bookseller thanked the Lord for saving him and his Bibles from the enemy.

Worshiping Our Guide

Quiet music: "I Love to Tell the Story"
Song: "Onward, Christian Soldiers!"
Theme chorus: "God of Great Power" (see page 5)
Song: "If God Be for Us" (page 117)
Bible reading: Deuteronomy 31:6
Prayer
Offering and announcements
Special music: "Only a Boy Named David"
Song: "Step by Step" (page 118)
Prayer

Bible Story

A Courageous Boy

(You may want to do today's Bible story as an interview. Practice the presentation ahead of time. You may want to use one teenager and three adults and let them present the interview before the children. Or use children who are good readers.)

Persons for interview:

Interviewer (narrator)

David, dressed in shepherd's clothes

Shammah (David's brother), dressed in a robe and headpiece and carrying a cardboard sword

Gar (Goliath's armor bearer), dressed as a soldier, carrying a shield

INTERVIEWER: Have you ever wished you could talk with some of the people who lived during Bible times? Would you like to hear Daniel tell of his experiences in the lions' den? Or talk with Peter about being led out of prison by an angel? Today we are going to talk to three fellows who will tell us about David and Goliath. Will you introduce yourselves?

DAVID: I am David, the shepherd boy who killed Goliath.

SHAMMAH: I am David's brother, Shammah. I was in the army of Israel when Goliath was killed.

GAR: I am Gar, Goliath's armor bearer. I carried the giant's shield.

INTERVIEWER: Well, David, you were too young to join King Saul's army. Why did you go to battle when Israel and the Philistines were at war?

DAVID: My three oldest brothers were in the army, and my father was worried about them. He sent me to the battlefield to see how they were doing, and to take some extra food. I was on an errand.

SHAMMAH: That's the way David always was. He was obedient to our parents and ready to help others.

DAVID: When I arrived at the battlefield, I left the food with the keeper of supplies and ran up to the battle lines and found my brothers. There were two mountains, side by side. The Philistines were on one, and we were on the other.

SHAMMAH: It may have been exciting for you, David, but the thought of war was frightening. Our enemies had a giant in their army, and we were afraid of him. Even King Saul was afraid. Goliath came down in the valley ever day and shouted, "Choose a man from your army and let him come down to me. If he is able to kill me, then we will be your servants. But if I kill him, you shall be our servants." He did this every day for forty days. He was huge, and not one of our soldiers was brave enough to meet his challenge.

GAR: Goliath was a monster. He was over nine feet tall, strong and powerful. He wasn't afraid of anything. Our Philistine army was sure that no one could kill him. We were sure we would win.

DAVID: While I was talking to some of the men, I heard the giant shout, and watched our soldiers run and hide. "Who does this ungodly Philistine think he is?" I asked. "How does he dare to defy the army of the living God?" The men told me that the king had offered a great reward to anyone who could kill him.

INTERVIEWER: David, you were not interested in rewards. You wanted to help win the war, didn't you? So you were willing to meet the challenge Goliath made. (Turn to Shammah.) Shammah, what did you think of your brother's courage?

SHAMMAH: My oldest brother was very angry. He said that David should have stayed home and watched sheep. He told David that he was naughty. All three of us knew that God had chosen him to be the next king, and we were jealous. We thought that he was trying to be smart.

DAVID: The scolding didn't cause me to change my mind. I explained to you and the other soldiers how I felt, and they told the king. When he heard that I was ready to fight the giant, he sent for me.

INTERVIEWER: Wasn't Saul surprised when he saw how young you were?

DAVID: Oh, yes! He said I was not able to fight with the great warrior. I told him how I had killed a lion and a bear while watching sheep. I said that God had helped me win over them and He would surely help me kill the giant. King Saul thought that I should have more protection for my body, so he gave me his own armor to wear, and his sword. But everything was too big. I had never practiced with a sword, so I returned them to him. I checked my slingshot and picked up my staff. Then I ran down in the valley. At the mountain stream I picked up five smooth stones and put them in my bag.

GAR: We saw you coming, and Goliath was very angry. He was expecting to see a soldier, not a boy. In his rough voice he shouted, "Do you think I am a dog that you come at me with sticks? I will kill you and give your body to the birds!"

DAVID: That's right. And I shouted back, "You come to me with a sword, a spear, and a shield. But I come to you in the name of the Lord Almighty, the God of the armies of Israel. You are challenging God. This day the Lord will deliver you into my hands, and I will take off your head."

SHAMMAH: You told Goliath that the armies would soon know that the Lord had won the battle without the sword and shield.

GAR: I saw the boy whirl his sling above his head. A stone flew through the air and plunged into the forehead of the giant. I laid down his shield and ran in terror. I escaped, but most of the Philistines didn't.

DAVID: As I ran forward and removed Goliath's head, everyone was shouting. When the enemies saw that their champion was dead, they fled. Our soldiers ran after them and killed thousands of men. The war was over, and God had won the battle.

INTERVIEWER: Shammah, you were David's brother and knew him best. Please tell us about him.

SHAMMAH: David was brave. I told you that he was obedient to our parents. He could be depended upon when he was asked to do anything. He was a musician and wrote many songs. David was well liked and very tenderhearted. He had many friends. He had a great faith in God. When Saul died, David sat on the throne, and he was a good king. There were times when he sinned, but he was known as a friend of God, and all Israel loved him.

Bible Story Application

To show His power over the enemies of His people, God helped David kill Goliath. David said he wasn't depending upon a sword and shield, but upon the Lord of hosts.

Ephesians 6:11-17 gives a list of pieces of armor the Christian should put on—the belt of truth, the breastplate of righteousness, the sandals of peace. We must hold up the shield of faith and believe as David believed. David didn't need Saul's big helmet. A heavy hat will not help us to defeat our enemies, but God provides the helmet of salvation through His Son. Last of all, we are to hold and use the sword of the Spirit, the Bible.

(Most first and second graders are still too literal-minded to understand the symbolism of the Ephesians passage. If most of your group are younger, you may want to omit this portion of the application. If you use it, you may want to use the visuals in the flannelgraph packet, "The Christian Soldier.")

Boys and girls usually don't have enemies who threaten to kill them. But street gangs can be very mean. And there are other kinds of enemies such as those who lie about us, take things, or cause trouble. Can you think of some times when you need God's help in winning victories over enemies? David's God is our God, and He will help us.

Activity Book

As students do the matching puzzle, you may need to refer to "Preview" in the "Learning Centers" section of the lesson. Review the Bible story as the children color the picture.

On the next page, help students find 1 Samuel 17

and write the missing words in the quotations. The word search puzzle has eleven words that remind us of David. Give help as needed as students fill in the blanks at the bottom of the page.

Craft Souvenir

Rock Paperweight

MATERIALS NEEDED FOR LESSONS 2 AND 3:
A stone that will lie flat and has a fairly flat-topped
   surface
Latex or enamel paint
Newspapers
Felt dot or small shank button
Colored chips such as those used in aquariums
Alphabet soup noodles
Green chenille wire
Glue
Flat toothpicks (optional)
Felt (for bottom of paperweight, optional)

PROCEDURE:
   Lay the rock on newspaper and paint. Let dry.

Near the side of one flat surface, arrange the chips around the button to make a five-petal flower. Glue in place.

Bend a small piece of wire to form a stem. Glue on the side, leaving room for the motto. Green chips may be added to the stem for leaves.

Write the student's name on the bottom of the rock and lay aside until next craft period.

NOTE: Toothpicks will be helpful when applying the glue to the chips and letters. Younger children will need help.

Next week the students can make the motto "God has all power" from the alphabet soup letters and glue the letters to the paperweight.

A Helping Prophet

2 Kings 4:8-37

Goals: That the student will know that God has power over death and that He wants us to be looking for ways to be helpful.

Student Responses: As a result of this lesson, the student should be able to

• Tell how the woman helped Elisha.
• Tell how Elisha was able to help.
• State at least one way in which he can be a helper.

Learning Centers

Preview

A Bible-times House

MATERIALS:
Cardboard box approximately 12 by 12 by 5 inches (or larger) with lid
Small square box with lid
Watercolors or tempera paint
Construction paper, modeling clay
Knife, scissors, glue, and pencil

PROCEDURE:
To make a Bible-times house, cut one door and two windows in the large box and one door and one window in the small box. Accordion-pleat a narrow strip of paper and glue to the outside of the larger box to represent stairs. Paint the house white.

Furnish the upper room with a paper table, stool, mat, and a piece of birthday candle fastened to the table with a drop of wax. Similar furnishing may be placed in the lower room.

When the children come to this center, show them the house. Say, "Today we are going to pretend to travel to a Bible-times house. Most houses then were only one-room apartments with a door and two windows. The walls were of stone or mud bricks and the floor was dirt with mats for covering.

"Many heavy rafters were fastened across the top to make a flat roof. Layers of mud and straw were spread over the rafters and pushed down with a stone roller. Over this sometimes a coating of white-wash was spread to make the roof as waterproof as possible.

"The furniture was simple—a low table, benches, low beds or mats, an oil lamp or candle."

Set the furnished room on top of the larger room. Show the furniture, but do not tell the Bible story.

Memory Ticket Office

"Jesus said unto her, I am the resurrection, and the life: he that believeth in me, though he were dead, yet shall he live." John 11:25

THINK
1. What does Jesus call himself in this verse?
2. What does the word "resurrection" mean?
3. Why is this verse important?

LEARNING GAME

Prepare the symbols below according to the instructions on page 5. Children can use them to learn the memory verse or to review it.

AWARD

Initial the tickets for those who memorized the verse.

Guidebook

Life-giving Miracles

The following are selected verses from five Bible stories. Briefly tell the stories and ask the students to read only those passages or verses for which you have time. One visual-aid Bible character is suggested for each story. (Use pictures, stand-ups, or flannelgraph figures from your files.)

Bible people who were brought back to life:
1. A big brother—John 11:11-14, 41-44
2. A widow's only son—Luke 7:12-15
3. A ruler's daughter—Luke 8:41, 42, 48-55
4. A dressmaker—Acts 9:36, 37, 39-41
5. An accident victim—Acts 20:9-12

Front View Adventure

Good Deeds Club

MATERIALS:

Puppet stage (See "Introduction.")
Three puppets (Two boy puppets and one girl puppet)
Grocery list and a small block of wood

(Mike enters, holding a grocery list.)

MIKE: Hey, where's everybody? I was sure Howie would be in the clubhouse. I'd better look at this list of things I have to get for Mom.

(Howie enters)

MIKE: Hi, Howie. How come you're late from school?

HOWIE: My teacher's little boy got hurt so she left early. I straightened up her desk for her. And I sharpened some pencils.

MIKE: Say, that's neat! You're always doing stuff for people. Guess I never notice things like that.

HOWIE: You wouldn't let old wilted flowers sit on a desk over the weekend, would you?

MIKE: Guess what? My dad is getting a pony for Mindy and me! He's all black. His name is Moonlight. But we have a problem. We're all going on a vacation this summer. Who's going to take care of him?

HOWIE: That's no problem. I can do that for you. I love horses. I helped Grandpa take care of horses last summer, so I know how.

MIKE: Great! I'll tell my dad. Say, can I borrow your bike? I gotta go to the store for Mom.

HOWIE: Sure! It's standing by the door.

(Mike leaves.)

HOWIE: Guess while I wait around, I'll review my Bible verse. *(Mumbles Ecclesiastes 9:10 as though memorizing.)*

MINDY: *(Enters, laughing)* Ah-ha, I caught you talking to yourself, didn't I?

HOWIE: I was just memorizing my Bible verse—"Whatsoever thy hand findeth to do, do it with thy might."

MINDY: Huh! I didn't know that was in the Bible. Where's it found?

HOWIE: Ecclesiastes 9:10. Christians are supposed to do good deeds. Mr. Willy showed us where it says that Jesus went about doing good. We are supposed to look for things we can do for others.

MINDY: Well, if the Bible says I should, then I guess I should try.

(Mike enters, breathing hard and holding a small block of wood.)

MINDY: Mike! You scared me. I thought you went to the store for Mom? What's the block of wood for?

MIKE: Dad said he'd go to the store for Mom. This belongs to Kinky. He wants to enter the Grand Prix car races and he is supposed to carve a car out of wood. He can't carve very easily; he has that crippled hand. I said I'd help him.

MINDY: Oh, so you're doing good things now, too. Howie, quote that verse for him.

HOWIE: Sure! "Whatsoever thy hand findeth to do, do it with thy might."

MIKE: Kinky's dad won't let him go to church anywhere. He has some weird ideas about Christians. I thought that while we worked on his car I might get an opportunity to talk to him about Jesus.

MINDY: Maybe you could invite him to Sunday school, too.

HOWIE: That's a good idea. It would be neat if he'd come to our church because you did this good deed.

MIKE: I got an idea. Maybe we could call our club the Good Deeds Club.

HOWIE: Listen! I heard my dad whistle. That means it's our supper time. Let's all go home. *(All say good-bye and leave.)*

Worshiping Our Guide

Quiet music: "Give of Your Best to the Master"
Song: "Step by Step" (page 118)
Theme chorus: "God of Great Power"
Song: "Loving and Kind" (page 119)
Bible reading: Matthew 28:18-20
Prayer
Offering and announcements
Special music: "Living for Jesus"
Song: "My God Is a Great God" (page 117)
Prayer

Bible Story

A Helping Prophet

Shunem was a town in the country of Samaria. Everyone who lived there was known as a Shunammite. Elisha, the prophet, often passed through Shunem when he was traveling from place to place serving the Lord.

One day a rich Shunammite woman and her husband saw the prophet and his servant coming along the dusty road past their home at the edge of town. She invited them to come in and have dinner. Since Elisha was a friendly guest and a servant of God, the woman told him to stop and eat dinner every time he passed that way.

One evening she said to her husband, "I can tell that Elisha is a holy man of God. Let's build a room on the roof of our house and when he comes this way, he will have a place to stay."

Her husband agreed, and soon construction work began. The servants made bricks, dried them in the sun, and carried them to the roof. When the room was ready, the woman brought in a table, a stool, a bed, and a lamp.

"This is a comfortable room," Elisha said when the woman showed him his sleeping quarters. When he lay down to rest, he thought of how good the couple were to think of his physical needs.

"I would like to do something for this woman in return for her kindness," Elisha thought. Then he told his servant to call her up to the room. When she stood in the doorway, he explained how much he appreciated her careful planning for his needs.

"What can I do for you in return?" Elisha asked. "Can I ask for a special favor from the king or the commander of the army?"

To this question the woman replied that she had a family around her, and that was enough. She was satisfied.

Later Elisha asked his servant, "What can we do for her?"

"I have an idea," said the servant. "As often as we have been in this home, I have never seen a child playing in the yard. Her husband is old, and she needs someone to keep her company."

When the woman was called back, Elisha told her that within a year she would have a son. The news was almost too good to be true. The woman was so surprised and happy she could hardly believe Elisha. Nevertheless, within a year, God sent a baby boy.

One summer day when the boy was old enough, his father took him to the field. He was too small to cut the grain, but he could pick up the loose stalks the servants missed. The sun was very hot, and it beat down upon his young head until finally he was overcome with heat. He complained of having a terrible headache. At last, his father told a servant to carry the child home to his mother.

"My little son is very ill," the Shunammite woman said, as she held him on her lap. "I have done everything I know to do for him, but I do not believe that he is going to get well." She was right! The child died at noon. With tearful eyes, the woman carried his little body up the stairs and laid it on the prophet's bed.

Calling to her husband, she said, "Send me a young man and your fastest donkey so we can go to the prophet's house."

Quickly she saddled the donkey. "Lead on," she said to the servant. "Don't slow down unless I tell you to." What a cloud of dust that must have made as the two of them hurried to Mount Carmel where Elisha was!

As soon as Elisha heard the sad news, he told his servant, Gehazi, to take his staff, run to the house, and lay it on the dead boy's face. The servant did just as he was told. Did the little boy come alive? No, and Gehazi returned to Elisha, saying that the boy did not awaken.

So Elisha himself went to the woman's house. When he climbed the stairs to his special room, there lay his little friend, limp and not breathing. Elisha knew that he did not have the power to put life into the young body, but God did. He shut the door, and then prayed. He stretched himself over the child, putting his mouth on the small lips, and his hands clasped over the cold fingers. The boy became warm. Then Elisha walked back and forth in the room, and as he walked he probably prayed. Again he put himself over the little one. This time the child sneezed! He sneezed seven times! And he opened his eyes!

"Gehazi, call the Shunammite woman!" demanded Elisha.

What a day it was for that mother! When she came in, Elisha said, "Take your son." The woman knelt down, and bowed to the ground. Then she picked up her son and carried him downstairs. He was alive and well!

Bible Story Application

The boy in our story died but the Lord who has power over death raised him from the dead. Several people of Bible times were raised from the dead. Nothing is too difficult for God.

Elisha trusted God. He believed in God's power. He was God's willing and cheerful helper. He watched for places where he could serve.

Are you a cheerful helper? Or do you wait to be coaxed? We can't do what Elisha did, but all around us every day are many things that we can do to help. Will you watch for times when you can help to make problems easier for your family, church, and friends? Can you list some ways in which you can help? (Read Galatians 6:10.)

Activity Book

On the first page of the pupil's book *Traveling With Bible People, Activity Book One,* pupils draw a picture of a Bible-times house and a picture of the furnishings in Elisha's room; complete an acrostic; and unscramble some words. Give help as needed as pupils fill in the blanks on the second page.

(Answers to the acrostic: prayed, love, did, sure, prophet, thankful.)

Craft Souvenir

Rock Paperweight

Complete the craft begun last week.

Give each two students a small handful of alphabet soup letters. Arrange the letters on the rock to make the motto "God has all power." Glue in place.

After the letters have dried, cut a piece of felt the same size as the rock and glue it on the bottom of the paperweight. (Optional.)

An Unfair Tax Collector

Luke 18:35-43; 19:1-10

Goals: That the student (1) will know that God has power to change lives and (2) will want to follow Jesus.

Student Responses: As a result of this lesson, the student would be able to

• Give examples of Bible people whose lives were changed when they followed the Lord. (See "Guidebook.")

• Tell how Zacchaeus changed and why.

• List ways our lives are changed when we follow Jesus.

Learning Centers

Preview

Taxes and Tax Collectors

PREPARATION:

Print two words, "taxes" and "publican," on separate cards with the definitions on the reverse sides. A picture of Biblical coinage would be helpful.

PROCEDURE:

1. TAXES—Money paid to support the government.

When your parents say they must pay their taxes, they mean that because they own property, or because they have a good income, they must give some of the money to the government to help support it.

People paid taxes when Jesus lived on the earth. Because Rome ruled over Israel, the people paid taxes to the Roman government.

2. PUBLICAN—A tax collector.

Publicans were hired by the Roman government to collect the tax money from the Jewish people. They overcharged the Jews and kept the extra money.

Most publicans were very unfair in their business. For example, they might decide to open a man's bun-

dle and search it. Then they would accuse him of smuggling the contents into the country unlawfully. For this the man would be forced to pay extra money which the publican would keep. Publicans became rich. The Jews hated them and wouldn't even let them attend religious services in the temple.

Memory Ticket Office

"If any man be in Christ, he is a new creature."

2 Corinthians 5:17

THINK

1. What does the word "creature" mean? (creation or person)

2. The Lord gives Christians the power to be like new persons. We try to be kind, honest, truthful, live clean lives, and love the Lord.

LEARNING GAME

Prepare the symbols below. (See page 5)

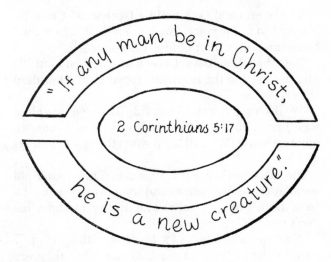

AWARD

Initial the tickets for those who memorize the verse.

Guidebook

"Who Am I?" Bible Drill

The following clues are about Bible people whose lives were changed when they became followers of the Lord. Use them as a quiz or as a Bible drill.

1. I am the woman from Jericho who hid two spies. My life was saved because I put a red cord in my window. I became a believer in the true God. Who am I? (Hebrews 11:31) (Rahab)

2. I was a tax collector. Jesus asked me to come and follow Him and be a disciple. Who am I? (Matthew 9:9) (Matthew)

3. I left Moab with Naomi to live with God's people in Bethlehem. Who am I? (Ruth 1:16) (Ruth)

4. I had evil spirits living within me. Then Jesus cast them out. I was one of the three women who planned to put spices on His body on resurrection morning. Who am I? (Luke 8:2) (Mary Magdalene)

5. Before I became a believer in Jesus, I went from place to place searching for Christians and putting them in prison. I became a missionary. Who am I? (Acts 8:3) (Paul)

6. I am the sinful woman who told Jesus that I had no husband and He knew that I had had five. I went back to the city and brought my friends to Jesus. Who am I? (John 4:7) (The woman at the well in Samaria)

Front View Adventure

Chad's New Name

"I have an idea! Let's build a treehouse," Chad Tobin said in a low voice. "We can make it into a clubhouse and have a lot of fun this summer."

The other three boys listened as Chad laid out his plan for getting the materials together and building the treehouse.

"We'll keep it a secret," he said. "The trees are close together in our back yard, and no one will ever see our treehouse. We will keep everything we do a secret."

The boys worked hard all week. They found old wood at the village dump and used tar paper for the roof. Dick brought nails, and Binky brought his dad's tools.

"Now we need hinges for the door," Binky said. "I found a set of them in our basement, but they are expensive ones. They're brass."

"Bring them, and don't tell your dad. He'll never miss them," said Chad.

When the clubhouse was finished, Chad spoke in a low voice saying, "Remember now—this place is a secret and what our club does is a secret."

Binky and Dick nodded their heads in approval. But Bret frowned and said, "It's okay as long as our secrets are honest and good. But if my dad ever finds out that we can't be trusted, it will all be off."

Chad was the leader and he was a fighter. Because he was bigger than the other boys, they were afraid not to do what he said. He was mean to little boys, and he was rough and rude to girls. His cousin said he was a thief. The neighbors called him "Chad the Bad."

One day when the boys were in their clubhouse, they had a quarrel. Dick accused Chad of stealing a radio he had brought in. Binky's dad missed the brass hinges and said that he had to bring them right back. Chad told the boys that to be members of the club, they had to lie and steal.

"I'm quitting this club," said Bret. "My dad says we'll get into trouble. Dick and I are going to join a fun club on Elm Street."

Bret and Dick liked the new club and had fun in the activities. Before they were dismissed, they sang songs and listened to a Bible story. For the first time Dick heard that Christ loved him so much that He died on the cross for his sins. After one of the lessons, Dick and Bret went to Mr. Noble, their leader, and said they wanted to become Christians.

In September the boys asked Chad and Binky to come to the new club. Chad laughed and said he was too big. But when Bret promised to take them to the ice cream shop, Chad said he would attend the club just once. When he won in the games because he was bigger than the rest, he decided to attend the following week. At first he didn't listen well during devotions, but when everyone else was quiet, he became more attentive.

One night Chad met Mr. Noble in the yard and said he liked the new club. He said he wanted to be a Christian like Bret and Dick. From then on, he had the Lord to help him be a better fellow and people began to see the difference.

"What's happening to Chad the Bad?" the neighbors asked one another. "He's not a troublemaker any more. He has certainly changed." From then on Chad had a new name—Chad the Glad.

"We must build a bigger clubhouse. Our club has grown so big that we no longer have room for everyone," said the Nobles.

When the new building was completed, a special dedication service was held. Many village people attended the afternoon service.

"Look at the sign on this clubhouse door!" exclaimed one of the neighbors. "It says, Brass Hinges Furnished by Chad the Glad."

Chad had earned the money to purchase the hinges from Binky's dad. He wanted them to remind him of how much he had changed.

Worshiping Our Guide

Quiet music: "Praise Him! Praise Him!"
Song: "He's Got the Whole World in His Hands"
Theme chorus: "God of Great Power"
Song: "There Is Power in Christ" (page 119)
Bible reading: 1 John 3:1-3
Prayer
Offering and announcements
Special number: "Zacchaeus Was a Wee Little Man" (by a small child)
Song: "What a Happy Day" (page 120)
Prayer

Bible Story

An Unfair Tax Collector

The time of the Passover feast was drawing near. Jews from every city and town went to Jerusalem in the springtime of each year to attend the religious event. Roads and streets were always crowded with travelers going to the temple to take part in the celebration. Jesus and His disciples were also on their way to the Passover. This was Jesus' last time to go because He knew that soon He would be crucified.

One of the cities Jesus and His disciples passed through was Jericho. As they drew near, a blind man named Bartimaeus begged Jesus to take away his blindness. Jesus did, and then Bartimaeus could see perfectly! This wonderful miracle caused the crowd to desire to get closer to Jesus and follow Him as He walked through Jericho.

Along the edge of the crowd walked a very short man with a black beard. He wore a costly robe, and on his head he wore an embroidered turban. Anyone noticing him knew he was rich.

"Let me through here!" said the little man. "I am short and I can't see above your heads. I would like to see this Jesus whom I have heard so much about."

"Who is this small man?" someone must have asked as the crowd pressed closer together.

"He is the chief commissioner of taxes here in Jericho. His name is Zaachaeus. He's a thief and a cheat," one of the town's people probably whispered.

"Don't let him through. He's rich because he is a crook."

Zaachaeus had heard a lot about Jesus. He had been told of the miracles Jesus had done and the wonderful things He taught. Now he was eager to see this One who had become so well known. But he was too short to see above the heads of the crowd, and no one would let him through.

"There's a sycamore tree along the roadside. I'll run ahead and climb into it," Zaachaeus thought, as he dashed around the mob. He found a comfortable branch where the view was good. There he sat and waited. He was curious and excited as he waited for Jesus to pass by.

Jesus knows everything. He knew all about Zacchaeus. When He came under the long branch of the tree, He looked up. "Zaachaeus, hurry and come down," He said, "for I am going to your house."

The little man lost no time getting out of the tree. Joyfully he took Jesus home with him as his honorable guest.

The Jewish people hated publicans. They felt that it was sinful to be their friends or go to their homes to eat. When they saw Jesus go into the publican's home, they complained and found fault with Him. They said He had gone to be a guest of a sinner.

The Bible does not tell us what Jesus said at Zacchaeus' table that day. But Jesus' presence and His words certainly had an effect on Zacchaeus. Standing up, he looked into the searching eyes of Jesus and said, "Half of what I own, I'll give to the poor. If I have taken anything by cheating, I will repay four times its worth."

"Today is salvation come to this house," Jesus said. Jesus forgave Zacchaeus. Then Jesus said, "I came to seek and to save the lost."

Zacchaeus became a true follower of Jesus. His family, his servants, and all who knew Him would see the difference. Jesus had given him power to live a new and different life, a life pleasing to God.

Bible Story Application

How did Zacchaeus change? . . . Why did Zacchaeus change? . . . Zacchaeus was a different man after he believed in Jesus and decided to follow Him. Jesus helped him to turn his life around. Even before Jesus left the house, Zacchaeus was thinking honest thoughts and wanting to do right. He was a new person.

(You may want to include the following in your discussion if you used the "Front View Adventure.") How did Chad the Bad change?

The Bible tells us that "If any man be in Christ, he

is a new creature" (2 Corinthians 5:17). That is our memory verse. Do you remember it?

How do our lives change when we follow Jesus? When we let Jesus take over our lives, we change our minds about God. We love Him, and we speak kindly about Him. We stop taking His name in vain. We talk to Him often in prayer. We have better thoughts. We do things for others. The Bible becomes a special book to us, and we want to read it. We ask the Lord to help us understand it and do what it says. We want to attend Sunday school and church faithfully each week. We like to think of Heaven and that we will see Christ some day. We tell others about Jesus the Savior.

We do not have the power to change our lives all by ourselves, but when we turn our lives over to the Lord, He has that power.

Activity Book

Pupils add the rhyming words to complete the poem about Zacchaeus, the publican.

You will need blue and red pencils for the puzzle at the bottom of the page. Pupils put a blue circle around four words that describe Zacchaeus before he met Jesus and a red circle around four words that describe Zacchaeus after he met Jesus. *(The words are disliked, dishonest, cheater, unfair; and forgiven, happy, fair, honest.)*

Most of the questions on the next page are "What would you have done?" questions, and each child should work out his own answers. After all have finished the activity, discuss the questions together and let some of the children read their answers.

Craft Souvenir

Stand-up Butterfly Motto

MATERIALS:
5½ by 7 inch white construction paper
Butterfly stickers (2 for each child)
Glue
Scissors
Blue felt pens
Blue construction paper

PROCEDURE:

Stick two identical butterfly seals together, back to back. Fold the wings together and press. Squeeze a line of glue along the folded edge and fasten to the lefthand upper part of the white paper.

With a felt pen, write "Christ can make life beautiful" on the paper.

Frame the motto by putting a drop of glue on each corner of the white paper and laying it on a slightly larger piece of blue paper.

A Faithful Traveler

Genesis 11:29-32; 12:1-9; 13; 17:1-8, 15

Goals: That the student (1) will know that God rewarded Abraham for his faith and (2) will decide to trust God's guidance for his life.

Student Responses: As a result of this lesson, the student should be able to
- Tell how Abraham was faithful.
- Define faith (in his own words).
- Say the memory verse.
- Thank God for *His guidance.*
- *Ask God for His guidance.*

Learning Centers

Preview

A Map Study

MATERIALS:
Large map showing Ur of the Chaldees and the Holy
  Land (Old Testament times)
Small cards and pins (or Plasti-tak)

PROCEDURE:
On the cards print these names: Ur, Euphrates, Haran, Shechem, and Bethel. Let the students place the cards on the locations with bits of Plasti-tak or by pinning.

"We are going to hear about a man named Abraham. God asked him to move to another part of the world. On the map we are going to find some of the places to which he traveled.

"Ur was a beautiful and modern city. Many of the people were rich. Some of the men carried golden daggers in their holsters, and some of the families ate their food from golden plates. This was the city in which Abram and Sara lived.

"Abram traveled along the Euphrates River. This is a long, wide river, the longest river in that part of Asia."

Memory Ticket Office

"And the Lord shall guide thee continually."
                                        Isaiah 58:11

THINK
  1. For how long has the Lord promised to guide us?
  2. Why is this verse important to you?

LEARNING GAME
  See page 5, "Preparation for Each Unit" for the use of the chalkboard in teaching the memory verses in this unit.

AWARD
  Initial the tickets for those who learned the verse.

Guidebook

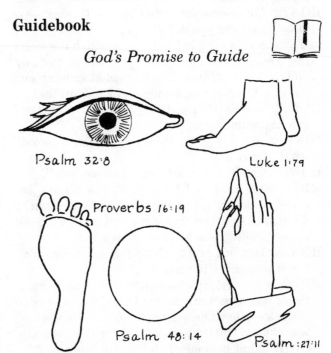

God's Promise to Guide

Psalm 32:8

Luke 1:79

Proverbs 16:19

Psalm 48:14

Psalm :27:11

Print the following Bible references on the paper

symbols indicated, and use as a Bible drill. (Refer to Bible drill rules on page 5.)

1. God guides with His eye. Psalm 32:8 (An eye)
2. God guides our feet in the way of peace. Luke 1:79 (Feet)
3. God guides us forever. Psalm 48:14 (A circle)
4. God guides our steps. Proverbs 16:9 (A footprint)
5. What our prayer should be. Psalm 27:11 (Praying hands)

Front View Adventure

Puppet Skit: "When Mindy Took Over"

Materials:
Two puppets and a puppet stage

Skit:
(Howie enters, whistling.)
HOWIE: I guess I didn't need to open up the clubhouse today. Everybody's gone away. *(Pause.)* Nope, no one is coming.
(Mike enters.)
HOWIE: Hi, Mike! I didn't think you would be back yet. You said you were going on a picnic with your family today.
MIKE: We did, and we're back. Dad and Mom took all the picnic stuff in the car and went ahead of Mindy and me.
HOWIE: You mean you didn't ride with your parents? What did you do? Walk?
MIKE: *(Laughs.)* Oh, no! You'd never catch me walking. Do you remember that two-wheeled cart my dad made for us? Well, Dad hitched Moonlight, our pony, to the cart and Mindy and I rode in that.
HOWIE: Sounds like fun. How about taking me for a ride sometime?
MIKE: Sure! But you'll have to promise not to do what Mindy did.
HOWIE: Oh-oh! What did your sister do now?
MIKE: Well, Dad said I should do the driving because Mindy is too young to guide Moonlight. I decided to take the short-cut along the river road to the picnic grounds. That's a nice trail.
HOWIE: Hey, it's pretty along the river—but isn't the trail narrow in places?
MIKE: Is it ever! But Moonlight is careful. Everything was okay until Mindy looked over the edge of the steep bank on her side. The wheel of the cart was about a foot from the edge. It was sort of scary.
HOWIE: What happened? Did Mindy jump out?
MIKE: *(Laughs.)* No! But she screamed. Then she grabbed the reins and started pulling on them. Poor Moonlight started to twist and turn, and push back. I thought surely we were going over the bank.
HOWIE: Wow! Then what!
MIKE: Well, I told Mindy that only one could be the driver. Then I put the reins into her hands and told her to drive the pony. That really scared her. She gave them back to me and sat quietly after that.
HOWIE: You know that makes a good lesson on trusting the Lord.
MIKE: Huh? You mean our frightening experience is a lesson? How?
HOWIE: Well, you were the one who should have been in charge. You would have taken Mindy safely to the picnic grounds, but she didn't trust you. She was going to take over.
MIKE: Oh, I get it. God wants to be in charge of our lives, and He will guide us safely. But we are like Mindy; we think we can do better.
HOWIE: Say, you're smart.
MIKE: You know, Howie, if Mindy hadn't given the reins back to me, we might have gone over the bank and been hurt—maybe killed. Or our plans would have been messed up.
HOWIE: That's it. If we don't trust the Lord and let Him guide us, our lives will be messed up, too. Guess no one else is coming to the clubhouse. Let's go. *(Both leave.)*

Worshiping Our Guide

Quiet music: "Footsteps of Jesus"
Song: "My God Is a Great God" (page 117)
Theme chorus: "Believe and Obey" (see page 5)
Song: "Step by Step" (page 118)
Bible reading: Hebrews 11:6
Prayer
Offering and announcements
Special music: "Savior, Like a Shepherd Lead Us"
Song: "Like a Shepherd" (page 121)
Prayer

Bible Story

A Faithful Traveler

We are learning about Bible travelers. The Bible tells us about a man who did a lot of traveling. His name was Abram.

Abram loved God and wanted to serve Him.

Abram's wife's name was Sarai. They were very rich, and they lived in the very rich city of Ur. Ur was located along the Euphrates River in Mesopotamia, the land of the Chaldeans. (Show on map.) The people there worshiped idols. But Abram remained true to God. He prayed to God and tried to do what God wanted him to do.

One day when Abram was all alone, the Lord came and talked to him. He said, "I want you to leave this city and move to another part of the world that I will show you. I will make of you a great nation, and all people will be blessed through you."

Reverently Abram listened to the voice of the Lord. Leave his home? He must have wondered. Go to a strange place? How would he know where to go? But God had promised to show him and to be with him.

Abram hurried home to Sarai and said, "God has just told me that we must leave this city. He has asked me to start a special nation. We will move away from Ur."

"Where are we going?" Sarai must have asked her husband.

"I do not know," he replied, "but God said that He would show me, and I believe His promises. We will leave soon, Sarai, and God will guide us along the way."

It was not a vacation trip. They were not coming back. They must take dishes and clay ovens, their weaving looms, and food. They would need their tents and mats. They would take their cattle with them. The servants and all the animals would need provisions, too.

With the help of the servants, the packing was finally completed, and they were ready for the long trip. Abram's riches of gold and silver and costly things were loaded on camels, and the caravan was on the way northwest along the great river. They did not go alone. Abram's father, Terah, and his nephew, Lot, and many servants went with them.

God led them along the rich, fertile land by the river until they arrived in Haran. They lived in Haran for several years, until Terah died.

After Terah died, the Lord told Abram to leave Haran and He would take him to the land He had promised. God promised to make of Abram a great nation, to bless him, and to make his name great. Abram could not completely understand God's plan for him and his descendants. He knew nothing about the new land to which he was going. But he believed God. And he did what God asked him to do.

Abram, Sarai, Lot, and the servants packed their things and left Haran. They were led south into the land of Canaan, to Shechem and then to Beth-el. Then they moved farther south. Because of a famine in the land of Canaan, they traveled to Egypt and lived there for a while. Later they returned to Beth-el. The servants pitched the tents and the family unpacked their possessions.

Soon after they had settled, trouble came between Lot's servants and Abram's servants. They quarreled over pasture land for the huge herds of cattle that belonged to Abram and Lot.

"Our servants must not quarrel," said Abram. "Let us divide the land, and we will separate. You may have the first choice of locations."

Lot chose the good land to the east and moved there with his family, servants, and herds. Abram took the land that was left.

After Lot was gone, the Lord called Abram to the top of a mountain where he could see for a long distance in every direction. God said, "Look to the south, to the north, then to the east, and the west. The land as far as you can see I will give to you and your children. Your family will increase so much that if you could count the stars or the sand of the sea, you would know how large your family will increase." After that, God led Abram and Sarai to Hebron.

When Abram was ninety-nine years old, God again told him that if he trusted and obeyed God, he would be the father of many nations, and his wife was to have a child. He changed Abram's name to Abraham, which means "father of many nations." He also gave Sarai a new name. She was called the beautiful name Sarah which means "princess."

God kept His promises to Abraham. He gave him a son, Isaac, even when both Abraham and Sarah were very old. Abraham's family eventually became the nation of Israel. From that nation came the Savior of the whole world. Even today Abraham is called the father of the faithful.

(If time permits, have students find Hebrews 11:8-12 in their Bibles. Ask a student to read the verses.)

Bible Story Application

Faith is believing even when we do not understand how something can happen. Abraham believed even though he couldn't imagine how God was going to lead him on the journey from Ur. He went out, not knowing where he was going. He believed that God would keep His promise to show him the way. He not only believed, but he obeyed.

Do you ever wonder what you will be when you are a teenager or when you grow up? The Lord has promised to show young travelers the way. He will guide you. He will help you to know.

We need God's guidance not only for the future, but

also for each day. If we pray to Him, have faith in Him, and obey Him, He will guide our steps. Psalm 27:11 is a good prayer to memorize and to pray. "Teach me thy way, O Lord, and lead me in a plain path." Isaiah says that God will guide us continually. (Isaiah 58:11) Abraham was rewarded for his faith, and you will be, too.

Now let's bow our heads and talk to God in prayer. First, let's thank Him for guiding us. Then let's ask Him to guide us in the future. *(Silent prayer.)*

Activity Book

Help the students find the places on the map. Refer to the large map used during "Preview." (If you did not use this learning center, you will need to spend more time discussing the map and the various locations.)

The code for the puzzle is the twenty-six letters of the alphabet. *(The answer is "A patient faithful man who had a great faith in God. He was very kind.")*

Students can use their Bibles as they fill in the blanks on the next page.

Since the mirror puzzle is solved by holding the page before a mirror, you may want to have one large mirror on the classroom wall and let students take turns using it to find the answer. Warn them that no one should tell until everyone has had an opportunity to read the answer.

Discuss the questions under "Thinking It Over."

Craft Souvenir

Stand-up Tent Booklet

MATERIALS:
Light brown construction paper

Flat toothpicks
Scissors, glue, and ball-point pen
Pattern of tent from pattern page

PROCEDURE:
(To save time for this project, pre-cut the tents.) Distribute four tents to each student. Fold each tent in half. On one tent cut about 1¼ inch along the bottom part of the fold and turn back for opening. Squeeze a thin line of glue along the top, side, and bottom of the left-hand side of the second tent and fasten it to the back of the front tent. Hold until it adheres. Continue this procedure until all tent sections are glued together. Now the tent (four parts) will stand.

Lay the tent flat on the table, front side up. On the under left-hand tent page write, "By faith Abraham left home to go to a land he had never seen. Hebrews 11:8."

On the under right-hand tent page write, "Abraham lived in tents. Hebrews 11:9."

Break toothpicks in pieces and glue stakes on the four corners of the tent.

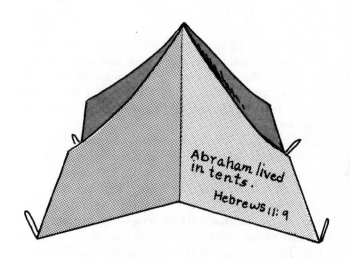

A Great Leader

Exodus 16

Goals: That the student (1) will know how God provided for a great leader and his people and (2) will trust God to provide at least one specific need.

Student Responses: As a result of this lesson, the student should be able to

- Tell the Bible story.
- Draw a picture of something he believes the Lord has supplied or will supply.
- Thank God for needs He has supplied.
- Explain the memory verse.

Learning Centers

Preview

A Walk in the Wilderness

MATERIALS:
Bible map of Sinai Peninsula showing the Wilderness of Sin
Picture of a wilderness

Have you ever taken a trip through a desert? You wouldn't care to stay there very long unless you had plenty of water and food. It's a lonely place the year around.

A wilderness is also a lonely place. The Israelites lived in the wilderness for many years after they left Egypt. One place was called the Wilderness of Sin. (*Locate on map and show where they had lived in Egypt and where they crossed the Red Sea.*)

This wilderness is hot and the air is dry. The ground is stony and rough, with slopes, hills, and mountains. There were no roads to be found when the Israelites traveled there. Here and there were clumps of trees and bushes, tough, thorny shrubs, clover, and wide-leafed grass called broom grass. Springs with good drinking water were scarce, and there was very little food for people.

Memory Ticket Office

"The young lions do lack, and suffer hunger: but they that seek the Lord shall not want any good thing."
Psalm 34:10

THINK
1. Why would lion cubs lack or suffer hunger? (The parent lions do not always find enough food for two or three growing cubs.)
2. What does "seek" mean? (Ask or depend upon.)

LEARNING GAME
Use the chalkboard to help the children learn the verse. (See page 5.)

AWARD
Initial the tickets for those who learned the verse.

Guidebook

Paste-on Mural

MATERIALS:
Shelfpaper of desired length
Typing paper, pencils, and a wide felt pen
Pictures for ideas (optional)
Bibles

PROCEDURE:
At the top of the shelfpaper with the felt pen, print the caption "God will supply all of our needs." Below the caption print the Bible references Philippians 4:19 and Psalm 23:1. (See illustration on page 30.)

At classtime ask the students to read the verses. Allow time for a brief discussion. Give each one a half sheet of typing paper and ask him to draw something he believes the Lord will supply or has supplied.

Print names on the drawings and hold until craft time when they can be finished.

Front View Adventure

Puppet Skit: "The Broken Wheel"

MATERIALS:

Three puppets

A paper banner on which is printed "Christian Middle School"

(Howie enters, whistling.)

HOWIE: *(Dreamily)* What a super duper day this is. Sure hope it's like this on Saturday 'cause I want to go to the parade. Oh, here comes Mike. I wonder what he wants.

(Mike enters, head down.)

HOWIE: Hi, Mike! You look as if you had lost your last friend. Why so sad on such a great day as today?

MIKE: You'd be sad, too, if you had planned to be in the parade with your pony and cart, and all your plans fell through.

HOWIE: Why can't you? Any kid can enter if he signs up.

MIKE: I signed up, all right. But one of the wheels on the cart broke, and Dad says it can't be replaced. You can't buy anything like that around here anymore.

HOWIE: Well, someone ought to have a wheel that could be made to fit. I thought you were going to represent our school in the parade?

MIKE: We were. But the parade is in just two days. We were going to decorate the cart and put a banner around it.

(Mindy enters, all excited.)

MINDY: Oh, Mike, your problem may be solved. Mr. Bates says there's a wheel something like ours in the dump.

MIKE: Great! Oh, but no one is allowed to take stuff from the village dump. If they caught us, we'd be fined. Anyway, that would be stealing.

HOWIE: I still think there will be a way to get that cart fixed in time. It will be fun to see Moonlight klopping down the street. I believe the Lord will help us if we ask Him. He says he will honor those who honor Him.

(All leave.)

(Howie and Mike reenter.)

MIKE: Guess what! We have the wheel, and my dad is fixing it right now.

HOWIE: Didn't I tell you? God promises to take care of our needs.

MIKE: See, it's like this: We found out that our pony is to be placed just ahead of our school band.

HOWIE: Even Moonlight will have the school spirit. It sounds like fun.

MIKE: The band teacher asked me if his little boy could ride in the cart with Mindy and me. I told him that it was without a wheel.

HOWIE: I 'spose you told him about the wheel in the dump?

MIKE: I sure did. He called the mayor and got permission for Dad and me to take it out. We got it free, too. The Lord sure helped us.

(Mindy enters with a banner.)

MINDY: Look what Mom made for us! Let's go home and decorate the cart! Dad says we should put tassels on Moonlight. Yea, Middle School! Come and help us, Howie.

(All leave.)

Worshiping Our Guide

Quiet music: "I Am So Glad"
Song: "Oh, How He Loves You and Me"
Theme chorus: "Believe and Obey" (See page 5.)
Song: "If God Be for Us" (page 117)
Bible reading: Psalm 37:3-5
Prayer
Offering and announcements
Special music: "God Will Take Care of You"
Song: "He's Able" (page 122)
Prayer

Bible Story

A Great Leader

(Arrange to have a short dialogue between teacher and a student.)

Teacher: _____ , our Bible story today is about the time when God led the Israelites into the wilderness after they had crossed the Red Sea. God chose Moses to be their leader.

Student: Moses was a good man, wasn't he? I think he was very kind.

Teacher: Yes, he was. The Bible says he was humble above all men who were on the earth. (Numbers 12:3) He was a great leader. The Lord gave him a great responsibility, for he led millions of people. That would be like the population in a large city.

Student: How did Moses get to be such a good leader.

Teacher: You will remember how as a baby Moses was hid in the river and the princess of Egypt found him. He lived in the palace until he was forty years old and received a good education. (Acts 7:22, 23) Later he watched sheep in the wilderness for forty years. While he was alone, God taught him many lessons.

Student: Then he was eighty years old when he became a leader. That's pretty old. What was Moses like?

Teacher: He had a great love for God. He didn't do things without talking to God. He was faithful in doing whatever God told him to do. He cared about his people. He encouraged them and prayed for them. Although he was a great leader, he was humble.

Do you remember how the Lord made a path through the Red Sea so the Israelites could walk across on dry ground? On the east shore they sang praises to the Lord.

Then they left the sandy beach and started toward the desert. God's cloud went before them to show the way and let them know that He was with them.

For three days they traveled without finding water. Then they found a spring, but the water was so bitter that they couldn't drink it. God told Moses how to make it sweet by a miracle.

Once, when it was very hot and the people were very thirsty and tired, the cloud led them to an oasis where there were seventy palm trees and twelve springs. Oh, what a lovely, restful camp site it was. When the cloud started to move ahead again, the people pulled up their tent stakes and loaded their belongings on camels and donkeys. Again they were on their way. They were led into the rough, wild Wilderness of Sin.

Again the people complained to Moses, and found fault. They said, "Where do we find food for our families? We are hungry! Why didn't we stay back in Egypt? We could just as well have died there as in this desert. In Egypt we had food." They had already forgotten that they had been slaves in that land.

To feed so many people would have taken tons and tons of food every day. Even using all of their camels and donkeys, they could not have brought enough food over the rough wilderness to feed the multitude every day. Only a miracle would save them from starving.

The Lord told Moses that He would send them meat every evening, and bread from Heaven every morning. That evening a great flock of plump quail flew into the camp. They were tame, and easily caught.

In the morning the dew was heavy like frost. When the dew was gone, the ground was covered with small white flakes the size of large seeds. The people kept saying, "What is it?" "What is it?" for they did not know what it was. "It is the bread the Lord has given you to eat," said Moses. When the people tasted it, it was delicious. They called the bread manna.

"There are rules to follow with the heavenly food," said Moses. "Every morning you shall gather as much as you will need for your families. No more! Do not try to store some for the next day because the leftovers will spoil."

The other rule was that each Friday morning they were to gather enough for the Sabbath day. On that day there would be no manna.

Many folk followed the rules carefully. Others did not. They gathered more than they needed and stored it. When they looked at it the next morning, they saw that it was wormy and spoiled. Some people went out on the seventh day to pick up manna, and none was on the ground. Those people had to go hungry. It was just as the Lord had warned.

Moses said, "The Lord has commanded that we take an omer (about two quarts) of manna and keep it for the generations to come, so they can see the bread God gave us to eat in the desert when He brought us out of Egypt."

So Moses said to Aaron, his brother, "Take a jar and put an omer of manna in it. It is to be kept for future generations." And Aaron did as Moses said.

For forty years the Israelites ate manna; they ate it until they came to the border of the land of Canaan.

Bible Story Application

Why did the Israelites think they were going to starve? They had seen God do many miracles in Egypt. They had seen Him divide the Red Sea so they could walk across on dry ground. They had watched Him destroy their enemies. They had the cloud above them day and night. Shouldn't they have believed God would feed them?

The Israelites were afraid because they really didn't believe God. They were hungry, but instead of complaining, they should have asked Him for help. His love for them was great, and He wouldn't let them starve. They were afraid because they didn't have faith in God. This always makes God unhappy. (Hebrews 11:6)

Moses had strong faith. He remembered all the good miracles of the past. How terrible it would have been if he had decided that the people should return to Egypt because they said they wanted to. The Lord rewarded his faith by sending manna and quail for forty years. God even took care of the people's clothing. Their clothes and shoes didn't wear out (Deuteronomy 29:5).

God is just as great today. Philippians 4:19 tells us that He will supply all our needs. *(Ask a child to read the verse.)* Remember our memory verse? "They that seek the Lord shall not want any good thing" (Psalm 34:10). God supplies our food—and much more. Do you need a warm jacket? Or school lunch money? Are you afraid of a tough fellow at school? Or a street gang? Is math or another study difficult for you? God is interested in all our needs. He wants us to pray to Him and to trust Him as Moses did.

Activity Book

After the students have filled in the blanks under "Let's Pretend," they can color the picture of the Bible story.

The four small crosswords at the bottom of the page are very simple. Give help if needed as students write the letters in the boxes.

The top of the next page is a familiar matching activity.

After students have filled in the blanks at the bottom of the page, discuss the questions. Students who want to may share with the class the three things they are going to pray about and trust God for.

Call attention to the fact that the name of each Bible traveler appears in large print on the first page of the activity book for each lesson.

If time permits, review the memory verse. You may want to use the chalkboard as suggested in "Learning Centers."

Craft Souvenir

Picture Mural

MATERIALS:
Crayons, paste or tape
Pie crust (optional)

PROCEDURE:
Finish the drawings that were started during "Guidebook" time. Paste or tape them to the shelf paper and fasten the mural to a wall.

Treat the students to pie crust "manna." Roll out a two-crust pie recipe and place on cookie baking sheets. With a table knife, cut the crust into long, narrow strips. Cut the strips the other way to make small squares. (Manna was round. If preferred, use a thimble as the cutter. The scraps need not be removed until the crust is baked.) Bake as you do regular pie crust, but watch closely. Keep in a sealed container until needed.

A Tall Young Man and the Lost Donkeys

1 Samuel 8:4 – 10:1

Goals: That the student (1) will discover how Saul's problem worked out to his advantage and (2) will determine to trust God to work out his problems.

Student Responses: As a result of this lesson, the student should be able to
- Describe Saul.
- Tell what Saul's problem was.
- Tell what wonderful thing happened to Saul.
- Say and explain the memory verse.

Learning Centers

Preview

The Little Donkey

MATERIALS:
Picture of a donkey
Bible picture of Jesus' triumphal entry

Most of you have seen a donkey at one time or another. Have you ever ridden on one? In what ways is it different from a horse?

A donkey is short. It measures from three to four and one-half feet to the shoulder. It has a gray or brownish coat and its ears are long. The hair on its mane is coarse and stands up. The donkey doesn't have a lock of hair over its forehead as the horse does.

In Bible times a man was considered rich if he had herds of camels, donkeys, and many oxen and sheep. He was thought to be very important if he rode a donkey. When people wanted to honor a king or reward someone special, they set him on a donkey and he rode through the city. The greatest one who did this was Jesus when He rode into Jerusalem.

In Bible times the donkey was used for traveling and carrying heavy loads. Pastures with fences around them were rare. Donkeys had to be tied or watched, or else the farmer trusted them to return to him at night.

Memory Ticket Office

"And we know that all things work together for the good to them that love God, to them who are the called according to His purpose."   Romans 8:28

THINK
1. Does the verse say that all things work good? What words did I leave out?
2. Does the verse promise that things will work out right for everyone?

LEARNING GAME
Use the chalkboard to help pupils learn the verse. (See page 5.)

AWARD
Initial tickets for those who memorized the verse.

Guidebook

Puzzle Verse Drill

MATERIALS:
One sheet and one narrow strip of construction paper
Pencil, wide felt pen, scissors
Spray adhesive and flannelgraph board

PREPARATION:
With felt pen print "TOGETHER" on the narrow strip and "FOR GOOD" on the whole sheet. Divide the sheet into six puzzle pieces. Number them and write on them the Bible references below. Spray (or use flocked or suede paper) and cut apart.

PROCEDURE:

Place the word strip on the board. Give the puzzle pieces to the students. As they find the verses, read them and arrange the pieces on the flannelboard. If desired, the students may work in pairs, with one student reading the verse and the other arranging the pieces.

The Lord causes things to work together for good for His children.

1. Psalm 37:23—He guides our steps.

2. Isaiah 58:11—He guides us continually.

3. 2 Peter 3:9—He is not slack in fulfilling His promises.

4. 1 Corinthians 2:9—He has promised more than we ever realize.

5. Psalm 107:8—We should praise Him for His goodness.

6. Galatians 6:9—We must not be weary but be patient.

Front View Adventure

Moonlight's New Home

MATERIALS:
Three puppets and stage

(Howie enters stage, whistling.)
HOWIE: I wonder where everybody is. It's sure been quiet here in the clubhouse.
(Mike enters, out of breath, nervous and carrying his hat.)

HOWIE: Well hi, Mike! What's the matter? You look as if you had lost your last friend.
MIKE: I didn't yet, but I'm going to. Guess what? My dad says we have to sell our pony?
HOWIE: You mean sell Moonlight? Oh no! You can't do that. You just got your pony cart fixed. Why does your dad want to sell him now?
MIKE: Dad doesn't really want to sell him because he knows how much Mindy and I like him. But—ah—well, you see, my Grandpa and Grandma sold their house and are moving in with us.
HOWIE: What's that got to do with selling Moonlight? I don't get it.
MIKE: Well, with our family getting bigger, we need a vegetable garden. Dad says we need Moonlight's fenced-in yard for garden space. Anyway, Grandpa likes to raise vegetables.
HOWIE: Can't you hitch Moonlight to a post some place?
MIKE: Oh, that would be mean to keep a pony tied up all of the time.
(Mindy enters, crying.)
MINDY: Ohhhhh, Mike, two boys came and looked at Moonlight, and they want to buy him. They just went home to ask their father if he will give them money to buy him. This is just awful.
HOWIE: Hey, let's not get too excited now. There must be a way. My Sunday-school teacher was talking about problems just last week. He says that even when everything bad seems to be happening to us, the Lord can make things work together for good when we love Him.
MIKE: But I can't see how selling our pony would ever be for good. If we sell him, we'll never get him back again.
(All leave.)
(Howie and Mike enter.)
HOWIE: What's new about Moonlight? Did you sell him?
MIKE: No, not yet. Maybe we won't have to. Mr. Miller says we can keep Moonlight on his farm.
HOWIE: Hey, that sounds super!
MIKE: We can even park the cart there. We can ride Moonlight any time we want to.
(Mindy enters, excited.)
MINDY: Mike, Dad says we can put our pony on Mr. Miller's farm. We're not going to sell him after all!
MIKE: *(Clap.)* Wow! Great!
MINDY: And listen—Grandpa says he will build me a treehouse above where the pony cart stood. And you can have a rabbit pen underneath.
MIKE: Well, it surely looks as if God caused things to work for the good after all. You were right, Howie. I guess we need to thank *Him.*
(All leave.)

Bible Story

A Young Man and the Lost Donkeys

The Israelites never seemed to be satisfied with what God had planned for them. They often asked their leaders to do something different even though they were warned that their plan would not work nearly as well.

One day the chief leaders came to the prophet Samuel and said, "We want a king to reign over us." They didn't need a king because they had the Lord as their wonderful guide and helper to fight their battles. They said they wanted to be like other nations around them and all other nations had kings to rule over them. This was exactly what God did not want them to be; He did not want them to be like other nations. He wanted them to be a special people.

Samuel was very displeased with the people's decision. He did the very best with the problem; he went to the Lord and prayed about it. The Lord told him that Israel wanted a king because they were disobedient and because they had rejected Him. "Listen to the people," said God. "Let them have their way. But you must warn them and let them know what a king who reigns over them will do."

Kish was an Israelite who lived in Gibeon in the land of Benjamin. He was an important man in his city, and he also was rich. He had a handsome son named Saul. Saul was very tall. In fact, he could easily be seen in a crowd because the heads of other men came just to his broad shoulders.

Saul's father owned many donkeys. When the donkeys were let out to graze, one of the servants usually watched them. But one day somehow the donkeys went far away before anyone missed them.

"Saul, we must find my donkeys," his father said. "Take a servant with you. When you locate them, round them up, and bring them back."

The fellows looked and looked for the lost donkeys. They walked across plains and around hills and hunted for the animals in grassy valleys. After three days of searching, Saul finally said, "Let's go back home. My father will be worried. Instead of worrying about the donkeys, he will be worrying about us."

The servant remembered hearing about the prophet Samuel. He lived in the town on the hill above where they stood.

"Look," said the servant, "in this town there lives an honorable prophet, a man of God. He is highly respected. Let's go there now. Perhaps he will tell us which way to go."

But Saul hesitated. Neither of them had presents to give the man of God in payment for his information. All they had was a small coin the servant had in his sack. That piece of money they would give.

Now the day before, God had spoken to the prophet Samuel. "Tomorrow at about this time of day," He had said," I will send you a man from the land of Benjamin. You shall annoint him as the king of my people."

Saul and the servant walked through the town on the right day. As they came to the gate, the Lord said to Samuel, "This is the man! I have chosen this man to reign over my people."

What a surprise Saul had when he asked the way to the prophet's house. "I am the prophet," said Samuel, "Come up and eat with me. Then tomorrow I will tell you things you must know." Samuel also said, "Don't worry about those donkeys you lost three days ago. They have been found."

Samuel had an even greater surprise for the tall man when he said, "You are the one all Israel is looking for." Young Saul was shocked and he was puzzled. He was from the tribe of Benjamin, the smallest tribe of Israel. Of what significance would his life be?

Samuel brought the two hungry men to a feast, and they ate with about thirty guests. Saul was given the most choice food and seated in the place of honor. As he ate his dinner, he must have wondered why he was receiving so much honor. He did not know that God had chosen him to be king of the people of Israel.

Very early the next morning the men started to go home. Samuel walked to the edge of town with them, and then asked Saul to send the servant on ahead. As they stood alone on the hillside, Samuel took a flask of oil and poured it on Saul's head. (This was the way kings were anointed in those days.) Then he kissed Saul and told him that the Lord had chosen him to be the captain of all Israel. Saul would be Israel's first king.

Then Samuel told Saul that after he left him, at a certain place he would meet two men. The men would tell him that his father's donkeys had been found and now his father was worrying about him instead of the donkeys. Samuel told Saul more things that would happen to him.

So Saul returned home. He told about meeting Samuel and what Samuel had said about the donkeys, but he did not tell what Samuel had said about his being the king.

Later Samuel called the people together and told them that God was going to let them have a king, and their king would be the tall young man called Saul.

Bible Story Application

What was Saul like before he became king? . . . He was tall and strong and handsome. He had been taught to be obedient and it seems he was not lazy. He was generous and kind, and probably most people liked him.

Have you ever looked for a ball that was lost, and while looking, you found something much more valuable? That is much like what happened to Saul. He went looking for donkeys, and found a kingdom. He was worried about little problems, but God had something great in store for him.

"All things work together for good" doesn't mean that all things that happen are good. But in all things God works for the good of the people who love Him and try to do His will. God uses problems in His plans for us. Like jigsaw pieces that fit together to make a beautiful picture, God's plans fit together to make our lives beautiful for Him.

Activity Book

You may need to refer to "Preview" in the "Learning Centers" section of the teacher's book for answers to the questions about the little donkey. The picture of the donkey may be colored with crayons or felt pens.

The word search reveals ten characteristics of Saul before he became king. (*Answers: handsome, generous, honest, worker, healthy, strong, obedient, tall, trusted, liked.*)

As the students do the matching quiz on the next page, they are to write in the blank the *letter* beside the right answer instead of the word or words.

Discuss Saul's problems as the children fill in the blanks at the bottom of the page. Then each child can fill in the blanks concerning his own problems.

Craft Souvenir

Mounted Puzzle

MATERIALS:
Used greeting card picture fronts of scenes, flowers, birds, etc.
Two identical cards for the teacher (optional)
Flowered or figured self-adhesive plastic
Large envelopes to hold kits
White construction paper
Scissors
Glue
Narrow felt pens or ball point pens

PROCEDURE:
Because of the various sizes of the greeting card fronts, it will be necessary to prepare individual kits for the students.

For each kit, prepare a piece of adhesive plastic the same size as the card. Cut the card into eight or ten puzzle pieces. Also cut a strip of white construction paper and on it print (or let the student print) the memory verse: "All things work together for good to them that love God" (Romans 8:28). Put all pieces in the envelope.

Let the student assemble the puzzle. Pull the paper backing away from the piece of plastic and mount the puzzle pieces on the sticky plastic. Glue the Bible verse strip to the card. If the card has printed greetings at the top, use the strip to cover them.

(OPTIONAL: The teacher may keep one identical card until all puzzles are mounted. The person who can match the card may be awarded a prize.)

As the children work on their puzzles, talk about the fact that like the jigsaw pieces that fit together to make a beautiful picture, God's plans fit together to make our lives beautiful for Him.

A King and a Frightening Letter

2 Chronicles 29 – 32; 2 Kings 18, 19

Goals: That the student (1) will know that Hezekiah's strong faith in God was rewarded and (2) will pray about his problems and know that God will answer.

Student Responses: As a result of this lesson, the student should be able to

- Tell why Hezekiah prayed to God and what he asked for.
- Tell how God answered Hezekiah's prayer.
- Answer the questions given in the section "Guidebook."
- Using the Scripture references given in the activity book, write why, when, and for what we should pray, and something he promises to pray for regularly.

Learning Centers

Preview

Walls for Defense

MATERIALS:
Picture of police and armed personnel
Bible pictures of walled cities

When there is trouble in one of our American cities, whom do we call upon for help? Sometimes the armed guard must be called in. If enemies from another country should attack us, who then would help us?

In Bible times, high walls were built around cities to protect them from their enemies. The walls were made of brick or stone. Some were of mud baked in the sun until it was hard. Some walls were very thick. the wall around the city of Jericho was so thick that houses were built on top.

The gates of the cities were heavy because they were made of thick wooden beams. Sometimes the beams were covered with metal. Strong bars were used as locks. Watch towers were built above the gates so the guards could see for a long distance. The gates were closed at night so spies could not enter. The walls around the city of Jerusalem had many gates.

Today we are going to hear about the great wall that surrounded the city of Jerusalem.

Memory Ticket Office

"He shall call upon me, and I will answer him: I will be with him in trouble; I will deliver him, and honour him."   Psalm 91:15

THINK
1. Who is speaking in this verse?
2. Before God answers our prayer, what must we do? (Call upon Him; ask Him.)
3. He will be with us in trouble. What two promises did He make in this verse? (Deliver us and honor us.)

LEARNING GAME
Once again use the chalkboard to help students learn the memory verse.

AWARD
Initial tickets for those who learned the verse.

Guidebook

Prayer Requests

Use the questions for discussion after the children have found the Bible verse and read it.

1. Psalm 6:9 – Does God always answer our prayers? (His answer is "Yes," "No," or "Wait.")
2. 1 John 3:22 – Why does God answer our

prayers? What two commandments has He given us? (verse 23)

3. Mark 11:24 – What does God want us to do when we pray?

If time permits, you may want to let the students at this learning center make prayer request booklets. You may prefer to substitute this activity for the craft souvenir suggested for today.

To prepare two copies of ten small prayer request booklets quickly and easily, lay a sheet of carbon paper between two sheets of typing paper. With ruler and pencil divide the top sheet in half the long way and into five equal lines across. Staple the ten ends of the 4½″ by 2¾″ booklets with one staple each *before* cutting apart.

Ask each student to write his prayer request on the booklet and give one copy to the teacher who can pray with him about the request during the week.

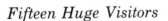

My Prayer Requests

Front View Adventure

Fifteen Huge Visitors

"This is wild animal country," said the missionary to his wife. "Do you suppose we will see a lion or maybe an elephant?"

"I wouldn't mind seeing them, but I would rather they didn't see me," she answered teasingly.

Late in the afternoon they stopped and put up their tent. Everyone was hungry and tired. Traveling after dark was not safe in that part of Africa. After supper and prayer time, the family lay down on their cots. The children went to sleep.

"Shhh! What kind of animal does that sound like?" asked Mrs. Missionary. "It's a hyena," said her husband. He went outside and shouted at the animal and then drove it away with a stick.

No sooner had they lain down again when they heard the roar of a lion coming toward the tent. The man and wife lay still and asked the Lord to keep them safe. The lion turned around and left, and soon his roaring sounded farther and farther away. Finally he was gone.

At midnight the missionaries were awakened by a strange movement of their tent. It seemed that the very ground beneath them was moving up and down. They wondered what was coming next through the tall elephant grass. The missionary arose from his mat, grabbed his gun, and stepped outside. There, in the African moonlight, surrounding the little tent were about fifteen elephants. They had been traveling single file, and when they saw the canvas shelter, they stopped to look it over. When the nearest ones saw the man, they lifted their trunks.

At first the missionary thought he would shoot. But what would one bullet do with so many? It would only make them angry. He quickly stepped back into the tent. In doing so, he tripped over the wobbly folded table and all the dishes and cooking pans fell to the ground with a crash.

"Oh! Oh! I've done it now!" he thought. "Now they will trample us all to death." But instead of charging, the elephants went on their angry way, pushing over trees and everything that was in their path.

The missionaries thanked God for sparing their lives. But they wondered what caused the elephants to leave in such a rage. Surely they were not frightened away by one man and a tent.

Worshiping Our Guide

Since today's lesson theme is prayer, place emphasis on prayer during your worship time. Use prayer songs and songs about prayer. You may want to make a few comments about prayer before the prayer time.

Quiet music: "A Mighty Fortress Is Our God"

Song: "Evening and Morning" (page 124)
Theme chorus: "Believe and Obey"
Song: "Whisper a Prayer" (page 124)
Bible reading: Psalm 55:16, 17
Prayer
Special: Teacher or child's report on an answer to prayer
Song: "Evening and Morning" (page 124) sung very softly with heads bowed and eyes closed.

"You did the right thing," said an elephant hunter when he heard their story. "Elephants' ears are sensitive to the clanging sound of tin. It frightened them away."

The missionaries went back to the United States for their furlough. While visiting in a lady's home, she told them that while doing her housework, she felt the need to stop and pray for them. So she knelt and prayed for their protection. The missionary checked his diary, and she checked the written date on her calendar. She had prayed at the very time the elephants had appeared around the little tent. How thankful the missionaries were that a lady in America had taken time to pray for them in Africa.

Bible Story

A King and a Frightening Letter

(Prepare a large card with the Bible quotation "He did that which was right in the sight of the Lord" (2 Kings 18:3) printed on it.)

A prince named Hezekiah grew up in the palace in Jersualem. His father was a wicked king who despised the Lord. When he died, Hezekiah became the new king of Judah. With such a bad father, what kind of king do you think Hezekiah was? The Bible says, "He did that which was right in the sight of the Lord." *(Hold up card.)* How do you think he learned to love and obey the Lord when he had such a wicked father? We do not know. Perhaps a prophet or his mother taught him.

When Hezekiah's father was king, he ordered the temple closed. But the year Hezekiah was crowned, he told the priests to open the doors, houseclean, and get everything ready for worship. Young Hezekiah also ordered all the idols to be destroyed. He wanted the people to worship only God. He ordered worship to begin in the temple and praises to be sung to God.

However, all was not easy for Hezekiah. Enemies lurked nearby to cause trouble. The country of Assyria had a great and powerful army and a wicked king named Sennacherib. He had come down with his soldiers into Judah and captured some of the fortified cities. The city of Jerusalem would be next!

"We are afraid of the Assyrians! They will attack us next!" said the people in Jerusalem.

Hezekiah was a wise king who depended upon God to show him what to do. He ordered the workmen to prepare the city and make it strong. They built the walls much higher and mended the holes. They even built another wall around the city. They blocked off the water from the springs outside the city so the enemies couldn't find drinking water (2 Chronicles 32:3-5). Oh how hard and fast the people worked!

When the work was completed, the good king gathered the army captains and leaders around him in the square at the city gate and encouraged them. He said, "Be strong and brave. Do not be afraid because of the king of Assyria. With us is the Lord our God to help us and fight our battles. Our enemy has only the human arm of flesh" (2 Chronicles 32:7, 8). The leaders were so glad that their king had such a great trust in God.

The day came when the Assyrian army marched up toward Jerusalem. The Assyrian soldiers were cruel. Whenever they won a battle, they tortured the leaders, killed the people they didn't take as slaves, and burned the city. Now they thought they would destroy Jerusalem.

Sennacherib sent three of his generals to Jerusalem to King Hezekiah. They called for the king, and he sent three of his officers to talk to them.

"Our king, Sennacherib, is wondering just whom King Hezekiah is trusting in," they said. "Your God will not help you. Do not listen to your king or let him persuade you to trust in your God. Don't you know what we have done to all the other nations? There is no God strong enough to deliver you out of our King Sennacherib's hands."

Some of the Jews were standing on the wall, listening. Hezekiah's officers didn't want them to hear the discouraging message the enemy general gave.

"Hush! Don't talk the language of the Jews," they said. "Speak so the people on the wall will not understand you."

But the general shouted even more loudly, "Hear the word of our great King Sennacherib. Do not trust Hezekiah. Don't let him persuade you to trust in your God. Come out and surrender. The gods of none of the other nations have been able to save their people from us. Your God can't either."

The people on the wall were silent. They did not answer the Assyrian general.

Hezekiah's three officers went to their king and told him all the Assyrian general had said.

King Hezekiah was troubled, but he trusted in God. He sent some of his men to Isaiah, God's prophet, to tell him what had happened and to ask him to pray.

Isaiah said, "Tell your master that the Lord says not to be afraid of what you have heard. God will take care of that Assyrian king."

King Sennacherib wrote a letter to King Hezekiah, and a messenger delivered it. It was a frightening letter. It contained more of the same threats and urged him and his captains to surrender.

After Hezekiah had read the letter, he took it and

traight to the temple of the Lord. He spread the letter out before the Lord. Then he knelt down and prayed. He prayed, "O Lord, God of Israel, You alone are God over all the kingdoms of the earth. Hear my prayer. Open your eyes and see. Listen to these words that Sennachrib has sent to insult You. It is true, O Lord, that the Assyrians have destroyed nations. They have destroyed the gods of those nations but those gods were only idols made of wood or stone. O Lord our God, deliver us from Sennacherib's hand, so that all the kingdoms of the earth will know that You alone are God."

The Lord heard Hezekiah's prayer and answered. He promised that the enemies would not come into the city, or even shoot an arrow against it.

That night the Lord caused 185,000 soldiers in the Assyrian army camp to die. Imagine that next morning finding 185,000 men dead! The Assyrians broke camp and left. Later Sennacherib's own sons killed him while he was in his idol temple.

Bible Story Application

"We're going to Washington, D. C.," said five-year-old Hal to his teacher. "I'm going to talk to the President of the United States!"

"You are? Did you get a formal invitation?" asked Miss Brown.

"No, I'm going to surprise him," said Hal. "I'll walk right up to his desk and say Hi."

"But just everyone can't meet with the President," said his teacher. "You have to plan ahead, and you must be invited."

If we were invited to have an audience with the President, we would wear our best clothes, and think about our manners. We would plan what to say, and maybe we would ask a favor of him.

The Lord is greater than all. He has given us a written invitation to come and talk to Him. He has said, "Call unto me, and I will answer" (Jeremiah 33:3). We can talk to God just as we are, wherever we are, and whenever we need to. He wants us to talk to Him and ask Him for what we need. Isn't that wonderful? But when we ask things of God, we must believe that He will answer (Hebrews 11:6).

Hezekiah was accustomed to praying. He had probably prayed ever since he was a little boy. Because he prayed often and had answers to his prayers, he knew that he could ask for help when he was in trouble. The Lord rewarded Hezekiah for his faith when he sent Sennacherib away and destroyed the enemy.

Activity Book

Refer to the "Preview" section of your teacher's book for information about city walls.

Ask different children to read the quotes in the cartoon at the bottom of the page.

Students will need to use their Bibles to look up the verses as they fill in the blanks. When the letters in the boxes are put together, they read, "God is in charge."

Discuss why we should pray, when we should pray, and for what we should pray. Pupils can find the verses in their Bibles and fill in the blanks. Each pupil will write his own answer concerning a particular thing or things he promises to pray for regularly.

Craft Souvenir

Elephant Stand-up Prayer Reminder

MATERIALS:
Heavy construction paper or lightweight cardboard
Scissors
Pencils and black felt pens
Elephant pattern from pattern pages of this book

PROCEDURE:
Before class time, cut a pattern of the elephant. Lay it on folded paper and prepare one animal for each child. The student may cut through both thicknesses and print "No problem is too big for God."

NOTE: You may want to lay the pattern flat (back to back) so the student does not need to cut through two thicknesses.

A Deacon Faces Danger

Acts 6, 7

Goals: That the student (1) will know that believers like Stephen must sometimes suffer for Christ, and (2) will determine to be loyal to Christ.

Student Responses: As a result of this lesson, the student should be able to

- Describe Stephen.
- Summarize Stephen's sermon.
- Tell how Stephen was loyal to Jesus.
- List some ways in which we sometimes have to suffer because of Christ.

Learning Centers

Preview

Rocky Israel

MATERIALS:
Pictures of structures and objects in which rocks were used in Israel: house, temple, wall, tower, tomb, sheepfold, olive press, grinding mill, altar, idol.

Israel is a land of many rocks. If we were to travel there today, we could see how rocky the hills are. The people of Israel used stones for all kinds of building purposes. They were a cheap material and very handy.

Rocks were used for good purposes, but they were also used for making idols. They were used for sling stones in time of war.

The Jewish people used stones as the means of capital punishment. When a Jew was worthy of death, he was taken away from the camp and killed by throwing stones on him. (Leviticus 24:13, 14)

Memory Ticket Office

"Yet if any man suffer as a Christian, let him not be ashamed; but let him glorify God on this behalf."
1 Peter 4:16

THINK
1. In what ways could a boy or girl suffer for being a Christian.
2. Should this cause a person to run and hide?
3. What does the word "glorify" mean? (Praise)

LEARNING GAME
Use the chalkboard to help the children remember the verse. (See page 5.)

AWARD
Initial the tickets for those who have learned the verse.

Guidebook

Tic-Tac-Toe Bible Drill

MATERIALS:
Chalkboard, chalk, and Bible references

PROCEDURE:
Draw the four tic-tac-toe game lines on the board. Divide the students into two teams: The MIKES and the MOONLIGHTS. A Mike teammate may draw a smiling face if he finds the Bible verse first. The Moonlight teammate may draw a horseshoe on the game square if he finds the verse first. The team to first get three symbols in a row wins.

1. Paul said that people would suffer for Christ. Philippians 1:29
2. God wants us to know He loves us very much. 1 John 4:9
3. God will help us. Psalm 46:1
4. Jesus said that people would lie about us. Matthew 5:12
5. We can talk to Him about our troubles. Hebrews 4:16

6. He will make us strong. Psalm 29:11
7. David said that God would make us strong. Psalm 118:6

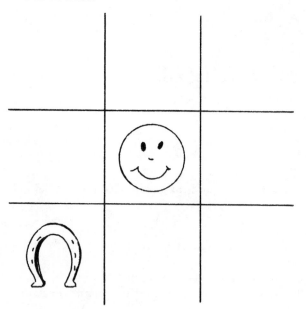

Front View Adventure

Mike's Problem

MATERIALS:
Two puppets
A sign fastened to a stick with "One Week Later" printed on it.

(Mike enters.)

MIKE: Hellooo! Anybody here? Wow! This clubhouse sure can be quiet when the gang's not around. Not even Howie is here.

(Howie enters.)

HOWIE: Hi, Mike. I had to go to the store for my mom. Say, how does your pony like his new home on Mr. Miller's farm?

MIKE: Oh, Moonlight thinks it's great. I thank God every night that we didn't have to sell him. But now I have another problem.

HOWIE: Another problem? What is it now?

MIKE: Remember that new kid who moved near us a month ago? His name is Von. He's kind of a nice guy in some ways. He likes sports and animals. He's been friendly, too.

HOWIE: I don't see any problem with that.

MIKE: Well, no—ah—well, he came up to my room a week ago and saw my Bible on my bed. That's when it started.

HOWIE: What was wrong with seeing your Bible on the bed?

MIKE: Nothing! Von didn't think so either. He looked at it and said that I had a nice Bible. He asked if I believed the Bible, and I said, "Sure." Then He asked if I was a Christian, and I said that I was.

HOWIE: That's neat. Then what happened?

MIKE: Von has been nasty ever since. Now he has some of the kids in my class on his side. Saturday they said I couldn't play ball on their team because they didn't want Christians.

HOWIE: I saw you weren't playing.

MIKE: He even got smart to Mindy. He said we were mean to Moonlight. That's not true, but some of the kids believe him.

HOWIE: The Bible says we are not to be ashamed of being Christians. Sometimes we have to suffer for Jesus. You know how He suffered on the cross for us?

MIKE: But what shall I do?

HOWIE: Pray about it. And keep reading your Bible. And be kind to Von and don't get mad. Mom says it helps to do a favor for guys like that. It's late. We'd better go. *(Both leave.)*

(The sign appears on stage. Howie and Mike return.)

HOWIE: Hi, Mike! How's it going with you and Von?

MIKE: He's nicer than he was. Mom said I should be kind even though he is rude. He needed more locker space so I let him use mine. Then his pet rooster got out the other day, and I found it for him. And guess what? I didn't get angry when he said some dumb things.

HOWIE: That's good. What are you going to try next?

MIKE: I'll invite him to our clubhouse. Next, I'm going to ask him to come to Sunday school with me. Thanks for your advice. It worked.

(Both leave.)

Worshiping Our Guide

Quiet music: "Take My Life and Let It Be"
Song: "There Is Power in Christ" (page 119)
Theme chorus: "Believe and Obey"
Song: "Oh How He loves You and Me" (page 122)
Song: "He's Able" (page 122)
Bible reading: Romans 8:31-32
Prayer
Offering and announcements
Special: "Wear a Crown"
Song: "Jesus Is My Answer" (page 125)
Song: "God of Great Power" (Unit 1 theme chorus)
Prayer

Bible Story

A Deacon Faces Danger

While Jesus was on earth, He had many long talks with His disciples. He said that He would be punished and He would suffer. When He was gone they were to continue to serve Him, but they, too, would be punished, and they would suffer because they were His followers (Matthew 10:16-20). He told them to be brave. Then He talked to the disciples about something they didn't quite understand at the time. He said the Holy Spirit was coming down from Heaven and He would give them the power and courage and the wisdom they would need (Matthew 10:20; John 14:16). After Jesus had died and gone back to Heaven, the disciples often met together to pray and to wait.

One day while they were all in one place, the Holy Spirit came down just as Jesus had promised. He came to live within them, to tell them what to preach, and to give them the power and courage they needed. Peter preached the first gospel sermon. About three thousand people believed what Peter preached about Jesus and were baptized. This was the beginning of the church.

The twelve apostles were kept very busy. Besides preaching and teaching, they were collecting money to buy food for poor Christians.

"We need helpers," said the apostles. "If we had men who would do these extra jobs, we could give full time to teaching and prayer. Let seven good men be chosen to have charge of this part of the Lord's work." The men were chosen and began their work. The names of the men are given in the Bible. One of them is Stephen. He had much faith and did wonderful miracles among the people.

(Give a student the following three questions to ask about Stephen.)

Student: Can you tell us what Stephen must have been like?

Teacher: The Bible says he was a man full of faith and of the Holy Spirit. He was a good teacher and preacher.

Student: Do you think Stephen had a lot of courage?

Teacher: Oh, yes! Stephen was very courageous. He had a strong faith in God. He was willing to suffer for the Lord if it was necessary.

Student: You said that Stephen did miracles. Tell us about that.

Teacher: The Holy Spirit, who lived inside him, gave him the power to do the miracles. When the enemies of Jesus saw these wonders happening and noticed how many were believing in Jesus, they were angry. *(Student may sit with class.)*

"We can't let this work go on," spoke the enemies roughly. "We must do something to upset and confuse this leader."

First they argued with Stephen but couldn't prove he was wrong. Then they lied to the people about him, saying he spoke against Moses and God. This was a plot to get Stephen before the Jewish council so they could sentence him to die. He could have defended himself and said the enemies were telling lies. He could have shouted back at them and tried to correct them. But instead Stephen remained calm. He knew that God was in control.

Finally the high priest asked if the things of which they were accusing him were true.

Stephen looked toward the crowd and said, "Brothers and fathers, listen to me!" Then he preached one of the finest sermons in the Bible. He spoke about Abraham's faith when he left Ur of the Chaldees to go to a land he had not seen. He told how Moses was used of God to lead the Israelites to their homeland in Canaan. He reminded his listeners of how their fathers of ancient times had refused to listen to God, but worshiped idols instead, and killed the prophets who told of the coming of Christ. He told his accusers that now they had killed Christ, the Righteous One.

This sermon made the Jewish leaders furious! They were so angry at Stephen that they gritted their teeth and said evil things.

At that moment in the council room Stephen looked up to Heaven and saw the glory of God and Jesus standing at the right hand of God.

When the Jewish leaders heard this, they shouted loudly and held their hands against their ears. Then they grabbed Stephen and dragged him outside the city wall.

"Pick up rocks and throw at him!" they probably screamed to one another. Some of them wore long, flowing robes and the long sleeves were in the way. They took off their robes and laid them down at the feet of a young man whose name was Saul.

One by one, the rocks hit against Stephen's body with a thud. He knew that soon he would die, but he was not afraid. He called upon God to receive his spirit. Finally the blows were so severe and painful that he knelt down and cried with a loud voice, "Lord, do not punish these people for this sin."

Stephen died of the blows from his enemies. But, though his body lay on the stony ground, the real Stephen went to be with the Lord.

Bible Story Application

Had Stephen done anything to deserve to be killed? No, of course not. We feel sad when we realize that evil people can behave so cruelly toward those who are righteous and fair.

What is the name given to those who die for a godly cause? ... Yes, they are called martyrs. *(Write the word on the chalkboard.)* Stephen was the first Christian martyr. Sometimes missionaries have given their lives in this way. *(You may want to give examples.)*

Probably most of us will not be called upon to give our lives in this way. But the Bible tells us that at times we will suffer in other ways if we are determined to be loyal to Jesus (Philippians 1:29). No matter where we go to live, there are those in the town who hate God. They do not throw rocks on us as Stephen's enemies did, but they may say mean things or lie about us. Stinging words can hurt in a different way. Mean tricks can be played on us to try to turn us away from being true to Jesus. But the Lord doesn't forget His followers. He will help us. He will cause us to win (1 Corinthians 15:57).

The Bible tells us that if we are asked to suffer for Christ, we are not to be ashamed (1 Peter 4:16).

David said he wasn't afraid what men could do to him (Psalm 118:6). Stephen wasn't either. And we don't need to be afraid if we belong to the Lord.

Stephen was loyal to the Lord. I want to be loyal to Him too. Don't you?

Activity Book

If you did not use "Preview" in the "Learning Centers" section of this lesson, you will need to share some of the information concerning the use of stones in Bible times before students do the activity. After you have discussed the use of stones, look at the poem. Included in it are nine ways stones were used in Bible times. Students may use the word bin if they need to as they fill in the blanks. When everyone has finished, read the poem, letting the students supply the missing words.

(Answers to the "Stephen" quiz at the bottom of the page are martyr, faith, teacher, preacher, courage, miracles, loyal, die.)

You may want to do "Answers From Acts" as a group or individually. If you do the activity as a group, ask the students to find the verse and one to read it aloud. Then all fill in the blanks. If you prefer that students work individually, give help as needed to younger children.

The code for the puzzle on the next page uses all the letters of the alphabet and the numbers from one to twenty-six. *(The answer is "death rather than give up his faith.")*

Use "Because" and "Think" as the students fill in the blanks at the bottom of the page.

Craft Souvenir

My Strength Box

MATERIALS:
One small empty safety match box (or similar drawer box)
Lightweight construction paper, typing paper
One reinforcement ring, scissors, glue
Alphabet-soup noodle letters

PROCEDURE:
Cover the outside of the box with construction paper. Glue ends.

Glue soup letters "My Strength Box" on the top. For decoration, a shell or flower may be glued beside the letters.

Cut a long strip of typing paper and accordion-fold it so it will lie in the drawer. On the left-hand end, attach a reinforcement ring. Print on the folds of the strip the following verses: 1 Peter 4:16; Psalm 118:6; and Psalm 46:1. Glue the other end to the bottom of the box, refold, and place inside so the reinforcement ring is on the outside.

Alternative: The letters on the box may be printed with a pen to save time.

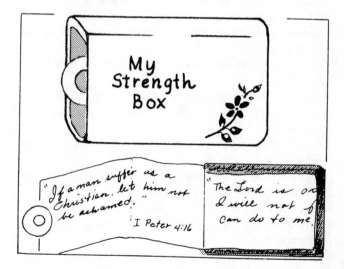

A Partner in a Deceitful Scheme

Genesis 25:20-34; 27; 28:1-5

Goals: (1) That the student will know that the Lord forgave Jacob but the results of his disobedience remained. (2) That the student will depend upon Christ to help him to be obedient.

Student Responses: As a result of this lesson, the student should be able to

- Describe Esau and Jacob.
- Tell what Jacob did that was wrong.
- List some of the results of Jacob's lie.
- Tell why it is better to do right even though God forgives us when we do wrong.
- Say the memory verse.

Learning Centers

Preview

A Special Treasure

MATERIALS:
A treasured inherited item (ring, picture, dish)
A card on which "birthright" has been printed

PROCEDURE:
(*Show the inherited item and explain why it is considered a treasure.*)

Are you the oldest child in your family? If you are, you probably have more responsibilities than your younger brothers and sisters have. You also have more privileges, such as staying up a little longer in the evening, owning a bigger bike, and choosing more of your clothes.

In Bible times, the oldest son in the family usually inherited the privilege of possessing a precious treasure. It was called a birthright. It was the right he received because he was born first. Because he had the birthright, he was to receive a double portion, or amount, of the inheritance. He also received special blessings. He had more power in making family de-

cisions. It was his right as he grew older to take his father's place.

If the son was in the king's family, he would be the next king. Every boy and man protected his birthright because he knew it was a special blessing.

Memory Ticket Office

"And thou shalt do that which is right and good in the sight of the Lord: that it may be well with thee."
Deuteronomy 6:18

THINK
1. How does the verse describe the two things we should do in the sight of the Lord?
2. What is promised if we do these?

LEARNING GAME
Print portions of the verse on strips of paper to be placed in a pocket chart. See page 5 for directions for making the chart.

AWARD
Initial the tickets for those who memorized the verse.

Guidebook

Treasure Chests

MATERIALS:
Six pieces of yellow construction paper
Felt-tip marker and pen

PROCEDURE:
Fold the papers in half and lay them so the fold is at the top. With the marker, design treasure chest covers. Lift the covers and print the following six Bible references. Pass the chests to the students and ask them not to look inside until it is their turn. Divide the class into pairs. One student may read

the statement and reference, and the other student may find and read the verse.

1. Our obedience pleases the Lord. – Matthew 25:21
2. Our obedience brings peace. – Philippians 41:9
3. Our obedience gives happiness. – John 13:17
4. Our obedience saves us from trouble. – Revelation 3:10
5. Our obedience brings peace from enemies. – Proverbs 16:7
6. It will go well with us when we obey. – Jeremiah 42:6

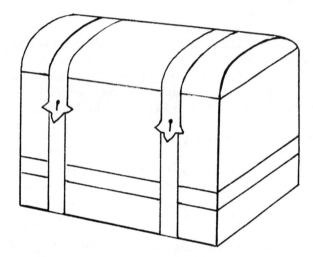

Front View Adventure

Dana's Disobedience

(Bring to class something nice that has been damaged through carelessness. It should be something that is still useful, such as a good book that a child has scribbled on, a repaired vase, or a scratched musical instrument. Explain that the item is useful, but it can not be the same as before, even though an effort was made to renew it.)

"It's total eclipse of the sun tomorrow, and I'm going to watch it," said Dana.

""Oh, no you're not," her mother said firmly.

"Why not? It sounds like fun. Then some day I'll write an essay about my experiences," the girl replied.

"You can watch, but you must not look directly at the sun. All radio and TV reporters warn us that people can ruin their eyes; it can cause blindness," warned her mother.

"That sure is a goofy idea," Dana retorted. "Just think how many miles away the sun is from the earth! No way could it damage my eyes. I'll not look at the eclipse all the time."

Dana called her friend, Cam, and she also said it was dangerous to watch the eclipse of the sun, except for a quick glance once in a while.

Dana's Sunday-school teacher visited in their home that evening, and she said it was dangerous. She said, "Dana, you plan to be a missionary some day. You must take care of your eyes so you can do your best work for the Lord."

But still the girl didn't mind. She went to the park where her mother wouldn't see her. She lay on the grass and watched the sun as slowly the moon came between it and the earth. She thought she was careful enough to get by because she looked away frequently and rested her eyes.

Can you guess what happened? The sun's hot rays burned her eyes so that she no longer had good forward vision. She had side vision and her eyes improved as they healed, but never again could she see as well as she did before. She asked God to forgive her, and He did, but for the rest of her life she must live with a problem caused by disobedience.

Worshiping Our Guide

Quiet music: "Trust and Obey"
Song: "Jesus, I Believe in You" (page 123)
Theme chorus: "Trust and Obey"
Song: "Like a Shepherd" (page 121)
Bible reading: 1 Corinthians 6:19-20
Prayer
Offering and accouncements
Solo: "My Jesus, as Thou Wilt"
Song: "Submission"
Prayer

Bible Story

A Partner in a Deceitful Scheme

(Involve a student for this short character study.)

Teacher: Our Bible story is about twin boys who were different. They looked different. They acted differently, and from the time they were small, they had different interests. Their parents' names were Isaac and Rebekah. Do you remember them?

Child: Isaac's father sent his servant to find a wife for his son, and he found Rebekah at a well. He brought her back on a camel.

Teacher: Yes, and God gave them twin sons. Their names were Esau and Jacob. Esau was born first.

Child: What was Esau like?

Teacher: He was healthy and strong. The Bible tells us that he had a lot of hair—not only on his head, but on his arms, hands, and legs. He loved the out-of-doors, and he loved to hunt. Because he was the older, he had the treasured birthright.

Child: What was Jacob like?

Teacher: Jacob was not at all like Esau. He didn't like hunting and roaming around out-of-doors. He preferred staying around their home. He was a quiet man and a hard worker. Jacob loved God, but he didn't like to wait for God's plan. (Child is seated.)

Isaac's favorite son was Esau, but Rebekah's favorite son was Jacob. The birthright usually belonged to the oldest son, but Esau was careless with his treasured possession. Before the babies were born, God had told Rebekah that some day the birthright would be given to the second son.

One day Esau came from the field, tired and hungry. Jacob was cooking a pot of tasty red beans, called pottage. The aroma was pleasing to Esau.

"Jacob, feed me, I pray. Let me have your red pottage for I am so hungry that I am about to faint," said Esau.

Jacob thought, "Oh! Here's my chance to get the birthright."

"Sell me your birthright, and I will give you my pottage," he said.

Esau quickly answered, "Look, I'm so faint from hunger that I'm about to die. I will sell it." His precious birthright, which gave him the right to have his father's special blessing and a double portion of the inheritance, was exchanged for a bowl of red beans.

Years went by and Isaac was old. His eyesight was very poor. He called Esau to him and said, "I am old. Go out and kill some venison and make me a tasty meal that I may die. Then I will give you my blessing."

Rebekah stood at the tent door and heard what Isaac told Esau. God had told her that Jacob would inherit the birthright as well as the blessing. But she decided to take things into her own hands. Her scheme was to be deceiving.

"Jacob, run quickly and bring two young goats for me. I heard your father tell Esau to get venison and make him a savory meat. After he eats, he will bless your brother with the special blessing." His mother spoke softly as she continued, "This must not happen! You must have the blessing. Get the goats and I will cook the meal. Hurry!"

Jacob reminded his mother that Esau's arms and hands were hairy but his were smooth. When his father felt of him he would know that Jacob had deceived him and would curse him instead of blessing him. But Rebekah only replied, "Let the curse be upon me. Just do what I say."

Jacob killed the goats and his mother prepared the meal. Then she took pieces of hairy goat skin and fastened them over her son's hands and arms. Jacob took the meal to his father.

"Here I am, Father," said Jacob.

"Yes, my son," said Isaac. "Who is it?"

"I am Esau, your oldest son. I have done what you told me. Here is your meal. Eat it and bless me," was Jacob's sly answer to his old, nearly blind father.

Isaac asked to feel of his son's hands and arms. They were like the older son's body, but the voice was Jacob's. So Isaac asked, "Are you really my son Esau?" Jacob lied and said, "I am." Isaac ate the meal and then blessed Jacob. After the blessing, Jacob proudly walked away from his father—and Esau came in from the field with his meal of venison.

"Who are you?" asked Isaac.

"I am Esau," replied the older son as he set the food before Isaac.

Both Isaac and Esau knew that Jacob had deceived his father, but it was too late. Isaac could not take back the blessing. For this, Esau hated Jacob and was determined to kill him after his father died.

Rebekah knew of Esau's plan. She sent Jacob away to stay with her brother. She hoped that he would need to stay only a few weeks, until Esau overcame his anger. But Jacob was gone for twenty years.

The Lord loved Jacob, but Jacob had many problems. He had to escape from his angry brother because of his dishonesty. He worked for his Uncle Laban and was not paid. Once he was given the wrong wife. Finally, when he returned to his father's land, he had a frightening experience. Esau met him, and with him were four hundred soldiers on horseback. Jacob was sure his brother had come to kill him, but when Esau saw his brother he forgave him. Jacob had to face many problems the rest of his life.

Bible Story Application

The sin of Jacob was not that he received the birthright and special blessing that belonged to his older brother, but that he was deceitful and lied. He should have waited to see how the Lord would work things out. If he had said, "No, Mother, I do not wish to deceive Father. Let us wait," probably the next twenty years of his life would have been different.

Was Jacob happy after he had his own way! No! He had many unhappy times. Once Moses said to the Israelites, "Be sure your sin will find you out" (Number 32:23). He meant that people cannot keep doing wrong and not be found out.

Did God forgive Jacob? Yes. He even changed his name to Israel, which means "Prince of God" (Genesis 32:27, 28).

God is ready to forgive us also. But it is much better to do things that are right, good, and obedient from the very start. That will save us a lot of future trouble. Jesus once told His disciples that when they knew to do right, they would be happy if they would do it (John 13:17).

Activity Book

If the children need help in working the crossword puzzle, they can use the words listed in the Word Bank. Each student will work on his own as he writes in "Dear Diary."

After the students have matched the pictures and sentences, review the Bible story as you check the answers together.

After the children have completed "Wanted, Your Advice," discuss the answers.

Give help as needed as the children find the Bible verses and fill in the blanks. Review the memory verse.

Craft Souvenir

Pencil Holder

MATERIALS:
Small frozen juice cans
Plain (not vinyl) wallpaper or construction paper
Braid
Scissors, pencil, and glue
Stickers or seals
Felt scraps

PROCEDURE:
Cut a strip of paper to cover the can. Glue the ends in place. Glue on braid at the top and decorate the sides with stickers. Cut a felt circle to fit the bottom of the inside of the can, and glue in place.

A King Who Disobeyed

1 Samuel 11:15; 18

Goals : That the student (1) will learn how King Saul's disobedience led to other sins and (2) will determine to behave wisely and obey promptly.

Student Responses : As a result of this lesson, the student should be able to

- List two ways in which King Saul disobeyed.
- Describe Saul after he became king.
- Give one example of how doing one wrong thing led to another.
- Say the memory verse.

Learning Centers

Preview

Kings, Crowns, and Thrones

MATERIALS:
Bible pictures of a king and a throne
A headband or turban trimmed with braid and studded with "jewels" from costume jewelry.

PROCEDURE:
We are going to hear about Israel's first king. It isn't likely that any of you have shaken hands with a king, or even seen one, except on television. The word "king" means "chief ruler." Every nation or tribe has a chief person, but few are called kings today.

When a man in Israel or Judah was chosen to be king, he knelt down and a priest or prophet annointed him by pouring oil on his head. He was then crowned king.

Crowns were not always the kind with points at the top like those we see in pictures. Some were headbands or turbans. They were usually decorated with beautiful braids and precious jewels. The crown was usually worn only when the king was sitting on his throne, or during special ceremonies.

The throne was a fancy chair with carvings, or gold plate or trim. Some thrones had ivory on them. The throne was elevated so the king was higher than the people who came before him. This helped him to show authority. Kings of Persia held short wooden or gold-plated rods in their hands. They were called scepters. A king sat on his throne when he was judging the people or making great decisions.

Memory Ticket Office

"But be ye doers of the word, and not hearers only, deceiving your own selves." James 1:22

THINK
1. What is another name for the Word?
2. Is it enough just to hear the Word?
3. How could we deceive ourselves?

LEARNING GAME
Pocket chart with the words and phrases printed on strips of paper. (See directions on page 5.)

AWARD
Initial the tickets for those who memorized the verse.

Guidebook

Sins Grow and Hurt
"They Disobeyed" Bible Drill

(Set dominoes on end, one behind the other so when the first one is pushed over, all will fall.)

Hazel bounced her ball on the kitchen floor. She had been told not to do this because she might break something. She thought that she would be careful, so she kept the ball low. But one time it bounced high. When she reached for it, she pushed it against the wall. The ball knocked down her mother's best wall plate and it broke. When her mother came home, Hazel told her that she had found the plate on the floor when she came home from school. What two disobedient things did Hazel do? (*Demonstrate with dominoes how one sin can lead to another.*)

If time permits, you may want to use this Bible drill concerning people who disobeyed the Lord. (See page 5 for Bible drill rules.)
1. Genesis 3:6 – The first to disobey.
2. Genesis 4:8 – A brother kills a brother.
3. Genesis 27:19 – A son deceives his father.
4. Genesis 32:1 – The Israelites disobey God.
5. 1 Kings 11:4 – A king forsakes God.
6. Matthew 26:73-75 – A disciple denies his Lord.
7. Acts 5:1-3 – A man and wife cheat the church.

Front View Adventure

Bragging Butch

MATERIALS:
Two puppets
Piece of blanket rolled like a sleeping bag

(Howie and Mike enter.)

HOWIE: Hi, Mike. I saw you come, riding on Moonlight.

MIKE: I brought back your sleeping bag that I borrowed to take to camp. Thanks a lot. I had a lot of fun. Had a neat counselor, too.

HOWIE: That's super! Did you make some new friends at camp?

MIKE: Oh, sure. *(Pause.)* We had a guy in our cabin named Butch. He was always bragging about himself. Everything we had or talked about, he would say "That's nothin – mine is better."

HOWIE: Didn't your counselor correct him?

MIKE: Yes, Chuck told him the Bible says that the person who boasts of a false gift is like clouds and wind without rain. He warned him that his boasting would cause him to do other wrong things. It did, too.

HOWIE: Tell me about it.

MIKE: I was telling the kids about my pony. Butch began to brag about his pony. He said Prancer was a beautiful black pony. He was so good that he could keep him in the garage. He said Prancer was nicer than Moonlight."

HOWIE: He probably is nice.

MIKE: His sister was at camp too, so we asked her if she ever rode Prancer. Beth said she was too big now. Prancer was the wooden hobby horse Butch played with when he was a little boy.

HOWIE: *(Both laugh.)* His bragging caused him to be deceiving, didn't it?

MIKE: I passed my canoeing test. Butch said that was nothing. He had won a prize in a row-boat race. He took me out on the lake in a row boat and it was awful; he couldn't row well at all.

HOWIE: That put a stop to his bragging, didn't it?

MIKE: No, it didn't. And it got him in trouble, too. He said he couldn't row well that day because a bee stung him under his arm and it hurt. You should have seen him walking around all afternoon with his elbow sticking out, away from his body. Chuck finally made him go to the nurse. She said there was no sign of a bee sting. Then he said he was just pretending.

HOWIE: I think I'd call that lying.

MIKE: Most of us had less than ten dollars spending money. Butch said that was nothing; he had twenty dollars. Later Beth said their dad had given each of them six dollars. Butch bought a lot of treats the first day. After that, he was always coaxing us to treat him. He didn't put anything in the camp offering plate either. But the last day he had a lot of money to spend.

HOWIE: Where did he get it?

MIKE: The leaders discovered that he was the one who had stolen money from a little kid.

HOWIE: The Bible says, "Be sure your sin will find you out." Even bragging can cause us to do other wrong things.

MIKE: Right! We all learned from Butch's experience. That night he asked God to forgive him for bragging, lying, and stealing. He also became a Christian. I've got to get Moonlight back to the farm. Let's go. *(Both leave.)*

(Note: A tape recording of a horse walking on a road would add interest.)

Worshiping Our Guide

Quiet music: "Savior, Like a Shepherd, Lead Us"
Song: "Whisper a Prayer" (page 124)
Theme chorus: "Trust and Obey"
Song: "There Is Power in Christ" (page 119)
Bible reading: Isaiah 50:7
Prayer
Special music: Instrumental number
Song: "Jesus Is My Answer" (page 125)
Song: "Thy Word Have I Hid in My Heart"
  (page 126)
Prayer

Bible Story

A King Disobeys
(An Interview with Samuel)

CHARACTERS:
Narrator
Samuel (A man, wearing a robe and a headpiece.)

NARRATOR: Have you ever wished that you could talk to some of the people who lived during Bible times? If you could, to whom besides Jesus would you like to speak? Would it be Moses, or David, or Paul?... Today we are going to pretend that Samuel is here. I will ask him questions that I think you might like to ask.

NARRATOR: Samuel, when you were a little boy, your mother took you to the tabernacle to live.

SAMUEL: Yes, Hannah gave me to the Lord and I grew up in the Lord's house. While there, the Lord told me He wanted me to be a prophet, a messenger for Him.

NARRATOR: One day the leaders of Israel told you they wanted a king. Why did they insist upon having their way?

SAMUEL: They wanted to be like other nations. I didn't want them to have a king, because I knew that some day they would be sorry. The Lord told me to warn them, but give them what they wanted. He chose Saul, and I annointed that tall young man as the first king of Israel.

NARRATOR: How did Saul do as a king?

SAMUEL: He had a good beginning. A cruel king named Nahash and his army came to fight the people in a town of Israel called Jabesh. They were so afraid that they said they would surrender. "I'll not fight you," said Nahash, "but my soldiers will put out your right eyes."

When Saul heard about this, the Spirit of the Lord came upon him and made him brave. He gathered together thousands of soldiers, fought the battle, and won. He saved many people's eyes.

NARRATOR: The people in Israel were happy about that.

SAMUEL: They respected their new king. They thought he was a hero. Later he made a bad mistake. Years ago when the Israelites were traveling through the wilderness after they left Egypt, the Amalekites were very cruel to them. God said He would punish them for the cruel things they did. God told me to tell Saul to fight the Amalekites. He was to see that everything the enemies owned was destroyed. Even the animals were to die. Saul did fight the Amalekites, but he disobeyed and brought all the good animals back to the camp and kept them.

NARRATOR: How was King Saul punished for his disobedience?

SAMUEL: I had to tell him the bad news. The Lord was not going to allow him or his sons to be king. God chose a shepherd boy to be the next king of Israel. I went to Bethlehem and annointed David.

NARRATOR: David didn't rule for a long time, did he?

SAMUEL: No, he didn't rule Israel for many years. When he was young, he killed Goliath. This wonderful victory thrilled the people everywhere. When Saul and his army marched back home after the war was over, the women came out and put on a happy demonstration. They sang and danced and played timbrels to honor him. "Saul has killed his thousands and David has killed his ten thousands", was their song.

NARRATOR: Saul didn't like to hear that, did he?

SAMUEL: He was angry. Then he became jealous. One sin added to another. "Hear what the women are saying about me," he grumbled.

NARRATOR: Didn't Saul ask David to come to the palace to live?

SAMUEL: Saul kept disobeying the Lord and wanting his own way. There were nights when he couldn't sleep because of his troubled thoughts. His servants suggested that they find someone who could play soft music for him to soothe his nerves. David could sing beautifully, and play a harp. So David often played and sang for Saul.

NARRATOR: Those were difficult times for David, were they not?

SAMUEL: Yes, Saul tried to kill David many times, but the Lord always kept David safe. Once when David was playing his harp, Saul drew his javelin and threw it at him. David dodged the spear and it pierced the wall behind him. After that, the king made many attempts upon the young fellow's life.

NARRATOR: Tell us more about Saul. You knew him so well.

SAMUEL: Saul was very good-looking, very handsome. Before he was king, he was kind and thoughtful and could be trusted. After he became king, he disobeyed the Lord's commands. He developed a temper, and insisted upon having his own way. He was jealous, and this led to the desire to murder. Once he was brave, but finally he became afraid.

Bible Story Application

Saul had a good beginning. But after he became king, he wanted his own way above the Lord's way. He allowed jealously to slip into his heart. This led to anger, and his anger and jealously led to a desire to murder. It seems that one sinful thing brought on another and another, until Saul's whole life was messed up. He became a miserable man. He knew how to do right but refused to do it. James 4:17 says this attitude is sinful.

Can you think of times when you did wrong and one bad thing led to another? ... Maybe you did something unkind to a friend when no one else was around. When you were corrected, you lied by denying that you did it. Then you became very angry at your friend because he repeated what you did or said. Then you no longer treated him as a friend.

Remember our memory verse? Who can say it? We are to be doers of the Word and not hearers only.

Activity Book

If you did not use "Preview" as a learning center today, discuss the material in that section before the children do the first activity in their books.

(*The answer to the decoded secret message is "It is very important that I obey the Lord."*)

(*The answers to the fill-in-the-blanks quiz on the next page are 1. nations; 2. Samuel, Saul, king (or captain); 3. right; 4. foolishly, keep (or obey); 5. sheep, oxen (or fatlings, lambs); 6. rejected; 7. jealous, ten thousands; 8. David; 9. harp, javelin; 10. afraid, Lord.*)

After the children have completed "The Message for Me," discuss the answers.

Craft Souvenir

String Puppet

MATERIALS:
Crayons, white construction paper
Ruler and black felt pen
Pattern of string puppet from pattern pages

PROCEDURE:
Trace the string puppet onto the paper. Print "Lord, help me to behave wisely" on the bottom. Color the puppet. With ruler and pen, mark the manipulating strings from the hands and feet to the top of the page.

Lord, help me to behave myself wisely

A Man Inside a Living Submarine

Jonah 1-4

Goals: That the student (1) will know how Jonah learned obedience and (2) will want to obey the Lord even when it is not easy.

Student Responses: As a result of this lesson, the student should be able to

• Tell what God asked Jonah to do.
• Tell how Jonah disobeyed.
• Describe the two ways in which God taught Jonah a lesson.
• List two good characteristics of Jonah and two bad ones.
• List times when obeying is not easy.

Learning Centers

Preview

The Whale and Map Study

MATERIALS:
A map of the ancient world
Picture of a whale (One can be found in the *National Geographic* magazine, August, 1984.)

PROCEDURE:
Today's Bible story is about a prophet who was told by the Lord that he was to go to Nineveh, but he decided to take a ship that sailed in the opposite direction. (*On the map, locate Nineveh and the costal city of Joppa. Locate Tarshish (Tartassus), probably the city in Spain to which the prophet expected to sail.*)

(*Show the students the picture of a whale.*) These sea mammals are warm-blooded, breathe air, have babies by birth, and grow to huge proportions. Some species are as much as sixty feet or longer. They have great heads and wide mouths.

The creature that swallowed Jonah was a fish. Be-

cause the Lord prepared it, it could have been even larger than a whale.

Memory Ticket Office

"If ye know these things, happy are ye if ye do them." John 13:17

THINK
1. Who spoke these words? (Jesus)
2. If we know how to obey Jesus, what shall we do about it?

LEARNING GAME
Use the pocket chart, three-inch tall stiff paper strips, and a felt marker. Divide the verse into words, phrases, and reference. Print them on the strips. As the verse is taught, remove the strips, one at a time, until the verse is memorized. Mix the strips on the chart and let the students put them in order.

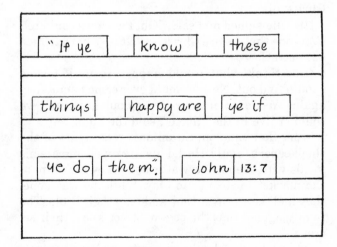

AWARD
Initial tickets for those who memorized the verse.

Guidebook

They Obeyed the Lord

Refer to page 5 for Bible Drill rules.
1. Luke 5:27, 28 – A publican obeyed the Lord.
2. Mark 10:28 – Peter obeyed the Lord.
3. Acts 11:20, 21 – Many in Antioch obeyed the Lord.
4. John 1:37 – Two disciples obeyed the Lord.
5. Matthew 8:27 – Wind and sea obeyed the Lord.
6. Luke 5:11 – Fishermen obeyed the Lord.
7. Matthew 16:24 – Christians are to obey the Lord.

Front View Adventure

Swamidoss

"Please, Sir, may I work for you?" asked a ten-year-old boy as he stood before a shopkeeper in faraway India.

"Where are your parents?" the shopkeeper asked. "I cannot hire a boy without knowing something about his family. What is your name?"

"My name is Swamidoss. My parents are from the same caste as you. They are poor, and they will be glad to have me earn my food and clothing," answered the boy.

The shopkeeper agreed to take the boy as a servant and provide him with food and clothing as his pay. That afternoon Swamidoss went to his new home on the west side of the village.

"We will have to have our family devotions at a time when we can send the boy to the market," said the shopkeeper. "Then he will not know that we are Christians."

His wife sighed and said, "Oh, I wish we could tell everyone that we are Christians. It is so hard to hide our secret."

"But think what would happen to us if people should find out. No one would ever come to our shop again. We would have to give up our home and we couldn't live in the village", said the man.

From that time on, Swamidoss was a part of the shopkeeper's family. He did his work well and ate his meals with them. Every afternoon they sent him to the market to shop or to play. While he was gone, they had their prayer time and read their Bible. The family agreed that the boy must not know their secret.

One night the shopkeeper was awakened from a sound sleep. At first he thought he was dreaming. He sat up and listened. He thought he was hearing an angel singing from the other side of the house. The angel was singing "Jesus loves me; this I know."

The shopkeeper left his bed and followed the voice to the other part of the house. It led him right to the servant boy's bedside.

Swamidoss was frightened half to death. He was so afraid that he couldn't speak.

"Where did you learn that song?" asked the man.

"In the mission school, Sir. Oh, I must tell you that I love Jesus. I am a Christian," Swamidoss answered with a trembling voice. "They told us such wonderful things, and read to us from the Bible. They told us about the true God and that Jesus is God's Son, and I know they are right."

"Boy, we love Jesus, too" said the shopkeeper. "We have been sending you to the market while we had our devotions. We were afraid you would tell the village people about us."

"I have sung softly and prayed every night," said Swamidoss. "But tonight Jesus seemed to tell me that I must sing more loudly, and I obeyed, even though I was afraid."

The shopkeeper said, "God must have helped me to awaken so that I would hear you. No more will you be sent to the market. From now on you will join our family in our prayer time." From that time on a happy Swamidoss became a part of a happy Christian family.

Worshiping Our Guide

Quiet music: "Trust and Obey"
Song: "Submission" (page 127)
Theme chorus: "Trust and Obey"
Song: "Step by Step" (page 118)
Bible reading: Luke 6:46-49
Prayer
Offering and announcements
Special music: "I'll Put Jesus First in My Life"
Song: "Thy Word Have I Hid in My Heart
   (page 126)
Prayer

Bible Story

Inside a Living Submarine

Far to the northeast of Judah was the great city of Nineveh. It was a splendid city where over half a million people lived. They were proud of their high wall with its many gates, and the palaces, and towers. But they were a very wicked people. And to make it even worse, they were teaching their children their sinful ways.

God decided to send a messenger to warn the people of Nineveh that because of their wickedness, He would destroy their city.

The Lord called His prophet Jonah to take the message. God said, "Arise and go to the great city of Nineveh. Preach against it. For I have seen its wickedness."

But Jonah did not want to go to Nineveh. He did not want to preach to those people who were the enemies of his country. He didn't want to obey God.

"I'll run away from the Lord," he said. "I'll go across the sea to another country."

Jonah hurried down to the seaport in Joppa. To his delight, he found a ship docked in the harbor. The sailors were loading freight, and the captain said they were sailing to Tarshish. This was in the opposite direction of Nineveh. Jonah thought this would take him far away from God, so he paid his fare and went below the deck. Soon he was asleep.

Of course God knew exactly where Jonah was. God loved Jonah but hated his disobedience. He decided to teach him that it is best to obey.

God sent a furious storm that swept across the sea. It caused huge waves to dash against the little ship. To keep the ship from sinking, the sailors began to thrown the cargo overboard. In their fear, they called upon their false gods to help them.

"Wake up, you sleepy head!" screamed the captain when he found the prophet below the deck. "The ship is about to break apart! How can you sleep? Get up and call on your God to save us! Maybe He will keep us from dying."

The sailors tried to find out who on board was the cause of all this trouble. At last Jonah confessed. He had run away from the true God. The storm was sent because of his disobedience.

"Throw me overboard! Then the storm will be over," said Jonah.

The sailors didn't wish to put their passenger into the sea. They tried hard to bring the ship to safety. But finally they lifted Jonah up and let him fall into the dashing waves. Immediately the wind ceased and the water became calm.

As for Jonah, God had prepared a great fish that sucked the prophet into its stomach. It was a terrible experience, and Jonah almost died. It was a long time to stay in a living submarine. During his conscious hours, he prayed, "I will pay that which I have promised. I will obey. Salvation comes from the Lord." Not long after his prayer, God caused the fish to throw Jonah out on the shore.

Again God told the prophet to go to Nineveh, and this time he obeyed. He went to Nineveh. The city was so large that it took three days to walk through it. Jonah walked through the great and wicked city, shouting over and over, "In forty days Nineveh will be destroyed. In forty days Nineveh will be destroyed." The citizens stopped and listened to Jonah. They believed the message was from the true God, and they began to be ashamed of their sins.

Someone ran to the palace and told the king, and he believed the message. He rose from his throne, took off his royal robe, put on sackcloth, and sat down in the dust. He told the people not even to taste food, but to put on sackcloth and pray and turn from their evil ways. He said, "Perhaps the Lord will spare our lives." Our loving Lord saw that the people of Nineveh were ashamed of their wickedness. He would not destroy the city after all.

Jonah went outside the city and built a shelter of leaves to sit under. He was waiting to see what would happen next. To shade Jonah from the scorching sun, God caused a gourd vine to grow up overnight and cover his shelter. The gourd vine made a shade to protect Jonah's head from the scorching sun. Jonah was very happy to have that gourd vine. But the next morning God sent a little cutting worm to nibble at the stalk until the vine withered and died. Next God sent a scorching wind. The hot wind blew and the hot sun blazed down on Jonah's head, and he almost fainted. "I'd rather die than endure this!" he cried.

Instead of rejoicing that the people had repented, Jonah was displeased and angry with God. He complained about the gourd vine wilting and taking away his shade.

"Do you have a right to be angry about the vine?" God asked Jonah.

"I do," said Jonah. "I'm angry enough to die."

Then God said, "You have been worried about this vine which you didn't even plant or help to grow. Think of the thousands of little children who would die if I destroyed Nineveh."

What do you think traveling with Jonah would have been like? You would have been able to really know Jonah. You would have learned that he believed in God and knew He was the great Creator. He wasn't afraid to die, so he had a strong faith in God. He said that salvation comes from the Lord. He was selfish and proud, and he had a temper. Later Jesus used the example of Jonah's being in the fish as the length of time the Savior would be in the grave (Matthew 12:40, 41).

Bible Story Application

Poor Jonah! The way he learned to obey God was

by being punished. Wasn't he foolish when he thought he could hide from God?

Things would have gone much better for Jonah if he had obeyed right away. When we know in our hearts what is right, the best way is to obey. Can you think of times when obeying was not easy? . . . Doing what God asks us to do brings happiness. Doing what we want to do instead of what God asks us to do brings trouble.

(*Ask the questions listed under "Student responses."*)

Activity Book

Review the Bible story as the students color the picture on the first page of their activity books. Remind them that the Bible does not say that the fish was a whale, only that it was a large fish that God prepared.

(*The answers to the puzzle are 1. Creator; 2. faith in; 3. prophet; 4. selfish.*)

On the next page the students are to unscramble the words and then fill in the blanks. If they have difficulty, they can look up the words in the Bible verses.

After everyone has filled in the blanks at the bottom of the page, discuss the answers.

Craft Souvenir

3-d Fish Plaque

MATERIALS:
Two 6 by 8 inch styrofoam meat trays
Blue and light-yellow construction paper
Fish from pattern page
Blue fine-line marker and ball-point pen
Exacto knife and scissors, glue
Braid (optional)

PROCEDURE:
Trace and cut out the fish, putting in the markings and eye.

Make a picture frame by cutting out the center of one tray with the knife or scissors.

Cut a piece of blue to fit the inside of the other tray. For 3-D waves, cut another blue strip with wavy edge. (This piece must be eight inches long.) Make a few wavy lines on both pieces with the marker. Glue the large piece on the inside of the tray.

For a sandy shore cut a one-inch strip of yellow paper. Along the lower edge print "It is best to obey God." Glue the strip over the *upper* part of the blue paper.

Squeeze glue on the three straight edges of the 3-D strip and attach to the outer edge of the tray. Hold, pulling it tight to take out the slack. Put a drop of glue on the fish and fasten it on the picture (partly under the wave). Glue the frame over the picture.

NOTE: To save time for smaller children, prepare the fish before class, and cut out the frame. Older children may glue braid around the inner edge of the frame. A tiny piece of corrugated cardboard may be fastened under the wave to hold it in place.

A Slave Who Ran Away

Philemon

Goals: That the student will know (1) that God forgave Onesimus when he became a Christian; (2) that He will forgive us; (3) that we need to forgive others.

Student Responses: As a result of this lesson, the student should be able to:
• Tell the story of Onesimus.
• Summarize what Paul wrote to Philemon.
• List times when he needs to forgive others.

Learning Centers

Preview

Map Study and Slave Life

(On a Bible map, locate the city of Colosse in Asia Minor and the city of Rome. Trace the two possible routes (sea or land) that Onesimus, Philemon's slave, traveled to reach Rome.)

Have you ever been asked to do a job for which you received no pay? Melvin's uncle asked him to pick up stones in the clover field. When he had finished, Uncle Jake thanked him for helping, but didn't pay him. That night Melvin told his parents that he had been a slave for his uncle. Was Melvin really a slave?

Not all slaves in Bible times were slaves because they had been captured by their enemies. Many times they were given in payment of a debt, or because they were very poor. A slave's child was a slave.

The jobs given to slaves were varied. The most common were serving as house boys or maids, or caring for the personal need of their masters.

During the time that Jesus lived on the earth, the whole world was ruled by the Roman Empire. Slavery was one of the terrible ways of the Romans. Many, many people were slaves. The law said that masters could be as cruel to their slaves as they wished. Slaves had no rights. If a slaves was caught stealing, or if he tried to run away, his punishment could be death.

Memory Ticket Office

"And be ye kind one to another, tenderhearted, forgiving one another, even as God for Christ's sake hath forgiven you."   Ephesians 4:32

THINK
1. What three attitudes does the verse tell us we should have toward one another?
2. Who forgave us and why should we forgive?

LEARNING GAME
Use the pocket chart with the words and phrases below printed on strips of stiff paper to help your pupils understand the meaning of forgiveness.

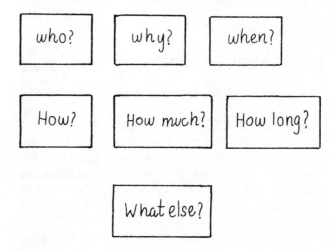

AWARD
Initial the tickets for those who memorized the verse.

Guidebook

Quicky Bible Drill

MATERIALS AND PREPARATION:
Construction paper, scissors, felt pen
Spra Mount or other adhesive spray or scraps of flannelgraph paper
Flannelboard

Cut the paper into card-size pieces. Print the following references and unfinished verses on them. Spray the printed sides of the cards, or glue pieces of flannelgraph paper aound the edges, and put them on the flannelboard.

PROCEDURE:

Ask a student to choose a card, read the unfinished verse and reference to the class, and conduct the drill. Only the one-word answer is to be read. The first student finding the answer may choose the next card and conduct the next drill.

1. Psalm 86:5 – "For thou, Lord, art good, and _____ to forgive." (ready)
2. Mark 2:7 – "Who can forgive sins but _____ _____ ?" (God only)
3. 1 John 1:9 – "He is _____ and just to forgive us our sins." (faithful)
4. Psalm 78:38 – "But he, being full of _____ , forgave their iniquity." (compassion)
5. Mark 2:10 – He has "_____ on earth to forgive sins." (power)
6. Luke 6:37 – "_____ , and ye shall be forgiven." (forgive)
7. Romans 4:7 – "Blessed are they whose iniquities are forgiven, and who sins are _____ ." (covered)

Front View Adventure

The Extra Radio

VISUALS FOR THIS STORY (*optional*):
Fold four pieces of heavy white paper in half and staple them together to make an eight-page booklet. Use black and red felt pens to make the following drawings and lettering: Page 1, a boy; Page 2, thirteen radios; Page 3, a bag; Page 4, black spot; Page 5, praying hands; Page 6, the word "forgiven"; Page 7, a bag; and Page 8, heart with the word "forgiven."

(*Page 1*) Leon counted as he took small radios out of a shipping carton. "Ten, eleven, twelve, thirteen! Say, there's an extra radio in this box," he said in surprise. He carefully counted them again as he set them in a neat row on the shelf in storage room.

(*Page 2*) "Hey, there really are thirteen, and it says on the box, 'One dozen Pocket AM/FM Stereo Radios.' Someone has made a mistake."

Leon thought about the extra radio until it was time to close the variety store. He decided that someone had counted wrong when he had packed the box. Mr. Swart wouldn't be charged for the extra radio. Even the shipping bill inside the box stated that there were only twelve.

(*Page 3*) Leon put the little radio in a paper bag with his school books, said good-night to Mr. Swart, and went home.

On Saturday when Leon went back to the store to help, Mr. Swart said, "Leon, did you find an extra radio in the carton when you unpacked it the other day? There should have been thirteen."

How do you think the storekeeper discovered that his helper had stolen the radio? The man who had packed the carton was the storekeeper's brother. He had packed an extra one as a gift, and paid for it himself. Then he had called Mr. Swart and told him the radio was a birthday gift for his daughter Carla.

(*Page 4*) How ashamed Leon was. "Please forgive me, Mr. Swart," he said. "What I did was wrong. I'll bring the radio back tomorrow."

(*Page 5*) Leon was scared to tell his parents what he had done. But he did. His father said, "Son, what you did was wrong. You asked Mr. Swart to forgive you. Now you need to ask God to forgive you."

(*Page 6*) That night Leon prayed, "Father, please forgive me for taking the radio. That was stealing, and it was wrong. Never again will I take anything that does not belong to me. Forgive me, I pray."

(*Page 7*)The next day Leon returned the radio. Carla did not know about the gift until she came home from a trip. She was disappointed that she hadn't received the radio before she left because she could have used it. But she forgave Leon.

(*Page 8*) She said, "Surely if the Lord forgave Leon, I should."

Worshiping Our Guide

Quiet music: "Holy! Holy! Holy!"
Song: "What a Happy Day" (page 128)
Theme song: "Trust and Obey"
Song: "Forgive One Another" (page 129)
Bible reading: Matthew 18:21, 22
Announcements and offering
Special number: "Wounded for Me"
Song: "Jesus Loves Even Me"
Prayer

Bible Story

A Slave Who Ran Away

Philemon was a man who lived in the city of Colosse. Philemon was a Christian. Perhaps he had heard Paul preach when Paul was at Ephesus. At any rate, Philemon had heard Paul's message about Jesus and had become a Christian. He was a wealthy man who lived in a large house. The church met in houses in those days, and the church at Colosse met in Philemon's home to worship.

Philemon was a generous man who loved and served God. He owned slaves who worked for him. (In those days owning slaves was common. The slave was considered a piece of property just as much as a house or a herd of cattle.)

One of Philemon's slaves was a man named Onesimus. Onesimus was probably young and strong. As a slave, he had to do everything his master commanded him to do. He probably didn't travel much farther than around the city of Colosse because he had much work to do for his master.

One day Onesimus ran away. We are not told why. Was he tired of working for his master? Did he want to go and come as he pleased? Did he want to see the world? Had he stolen something from his master? Was he sent to the faraway city of Rome on an errand and just decided to stay there? We do not know, but we do know that he ran away.

"Now I am a free man," Onesimus probably said to himself. He was his own boss and he could do anything he wanted to do. We do not know what Onesimus did, but he eventually traveled to the big city of Rome.

And in the city of Rome, he met Paul. The Bible does not tell us how Onesimus and Paul met. Paul was a prisoner in Rome. But he was allowed to stay in his own house, not in a jail. Perhaps in Rome Onesimus met Epaphras, a Christian and friend of Paul who was also from Colosse, and Epaphras brought Onesimus to Paul. We do not know.

But we do know that Paul taught Onesimus about Jesus, the Son of God. And Onesimus became a Christian. Onesimus told Paul that he had run away from his master back in Colosse. "Why I know him," Paul must have said. "Philemon is a good Christian man."

Onesimus was a helper for Paul, and Paul thought of him as a dear Christian friend. But of course both Paul and Onesimus knew that Onesimus must return to his master. Now that he was a Christian, he must go back and ask Philemon to forgive him for running away. No doubt he was afraid, for masters punished runaways severely; sometimes they even killed them.

"I will write a letter to Philemon and send it with you," said Paul. "I will make it safe for you."

Paul wrote to Philemon, and we have the personal letter right here in our Bible. (*Show book of Philemon.*) Paul asked Philemon to take back his slave. He said that if need be, he would pay back any debt Onesimus owed him. The slave was a Christian now, and he should be treated as a Christian brother. This meant that Philemon should forgive him and not punish him. Paul told Philemon that he would like to have kept Onesimus with him as a helper, but he knew Onesimus should return. Paul said that now Onesimus would not be just a servant to Paul but a Christian brother, that once he had been unprofitable but now he was profitable.

As Onesimus traveled back home to Colosse, he carried with him Paul's letter.

The Bible does not tell us what Philemon thought or said or did when Onesimus returned and handed him the letter. What do you think he did? (*Discussion.*)

Bible Story Application

God had forgiven Onesimus of his sins. Now Philemon needed to forgive him. Since God forgives us of our sins, we need to forgive others. In fact God will not forgive us if we do not forgive others. And we must do it over and over again (Matthew 18:21, 22). This is not always easy to do. Sometimes it can be difficult to say, "I forgive you," and mean it. But when we think of all that Christ has done for us, we want to be obedient to His commands.

Can you think of some times when you need to forgive others? (*Discuss*)

Activity Book

The first activity is a maze puzzle taking Onesimus from Philemon's home to the city of Rome.

At the bottom of the page, the student can consider some of the characteristics of Onesimus both before and after he became a Christian.

As the children do the activity on the next page, give help as needed to students who have difficulty finding the verses or reading them.

After everyone has completed the "Quicky Puzzle," check the answers together.

Ask the students to give some thought to the suggested prayer at the bottom of the page before filling in the blanks. Remind them that this may be a prayer they want to say at home this week.

Craft Souvenir

Stand-up Double Motto

MATERIALS:
Red and light shades of construction paper
Typing paper or colored paper
Ruler, glue, and felt-tip pens or crayons
Typewritten verses: Psalm 86:5 and Ephesians 4:32

PROCEDURE:
Copies of the unfinished motto should be prepared ahead of time; one for each student.

Cut the construction paper into 6 by 11 inch pieces. Follow the dimensions in the sketch for putting in the three dotted folding lines.

Print "God forgives" at the top of one 4 by 6 inch section and "Forgive Others" on the other section, only upside down (*see sketch*). Students may use pens to draw over the letters.

On the lower half of the "God Forgives" motto, glue the verse Psalm 86:5 and a small red heart.

On the lower half of "Forgive Others" motto, glue the verse Ephesians 4:32 and draw two stick men holding hands.

Fold on the dotted lines and glue the one-inch section to the inside of the opposite edge so the motto will stand.

A Praising Prophetess

Exodus 14:17—15:21

Goals: That the student will know that Miriam served the Lord by praising and (2) will decide on ways he can use his talents to praise the Lord.

Student Responses: As a result of this lesson, the pupil should be able to do the following:
• Tell the Bible story.
• Describe Miriam.
• Say the memory verse.
• List three ways he can praise the Lord.

Learning Centers

Preview

MATERIALS:
A tambourine and a Bible dictionary

PROCEDURE:
If we could travel to an Arab country today, we might hear musicians play small instruments called dufs. A duf is a round wooden hoop with animal skin stretched over it. Clanging metal discs hang loosly from the sides. It is similar to our tambourine and the Jewish timbrel. The timbrel was not used in the temple worship service but was played at special praise and thanksgiving times. The women usually played the timbrels.

Other musical instruments used for worship were cymbals, psalteries, harps, and trumpets. (2 Chronicles 29:25, 26) The Jewish harps were of various shapes and sizes. Some were rounded and others were triangular. Strings numbered from two or three to over thirty. Most Bible-times harps had seven or eight strings. The psaltry also had strings, but it was smaller.

Women in our Bible story danced as they played. Most people who go dancing today are thinking about how they dance and of those with whom they are dancing, but people in Bible times who praised God in dance were thinking about the Lord and how holy and good He is.

Often when we hear an orchestra, choir, or a soloist play or sing to honor the Lord, we stand or clap to show our praise. Bible people expressed praise by dancing.

Memory Ticket Office

"Enter into his gates with thanksgiving, and into his courts with praise: be thankful unto him, and bless his name." Psalm 100:4

THINK
1. What two attitudes in this verse are we to have toward God?
2. What is another word for "bless"? (honor)

LEARNING GAME
Teach with the use of the chalkboard. (See Introduction, page 5.)

AWARD
Initial the tickets for those who have memorized the verse.

Guidebook

What the Psalmist Says About Praise

MATERIALS:
Seven pieces of lightweight cardboard
Magic marker and pocket chart (See "Introduction," page 5.) (Alternative: chalkboard)

PROCEDURE:
Print on the cards the words WHO? WHY? WHEN? HOW? HOW MUCH? HOW LONG? and WHAT ELSE?
The following verses may be used as a Bible drill or Bible study. Place each word in the pocket chart

before the question is asked and the reference is given.

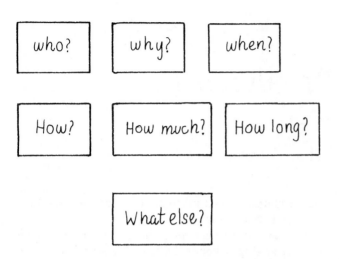

1. Who should praise the Lord?—Psalm 148:11, 12
2. Why should we praise the Lord?—Psalm 48:1
3. When should we praise the Lord?—Psalm 92:1,2
4. What is one way in which we can praise the Lord?—Psalm 34:1
5. How long should we praise the Lord?—Psalm 52:9
6. How much should we praise the Lord?—Psalm 9:1
7. What else should praise the Lord?—Psalm 148:2-10

(From these verses the students select created things that praise the Lord.)

Front View Adventure

Sounds of Praise

Plan a short praise and thanksgiving program using as many students as possible. Stress the importance of reverence throughout the program and encourage students to do their parts as unto the Lord. Keep the parts short but the service unhurried. The following are suggested numbers:

1. Vocal or piano solo
2. Children's choir
3. Poem
4. A special by a teacher
5. Recording of a hymn
6. Scripture reading
7. A sharing bag: Ask a student to bring a bag or box containing items for which he is thankful. These may be his Bible; pictures of his parents, church, family; flag; eye glasses; Sunday-school paper; fruit; and one favorite toy. It is best to limit the items to not more than ten things.

Bible Story

A Praising Prophetess

The Israelites had been slaves in Egypt for many years. Pharaoh, the ruler of the land, had been forcing them to work very hard without wages. Finally God was ready to free them. He chose a faithful leader named Moses to help them escape. It took many miracles and much suffering before they were set free and could leave the country.

"Look at the long line of people behind me," Moses must have thought as he looked back. "There are millions of Israelites traveling on this highway. The Lord has chosen me to be the leader. It is a great responsibility." When he looked above his head, he saw a sight that no one had ever seen before. God had sent a pillar of cloud to show Moses where to lead the multitude; God was with them guiding them.

As the Israelites marched along the desert highway, they probably cheered each other by saying, "Praise to the Lord! We are free from slavery! No longer do we need to work without pay. God has helped us escape from Pharaoh and the slave drivers. We do not know where we are going, but Moses is at the head of the line and we are trusting the Lord."

Moses' family probably walked with him up near the front—his older brother Aaron and his older sister, Miriam, and his other relatives.

The older people remembered Moses when he was young. They probably told how his mother had laid him in a waterproof basket and hidden him on the Nile River. Someone may have said, "Miriam was Moses' baby sitter. She was a wise little girl. When Pharaoh's daughter found him, she offered to bring a Jewish mother to be his nurse. The nurse she brought was his very own mother."

When the pillar of cloud moved ahead, the people followed. When it stood still, they rested and put up their tents. Finally the pillar of cloud stood beside the Red Sea. The people gathered in a level place and waited.

In the meantime, Pharaoh had called his captains to the palace and told them that he had changed his mind. He had decided that he must bring back his slaves. He said the Israelites were trapped, and he was sending his army to force them to return to slavery. He would go with them.

Can you imagine how frightened the Israelites were when they saw a cloud of dust and knew it was the Egyptians racing toward them? And they were coming in six hundred choice chariots! The Israelites were terrified! They even told Moses that it would have been better if they had never left Egypt.

"Don't be afraid," said Moses. "Stand firm and see what the Lord will do. You will never again see Pharaoh and his army. The Lord will fight for you."

Then the Lord did a wonderful thing. At His command, Moses lifted his rod and waved it toward the sea. All night God sent a strong wind to blow across the deep water. The sea was parted, causing the water to stand on either side and leave a dry path to the opposite shore. It was a miracle! The pillar of cloud turned and went behind them, giving light for the Israelites but darkness for the Egyptians. Moses led the way and the Israelites walked along the dry path between the walls of water to the other shore. With His great power, God held the water in place.

Pharaoh and his army dared to follow. They went down on the path with their chariots and horses, captains and riders. They couldn't catch the Israelites because the Lord caused the chariot wheels to fall off. When the last Israelite was safely on the other side, the Lord let the water fall back into place, drowning Pharaoh and his army in the sea.

"We are safe! We are free!" the Israelites must have shouted. When they saw the Egyptians destroyed, they thought they would trust the Lord forever. They burst into a song of praise and thanks as one great choir. We can read the hymn of praise in Exodus, Chapter 15.

Miriam's heart was full of praise for what the Lord had done. She hurried to her tent and brought a timbrel to play as she sang. Soon all the women followed her and played and sang. The words were, "Sing ye to the Lord, for he hath triumphed gloriously; the horse and his rider hath he thrown into the sea."

Miriam is called a prophetess. She was grateful to God and praised Him with music. Miriam must have been a leader of women, teaching them to serve by praising.

Bible Story Application

The neighbors invited Wayne to go swimming with them, but he needed to leave before the rest of the family had their evening meal. His mother fixed his plate of food and waited for him to ask the table blessing. When he didn't bow his head and thank the Lord for his food, she said, "Wayne, this is the third time you've neglected thanking God before you ate. Don't you think you ought to?"

"Nope! The Lord knows I'm thankful. I don't need to say it every time."

The next day was Wayne's parents' anniversary. He had saved his spending money to buy a picture for them. They opened the gift and set it on the table. Neither of them said anything about it.

At last Wayne said, "Mom, don't you and Dad like the picture? You didn't thank me for it."

His mother answered this way: "Yes, we liked it a lot. But you knew we were thankful, so we didn't think it was necessary to say thanks." Wayne understood. He learned a lesson he never forgot.

The Lord never gets tired of hearing us praise Him. King David said we owe the Lord our praise (Psalm 29:2). The very best way to serve the Lord is to praise Him.

Activity Book

Refer to "Preview" in the "Learning Center" section of this lesson as the children discuss and color the pictures of musical instruments of Bible times.

We are told little about Miriam but we can list a few characteristics.

Give help as needed as the students do the puzzle on the next page. *(The secret message is "For He is worthy." If students write "stood" for No. 8 instead of "went," ask them to think of another word that will fit.)*

The Scripture passages provide the answers to be written on the blanks.

At the bottom of the page, each child can think of three ways he can praise the Lord as he serves Him, and write them on the lines.

Craft Souvenir

Praise Buttons

MATERIALS:
Unwanted pin-on buttons
Enamel, paint brush, and newspaper

Black felt-tip pens (Permanent kind is best)
Smiling-face stickers or others

PROCEDURE:

Paint the buttons and allow twenty-four hours to dry.

Decorate the button by putting the sticker on one side. If the sticker has a border, it may be trimmed.

Use the pen to print "PRAISE THE LORD" or "LET US PRAISE THE LORD." The length of the motto will depend upon the size of the button. For the very large buttons, an extra sticker may be added.

ABC'S for Teaching Children

A – Always give your best.
B – Be a friend.
C – Challenge to high goals.
D – Delight in students' achievements.
E – Exalt the Lord in their presence.
F – Frown on evil.
G – Give your students love.
H – Hear their problems.
I – Ignore not their childish fears.
J – Joyfully accept their apologies.
K – Keep their confidence.
L – Live a Christ-like example before them.
M – Motivate students to memorize Scripture.
N – Never ignore questions.
O – Open your home to visits.
P – Pray for each boy and girl by name.
Q – Quicken your interest in each child's spiritual growth.
R – Remember the needs of your students.
S – Show them the way of salvation.
T – Teach them to respect God's house.
U – Understand that they are still young.
V – Visit them in their homes.
W – Wean them from bad company.
X – Expect them to obey.
Y – Yearn for God's best for them.
Z – Zealously guide them in Biblical truths.

A Rewarded Lender

1 Samuel 1:1-28; 2:1-26

Goals: (1) That the student will know that Hannah's sacrificial gift was rewarding. (2) That he will want to give to God and will realize that he cannot outgive God.

Student Responses: As a result of this lesson, the student should be able to do the following:
- Tell the Bible story
- Describe Hannah
- Say the memory verse.
- Tell why it is more blessed to give than to receive.
- List two ways he will give to the Lord because he loves Him. (Activity Book)

Learning Centers

Preview

A Worship Service

Before the temple was built, the tabernacle was the place of worship. The tabernacle tent wasn't as beautiful as the temple, but the worship services were the same.

In the court stood a flat altar made of wood, covered with brass. The priest was never to let the fire go out from under the altar. Twice a day he offered an animal sacrifice on the altar for the sins of the people.

When a person knew he had sinned, he picked either a lamb, a goat, or a bullock and brought it to the tabernacle. He made sure the animal was healthy and its body was in perfect condition. When he came to the court, he laid his hand on its head to show that he had put his sin there. Then it was killed and the priest burned it upon the brazen altar. God then forgave the person of his sin.

The lamb didn't take away his sin. It was a sign that some day Christ, God's perfect Son, would come and bleed and die on the cross for him. We no longer need to sacrifice animals because Jesus is the Lamb of God who was slain for us.

Sometimes a person would bring an offering to show that he was thankful for what the Lord had done for him.

There were special worship times. The Passover was the time when everyone came to celebrate the night when the oldest son of the family was spared from death in Egypt. The Day of Atonement came just once a year. On that day the high priest offered a sacrifice to God for his own sins and for the sins of the people. This was the only day in the year when he went into the Holy of Holies, the most sacred part of the tabernacle (later the temple).

Memory Ticket Office

"Remember the words of the Lord Jesus, how he said, It is more blessed to give than to receive."
                                                      Acts 20:35

THINK
1. Why do you think it is rewarding to give?
2. Since Jesus said it, should we not believe these words and try them often?

LEARNING GAME
  See page 5 for information for pocket chart.

AWARD
  Initial the tickets for those who have learned the verse. (See page 5 for information for "passport" award.)

Guidebook

Three Givers

MATERIALS:
A box of safety matches
Common matches and a candle

The Lord is pleased when we give cheerfully and when we give our best. Giving doesn't refer only to money. It includes time, talents, and possessions.

1. This safety match is very particular about the kind of surface I strike it against to ignite it. (*Demonstrate on substances other than the box.*) When it is lit, it doesn't give much light. Some people who give are like the safety match. They must be coaxed to use their talents, and they often give very little.

2. The common match willingly ignites on one of many substances. (*Demonstrate.*) But it also burns out very quickly. Some people who give are like the common match. As soon as they are asked to give or help, they willingly accept. They may give a little more than the first giver, but soon get tired and quit.

3. The candle ignites quickly and burns with a steady light until all of the wax is gone. Some people are like the candle; they cheerfully accept when they are asked to help. They give everything they can and they give of themselves.

Have pupils find and read these verses:

We can know our work will be rewarded. – Hebrews 6:10

We can know our money offerings will be rewarded. – Malachi 3:10

We can know our praying will be rewarded. – Matthew 6:6

Front View Adventure

The Earned Coin

"I enjoy the smell of burning wood," said the tall, thin man as he pulled a chair close to the fireplace. "Are you burning cedar?" he asked.

"Yes. And maple logs," answered the quiet hostess.

The man reached for the iron rod and lifted the burning wood making the hot flames sparkle and dance. He was glad his schedule permitted him to stop to visit this family since they were his good friends.

"I must review some important papers," the man said. Then he took a notebook from his case, leaned forward, and began to read.

"Clunk! Clunk!" came the sound of a noisy toy down the hall. In a moment a little girl, wearing a long dress dashed into the room. She was pulling a homemade doll cart with wooden wheels. Under the blanket was her rag doll.

"Uncle Abe, please tell me about something nice you see when you travel," said the child.

"Well, Bess, I see a lot and have many experiences every day. Suppose you tell me something nice about yourself first," Uncle Abe replied.

Bess clasped her hands tightly together. "I have a money bank. Our Sunday school is saving coins to help a missionary," she exclaimed. Then she dashed out of the room, leaving her doll in the care of Uncle Abe. When she returned, she held a painted box with a slot in the top.

"I have twenty-eight pennies," she said. "We have a whole year to save our offering. But the time is almost up."

Uncle Abe reached into his pocket and took out a shiny coin. Taking the bank, he started to put the coin through the slot.

"Oh, no," cried the child. "Teacher says we must earn all the money we put in. She says Jesus will bless us a lot if we do our best. I have carried firewood and done a lot of things to earn my money."

The next morning the tall man set his suitcase by the door. Soon he would catch the train to go to Washington.

"Bess, are you going to the train depot with me? I need your help to carry my suitcase," Uncle Abe said with a smile.

After breakfast the two of them walked toward the depot – a tall man and a tiny girl. They were carrying a case between them. The man was holding onto one handle and Bess was trudging along, holding onto the other.

"Here is a coin for helping me. You have earned it. Put it in your bank for the missionary," he said.

Bess was very happy that Sunday when she gave the teacher her coins. She said that she had earned all of them.

"Wherever did you get this coin?" asked the teacher when all the banks had been opened and the money had been counted.

To Bess' surprise, the teacher told her that she had brought five dollars and thirty-one cents. The shiny coin from Uncle Abe was not a penny but a five-dollar gold piece.

Praising Our Guide

Quiet music: "There Shall Be Showers of Blessing."
Song: "Giving to Jesus" (page 132)
Theme chorus: "Serve, Serve, Serve the Lord." (See page 6)
Song: "Jesus Is My Answer." (page 125)
Bible reading: Luke 6:38
Prayer
Offering and Announcements
Special music: "All for Jesus"
Song: "Serve the Lord With Gladness." (page 131)
Prayer

Bible Story

A Rewarded Lender

CHARACTERS FOR INTERVIEW:
Narrator
Hannah (dressed in a simple robe and scarf)

We are going to interview Hannah, but first let's learn a little about her family.

Hannah lived in the hill country in the town of Ramah. Her husband, Elkanah, was a godly man who tried to follow the ways of the Lord.

Hannah was a quiet person who probably didn't complain very often. When a problem arose, she talked to the Lord about it. She did her housework faithfully. She loved children but didn't have one of her own. This made her very unhappy. She longed to have her very own baby to hold, and to love, and to watch grow.

In those days, men often had more than one wife. Elkanah had taken a second wife, Peninnah, so there were two ladies living in the house. Peninnah had several children. She teased Hannah a lot about not having a baby. She may have said, "Don't you wish you had a baby like mine?" Some of her remarks may have been cruel. This made Hannah very sad.

Every year Elkanah and Hannah went to the tabernacle to worship and to offer sacrifices unto God. On one journey Hannah seemed especially sad. She cried and wouldn't eat her dinner. Elkanah tried to discover why she was weeping, so he asked, "Why do you cry? Haven't I been good to you? Am I not better to you than ten sons?"

HANNAH: I was weeping because I did not have a son. When the meal was over, I went to the court of the tabernacle to worship. I knew there was only One who could help me. I cried and I prayed to the Lord. I told the Lord about my unhappiness and asked Him to give me a son. I promised to give the child back to Him for the rest of his life.

NARRATOR: Eli, the priest, was watching, wasn't he?

HANNAH: Yes! I was praying in my heart. He saw my lips moving but did not hear my voice, so he thought I was drunk. He understood when he saw that I was sincere. I explained that I was telling the Lord about my problem and truly worshiping.

NARRATOR: The Lord honored you by answering your prayer, didn't He?

HANNAH: Yes, He did, and in a wonderful way, too. By the next year I had a baby boy. I named him Samuel. When it was time for the yearly sacrifice, my husband took Peninnah and her children back to the tabernacle to worship. I didn't go.

NARRATOR: You stayed home with Samuel, didn't you?

HANNAH: Yes. When he was big enough to feed and dress himself, I took him to the tabernacle. After we had offered our sacrifices, we took Samuel to Eli and left him there. God had given him to me; now I was giving him back. I spent some time talking to the Lord before I left. I told Him that my heart was rejoicing and He was my salvation. There is no God like Him, or as holy.

NARRATOR: I'm sure you missed your little boy. Did you get to see Him very often?

HANNAH: I missed him a lot. I missed his sweet smile and childish chatter. I had given my dearest treasure to the Lord. (Pause) Yes, I saw Samuel once each year when we brought our yearly sacrifice to the tabernacle. Each time we went, I took him a new coat I had made. He grew so fast.

NARRATOR: In what ways do you feel the Lord rewarded you for giving Samuel back to Him?

HANNAH: He rewarded me by giving me five more children—three sons and two daughters. Also I knew that Samuel was serving the Lord and this was a great reward. When he grew to manhood, he became a fine and faithful prophet.

Bible Story Application

Hannah's first gift to the Lord was herself.

Once a poor congregation gave money to the church in Jerusalem because they were in great need. They sent the money with Paul. The Bible says they first gave themselves (2 Corinthians 8:5). Our very best gift to the Lord is ourselves.

Hannah gave her son willingly, and she was rewarded. When we give because we want to, the Lord promises to reward us (Hebrews 6:10).

Even though Hannah gave her great treasure, she couldn't give more than the Lord gave back to her. When we give, whether it is our offering, time, or talents, He will reward much more (Luke 6:38).

What gifts can you give to the Lord? *(Discuss and list on the chalkboard. Include time, talents, and money. Review the memory verse and discuss why it is more blessed to give than to receive.)*

Activity Book

If you did not use "Preview" in the "Learning Centers" section of this lesson, you may want to present the material about Jewish sacrifices before the students begin the first activity. Of course the Scripture references provide the answers.

The code for the puzzle at the bottom of the page is the alphabet numbered backwards.

The children should be able to fill in most of the squares on the next page without looking in 1 Samuel: 1 and 2 to find the answers.

After the students have completed "Check Up," discuss the answers.

Craft Souvenir

Folder Greeting Card

Because the lesson has been on giving, encourage the students to make this craft as a gift.

MATERIALS:
Two 6″ by 8″ Styrofoam trays
Used greeting cards
Tacky glue and scissors
Package shipping tape
Artificial flowers
Yarn and darning needle
Lace or dress trim (optional)

PROCEDURE:
Lay the trays side by side, right sides up.

Cut out the printed greeting (poem) from the card. Glue it to the tray on the right. Tape a tiny arrangement of flowers to the tray on the left. A Bible verse may be glued underneath the flowers.

With threaded needle, punch holes on the left side edges and pull the yarn through. Tie the yarn in bows on the outside of the folder. (The folder will stand up.)

Glue a pretty card front to the front cover of the folder.

(The inside edges of one or both trays may be decorated by gluing lace or trim on before the folder is put together. Narrow trim may be put around the poem.)

A King and The First Offering Box

2 Chronicles 22:10—24:14; 2 Kings 12:1-16

Goals: That the student (1) will appreciate the sincerity with which Joash and the people of Judah gave to the Lord, and (2) will decide to give to the Lord with the attitude of serving.

Student Responses: As a result of this lesson, the pupil should be able to do the following:
• Tell the Bible story.
• Tell why we give our offerings.
• Describe the kind of giver we should be.
• List two things we can give besides our money.

Learning Centers

Preview

The Temple

MATERIALS:
Pictures of the local church building and of Solomon's temple.

If someone said, "I have not been inside your church building. What is it like?" how would you describe it? *(Brief discussion)*

While Solomon was king of Israel, he arranged for God's splendid temple to be built. When it was completed, it was a most beautiful and magnificent structure! Would you have liked to have seen it? Let's take an imaginary tour.

As we come into view of the temple, our guide tells us that it is made of stone and lined with cedar wood. Look how it shines in the sun! It is covered with pure gold!

We enter the court and pass a great altar made of brass. Here is where the animals are sacrificed each day.

Next, we see the laver. It contains water. This is where the priests wash their hands and feet before offering sacrifices.

Now we climb a few steps and walk through a tall, arched door and look inside. "Oooo!" we exclaim as we look around. The room we are in is so splendid that we do not care to even whisper. The walls and floor are covered with gold. The walls and doors have carved designs of beautiful cherubim and flowers—all covered with gold. The room has three pieces of furniture: a candle stand with seven candles, and the lights are never to go out; a table with twelve loaves of bread; and an altar of incense. They are all overlaid with gold.

Our guide tells us we cannot enter the next room. But we do see the beautiful blue, purple, and scarlet curtain that divides the two rooms. It has the most beautiful embroidery work we have ever seen. The special room is also covered with gold. Below golden-winged cherubim stands the golden chest called the ark of the covenant. This room is where the glory of God is.

We'd love to stay, but we must tiptoe across the golden floor and leave so we can visit out next learning center.

Memory Ticket Office

"Every man according as he purposeth in his heart, so let him give; not grudgingly, or of necessity, for God loveth a cheerful giver." 2 Corinthians 9:7

THINK
1. What kind of giver does the verse say God loves?
2. What two ways does God not want us to give?
3. Can you put in your own words the part that says "according as he purposeth in his heart?" (Give the amount you choose, but give it because you want to.)

LEARNING GAME
Use the pocket chart to teach the memory verse. Cut construction paper strips. Divide the verse into

six phrases. Print each phrase and an illustrated sketch on each strip as follows:

Every man (a stick man)
according as he purposeth in his heart (heart)
so let him give (offering plate)
not grudgingly (sad face)
or of necessity (scowling face)
for the Lord loveth a cheerful giver (smiling face)
2 Corinthians 9:7

Everyman	🯄
according	♡
so let him	⬭
not grudgingly	☹
or of necessity	☹
for the Lord	☺
2 Corinthians 9:7	

AWARD
Initial the tickets for those who have learned the verse.

Guidebook

Bible Drill About Giving

Before the session, wrap a gift box and cut a slot in the top. Fasten pieces of string to strips of folded paper on which have been written the following questions and references. Put the papers in the box with strings extending to the outside. Let the students take turns drawing the slips. Read the question and reference and conduct the drill.

1. Who is to give gifts to the Lord?—1 Corinthians 16:2
2. What determines how much we give?—1 Corinthians 16:2 (as God hath prospered him)
3. How are we not to give?—2 Corinthians 9:7
4. Who gave the best gift?—2 Corinthians 9:15
5. What is the best gift we can give to God?—Proverbs 23:26

Front View Adventure

Lessons From a Coin

Give each student a shiny penny. You may wish to make a large replica of the two sides of the coin for class use as you talk about the coin.

1. *Mr. Lincoln's picture.* He was an honorable president who contributed to the Lord's work.
2. *Date.* This tells how many years since Christ was on the earth.
3. *Liberty.* In our country we have freedom to give to God's work.
4. *In God We Trust.* A wonderful motto found on all United States coins.
5. *United States of America.* This tells to what country the penny belongs.
6. *E Pluribus Unum.* This means "one out of many." It is the motto of the United States. We have five coins for common use. This is a blessing. If we had no other coins than the penny, we would need to carry and count eighty-five coins if we we wanted to give eight-five cents!
7. *One cent.* This is the value of the coin. It is very small, but when many, many pennies are put together, they make a dollar. Many dollars make one hundred dollars. But first we must start with the little one cent.

(NOTE: If you live in another country, use the coin smallest in value and refer to the inscriptions on it.)

You may think that you are small and cannot do much for the Lord. But children can do a lot. One child decided to pray for his class. One by one, each member of the class accepted Jesus as Savior. But it started with just one child.

Worshiping Our Guide

Quiet music: "Give of Your Best to the Master."
Song: "Giving to Jesus" (page 132)
Theme chorus: "Serve, Serve, Serve the Lord."
Song: "Oh How He Loves You and Me."
Bible reading: Colossians 3:23,24
Prayer
Offering and announcements
Special: Charade with children showing serving
Song: "We Can Reach Around the World." (page 133)
Song: "God of Great Power" (Theme chorus for Unit 1)
Prayer

Bible Story

A King and the First Offering Box

Sometimes, when people are very selfish, they also want to become very important in the world. The selfishness grows and grows, and the desire becomes stronger. Finally, terrible wickedness comes into their lives. Then they decide to do terrible things.

A very selfish grandmother in the Bible watched as her son was crowned the king of the kingdom of Judah. Her name was Athaliah. But the young king reigned only one year and he was killed.

"My son, is dead! This is my opportunity to be the queen," Athaliah cried. "But how can I, when the law says that the oldest son of a king shall be the next to reign? Ahaziah has several sons."

Athaliah formed a cruel and terrible plan. She ordered all of her grandsons to be killed. The armed guard searched until the boys were found, and one by one, they were put to death.

But not all of Athaliah's grandsons were killed. Oh, no! One little prince was saved. When his good aunt heard of the fearful thing that was happening, she hurried to the palace. She grabbed the little boy in her arms and urged his nurse to follow her.

"Let us rush to the temple," Aunt Jehosheba called to the nurse from over her shoulder. "It's the only safe hiding place for the little prince."

Jehosheba was married to Jehoiada, the priest. The godly couple hid little Joash and his nursemaid in the bedchamber of the temple for six years. Queen Athaliah never guessed that her youngest grandson was waiting until he was old enough to be crowned the rightful king.

The priest was faithful. He wanted Joash to become a good ruler, so he taught the boy much about the true God. Joash must grow up to trust, obey, and serve the Lord in order to be a good king.

When Prince Joash was seven years old, the priest called the captains and leaders to Jerusalem. He told them that Joash was hidden in the temple. He informed them that the proper king should reign, and the time was ready. He gave the captains weapons and told them where to stand as guards. He explained what they should do.

When everyone was ready, Jehoiada brought the prince to the door of the temple. There, they annointed him with oil and set him apart as king. They put the crown on his little head, a royal robe over his shoulders, and Joash became the ruler.

Everyone was happy. Athaliah had been ruling for six years and the people hated her wicked, cruel ways. Now they would have a good king. They played music, sang, and clapped their hands. They shouted, "Long live the king!" "Long live the king!" The noise reached Athaliah's palace, and she came to see what was going on.

"Treason! Treason!" she shouted in surprise and anger. She called little Joash a traitor and unfair, when all the while Athaliah was the traitor. The soldiers captured her at a gate of the city and there she was killed.

At first Joash was too young to rule a kingdom alone, so Jehoiada helped him. The altar that had been built for worshiping idols was torn down. The false priests were killed. People who had been worshiping false gods returned to the temple to worship and serve the Lord. Once again the city of Jerusalem was quiet and peaceful.

One day Joash called the priests and leaders together and said, "The temple needs to be repaired. We must ask folk to give money so we can hire workers. They will need materials to work with, too." He told them to go to the cities of Judah and collect the people's offerings. But this plan didn't work. The temple leaders were too slow in getting started.

"Let us make a chest," said the good priest Jehoiada. "We can bore a hole in the top of the box so the givers can drop their offerings into it when they come to worship." King Joash liked the idea. He commanded that a wooden chest be built and placed at the temple gate.

The plan worked beautifully. An announcement was sent to all Judah to bring their offerings. Moses had said long ago that every man who was twenty years old or older should give half a shekel for the upkeep of the temple building (Exodus 30:12-16). The princes and all the people were happy to give to repair the Lord's house.

As worshipers walked through the gate, they cheerfully dropped their offerings through the slot of the wooden bank. When the chest was full, the money was counted and emptied into bags.

The money was used to pay carpenters and men who knew how to hew stone. Repairmen mended the cracks in the broken walls. Gold and silver vessels were purchased and brought for the worship services. Finally the building was made to be the beautiful temple they had once known it to be.

Joash was brought up well and taught to worship God. He was a good king as long as the priest who helped him was alive. But when Jehoiada died, Joash didn't follow the Lord any more. He listened to poor advice from the leaders of Judah who had never really given up their idol worshiping. He even told the people to throw stones on the son of good Jehoiada when he begged the people to return to God (2 Chronicles 24:20-22).

Bible Story Application

Almost every Sunday school has some kind of money container with a coin slot where we can drop an offering. The wooden chest is the first such bank mentioned in the Bible. It was King Joash who commanded that it be placed at the temple gate. Both he and the people knew they were serving the Lord by giving.

Giving is a very important way to serve God. Our offerings are used to pay the minister so that he can keep serving the Lord. *(Discuss other ways in which offerings are used.)*

The apostle Paul said that Christians are to give because we want to give, not because we feel we must, or so people see we are giving. When we give with the right attitude, we feel happy inside. The Lord loves a cheerful giver (2 Corinthians 9:7).

We cannot please God if we do not give something. If we have a lot, we should give accordingly. This is because God wants us to have the opportunity to serve in this special way.

We must always remember that what we have isn't really ours. When we give an offering, we are giving back to God a part of what was His all the time.

Giving money isn't the only present we can give to the Lord. The very best gift we can present to Him is ourselves—our love and our time.

Activity Book

Talk about the Bible story as the children color the picture. The letters already on the blanks will help the children to complete the words. After the child has connected the dots, he will have drawn a money chest. He can then find the Bible verse and fill in the blanks.

Let each student work on his own completing the True or False Quiz. After everyone has finished, check the answers together.

After the students have filled in the blanks at the bottom of the page, discuss the answers.

Craft Souvenir

Cheerful Giver Bank

MATERIALS:
Yellow felt or heavy paper
White glue
Scissors, narrow black felt tip pen
A cup for a pattern

PROCEDURE:
Use the cup or similar object to draw two circles on felt. Cut the circles and cut a coin slot near the top of one. With a pen print "Give Cheerfully" under the slot. Draw a smiling face on the other circle. Squeeze a thin line of glue around the inside edge of one circle. Put together and hold firmly until the glue holds.

The children may want to use these "banks" to save money for a particular mission or other project.

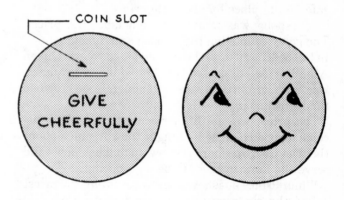

The Vanishing Evangelist

Acts 6:1-6; 8

Goals: That the student (1) will remember Philip as a zealous Christian who brought lost souls to Christ and (2) will be determined to share his faith in Christ with his friends.

Student Responses: As a result of this lesson, the pupil should be able to do the following:
- Answer questions about the Bible story.
- Tell three things he knows about Philip.
- Tell why we should tell others about Jesus.

Learning Centers

Preview

Map Study and the Chariot

MATERIALS:
Map showing Israel, Egypt, and Ethiopia
Picture of a chariot

PROCEDURE:
Trace the route the Ethiopian eunuch may have traveled enroute to Jerusalem from his country. Also locate the city of Samaria and the route Philip could have traveled to reach the desert below Gaza.

If someone told us he had ridden in a chariot, we could just imagine a beautiful wagon or cart trimmed in gold, with velvet padding and plush cushions. But most chariots the Bible speaks about were not elegant.

A chariot was a box-like cart with two wheels. It was built high in the front and on the sides, but it was open in the back. It held one, two, or three people and was drawn by horses or mules. In some places the chariots were carried on the shoulders of slaves.

Some chariots were used for travel, as in our story. But mostly, they were used for war. Some nations, especially the Canaanites, put sharp swords on the outside of the wheels. Then they raced their horses into the enemy camp and the swords would cut as the wheels turned. Soldiers would be cut to pieces as they tried to flee from the speeding race horses with chariots.

Memory Ticket Office

"Howbeit Jesus suffered him not, but saith unto him, Go home to thy friends, and tell them how great things the Lord hath done for thee."

Mark 5:19

THINK
1. What does "suffered him not" mean? (Would not let or allow)
2. What does this verse encourage you to do?

LEARNING GAME
Divide the verse into about eight sections. For a change, print the sections on flash cards cut in the shape of chariots. Let the students hold them as the verse is memorized. As soon as a student can quote the verse, he may eliminate his section.

AWARD
Initial the tickets for those who have memorized the verse.

Guidebook

"Tell Others" Bible Drill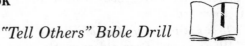

1. Jesus tells us to tell others about Him.—Mark 16:15
2. What should we tell?—John 3:16
3. What should we not be?—Romans 1:16
4. One way we can tell our family—Ephesians 6:1
5. One way we can tell our friends—1 Timothy 4:12
6. Another way we can tell people—1 John 4:7

Front View Adventure

The Good News Package

MATERIALS:

Howie's clubhouse but change the backdrop slightly

Four puppets: Howie, Mike, Mindy, and Lisa. (If necessary, interchange Howie by using a girl's hat or scarf and glasses.)

Narrator

Small package and printed sign: "One month later"

(Mindy and Lisa enter.)

LISA: Hi, Mindy. I've not been here for a while. Hey! Our clubhouse is looking great. Who's been doing all the work?

MINDY: Several of us. My mom made the curtains. Say, did you see old Mr. Barney when he came into town today? Wowee, was he ever dirty!

LISA: I didn't see him, but my dad did. He said that he looked so sad, and he was very dirty. He must be really poor. He comes to town only when he needs some groceries.

(Mike enters,)

MIKE: Hello everybody. Guess who I saw come to town today!

(Girls say together "Old Mr. Barney.")

MIKE: Right! Poor old man. He went to the post office for his mail, and there was nothing. Absolutely no mail. Imagine anyone not getting mail in a whole month!

MINDY: He must not have any relatives or friends.

LISA: My dad says he has a parrot but it doesn't talk.

MIKE: It sure must be lonely up on that hill. I wish we could do something to make him a little bit happier.

MINDY: I have an idea. Why don't we mail him something from our clubhouse kids? Maybe a letter, or....

LISA: Maybe a little package. Would he ever be surprised!

MIKE: That sounds like a good idea, Lisa. Mr. Barney needs to know that Jesus wants to be his friend. What could we put in a package?

LISA: I have a little picture of Jesus, the Good Shepherd. We could send that for one thing.

MIKE: Hey, do you 'spose he'd read our Sunday-school paper? Maybe we could put in our church bulletin.

LISA: How about a treat? Let's not tell him where the package came from.

MINDY: I wish we could send him a Bible. He needs to read God's Word. I know! Howie has a little New Testament he never uses. Maybe he will put that in. Let's go home and get our stuff together.

(All leave and Howie enters with package.)

HOWIE: Well, here's the package ready for me to mail. *(Motion with hand for each article named.)* Picture of Jesus, Sunday-school paper, New Testament, bulletin, and a candy bar. I'll go and mail it right away. *(Leaves)*

(Lift the sign to the stage and lower.)

(Howie enters.)

HOWIE: Mr. Narrator, sending that package was a good idea. Tell the folk what happened.

NARRATOR: I surely will, Howie. Our minister said that Mr. Barney rode past our church the other day and stopped to ask what time Sunday school and worship started. He said he was going to come to church before long. Your package must have had some effect on him. I suppose it started him thinking about Jesus—and let him know that people care about him. I'm mighty proud of you kids for letting other people know about Jesus.

Bible Story

The Vanishing Evangelist

After Jesus went back to Heaven the apostles waited until Jesus sent the Holy Spirit. And the church began. Many people believed in Jesus and became Christians. The apostles preached and as crowds grew bigger, more believers were added. Among them were many Christians who needed help.

"We must have more help so that we have more time to preach," said the apostles. "Choose seven faithful men who can take care of the poor members." Seven men were chosen. We call them deacons. One of these men was Philip.

The Pharisees and other Jewish leaders hated those who believed that Jesus is God's Son. Because of this, they did everything they could do to stop the Christians. They punished them, put them in prison, and stoned Stephen. This caused believers to leave Jerusalem and move to other places. The Bible says they were scattered. Philip went north to the city of Samaria. Crowds gathered in the big city and listened as he preached to them about Christ. He told them that Jesus could save them from their sin if they would believe in Him and obey Him. Many listeners loved to hear the good news. The attendance at the meetings was large. The Lord used Philip to do many miracles. Sick people were getting well and cripples were walking again. There was great joy in the city because of what was happening.

Everything was going well, and Philip was preach-

ing every day. Then something different happened. The voice of an angel said to Philip, "Go south to the road from Jerusalem to Gaza." What a strange place to be told to go! The land beyond Gaza was desert. There were no little towns where Philip could preach. He must have wondered why the Lord was asking him to leave the city where the attendance was so good and where he was accomplishing so much for God.

In the desert, the sand was hot and Philip was alone. As far as he could see, no one was in sight.

Then at a distance he could see something moving along, slowly. It was a chariot and someone was seated in it. He appeared to be looking at something.

"Go up to it," said the Lord. Philip obeyed and ran until he caught up with the chariot and walked beside it. The rider was reading from a scroll. He was from the country of Ethiopia, and was returning to his land where he was the treasurer for Queen Candace. He had been to Jerusalem to worship in the beautiful temple. He had heard about God but he did not know about Jesus. On his way home he was reading from the Old Testament book of Isaiah.

Philip ran up to the chariot and asked, "Do you understand what you are reading?"

"No! said the man. "How can I unless someone explains it to me?" Then he invited Philip to come up into the chariot and sit with him.

Now Philip knew why he had been sent to the lonely desert. He climbed up and sat beside the man. The place where the Ethiopian was reading was Isaiah, Chapter 53. The verse he placed his finger on was "He was led as a sheep to the slaughter; and like a lamb dumb before his shearer, so opened he not his mouth."

How pleased Philip was to be the teacher. He explained to the man from Ethiopia that this was Jesus, God's perfect Son, who willingly died on the cross. Jesus did not murmur or complain when cruel soldiers beat Him, mocked Him, and then nailed Him to a cross. He told how Jesus arose from the grave and has promised to come back some day.

The two men rode along together until they came near some water—a lake, a pond, or stream. Then the Ethiopian said, "Here is water. Why can't I be baptized?"

"If you believe with all your heart, you can," Philip replied.

"I believe that Jesus Christ is the Son of God," was his answer.

The Ethiopian commanded the chariot to stop. He and Philip went down into the water, and he was baptized. When they came up out of the water, the Lord took Philip away. He vanished, or disappeared, out of the man's sight.

What happened to the Ethiopian treasurer? He rode south in his chariot to his home. He went on his way a happy man. Now he had good news to tell his family and friends, for he was a follower of Jesus!

Bible Story Application

People are always ready to tell others about that which means most to them.

Robin has a baby brother of whom she is very fond. Students and teachers know all about the darling baby and his cute actions.

Jim's uncle is a professional football player. All year long Jim keeps everyone informed as to where his uncle is playing next, and what he does.

Philip talked about the Lord wherever he went. He loved the Lord and enjoyed serving Him. He was like Robin and Jim; he wanted to tell as many people about Christ as he could.

This is the way the Lord wants us to be. He wants us to serve Him by telling others about Him—about the great things He has done for us and the great things He can do for them (Mark 5:19 and 1 Chronicles 16:8, 9).

Activity Book

Discuss the material about chariots in the "Preview" section of the lesson before the children draw the two types of chariots. Provide pictures of chariots.

(The nine other words that describe Philip's character and what he did are evangelist, willing, obedient, teacher, preacher, helper, wise, prayed, friendly.)

Students unscramble the words to complete the sentences. *(The answers are 1. Samaria; 2. miracles; 3. desert, Gaza; 4. Jerusalem, worship; 5. Isaiah—this spelling instead of the one in the King James version; 6. Scripture; 7. baptized; 8. believe; 9. Spirit, more; 10. rejoicing.)*

Each student can fill in the answers in the "cartoon" at the bottom of the page. Discuss the importance of telling others about Jesus.

Craft Souvenir

Paper Plate Kaleidoscope

MATERIALS:
Two six-inch paper desert plates
Two four and one-half inch white tissue paper circles
Colored cellophane or tissue paper
Scissors, glue, and colorful felt-tip pens

PROCEDURE:
Before classtime cut a 3½ inch circle from the center of the plates. Cut the tissue circles.

Turn one plate upside down. Squeeze a line of glue around the inside edge. Lay one tissue over this and carefully stretch until taut.

Cut the cellophane into tiny circles, triangles, ovals, and others. (Candy wrappers can be used too.) Lay several pieces on the tissue to form a design. Squeeze another line of glue around the inside and outside edges of the plate and lay the second plate over it. Press firmly. Turn the double plate right side up. With felt pen, print "Tell your friends what great things the Lord has done for you" (Mark 5:19).

The outer edge of the plate may be colored with the pens.

The cellophane design will not stay in place, but the students will like to scatter them and look at the colors through the light.

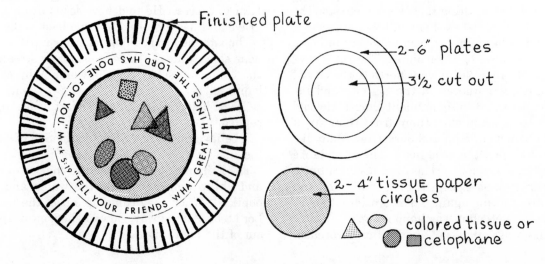

Paul's Quiet Helpers

Acts 18; Romans 16:1-3

Goals: (1) That the student will become familiar with three Bible characters who served the Lord by serving others, and (2) that he will seek small ways in which to serve the Lord.

Student Responses: As a result of this lesson, the student should be able to

- Tell how Priscilla, Agrippa, and Phoebe served the Lord.
- Tell why serving in small ways is important.
- List (or check in the activity book) three small things he will do this week to serve the Lord.
- Make something to give away. (Craft)

Learning Centers

Preview

Visiting a Tentmaker

MATERIALS:
Pictures of tents of the Near East

PROCEDURE:
Does your family own a tent? ... What are the greatest number of days you have lived in a tent? ... Would you like to make a tent your permanent home?

People of the world have lived in tents for several thousand years. They were the homes of such great men as Abraham, Isaac, Jacob, and Moses. Million of people have lived in tents. Tents have kept folk warm or cool. They have protected families and travelers from rain, wind, or blowing sand.

Tents in Bible times were made by spinning camel or goats' hair together with fiber from a plant something like hemp. This material was spun into spools of heavy, tough cords or string. The cord was then woven into long strips about a yard wide. The job of spinning was done mostly by the women. The men sewed the strips together and made the tents. Strips were convenient because when one wore out, it could be replaced by a new strip. Even today many tents are made by this method.

We like to move into newly built homes with new roofs that do not leak. But what do you think it would be like to move into a new Bible-times tent? It would be comfortable until it rained. The water leaked through the tiny holes until the material was watersoaked. Then the material swelled and the holes were sealed shut.

The tent house was made by propping up a long length of the goat-hair cloth, and living underneath. The area at the back was closed in with a screen of goat-hair cloth or reeds and twigs woven together. A curtain divided the tent into two rooms. One was an open porch where visitors could be received. The other was for the women and for household chores.

Memory Ticket Office

"His lord said unto him, Well done, thou good and faithful servant: thou hast been faithful over a few things, I will make thee ruler over many things: enter thou into the joy of thy lord." Matthew 25:21

THINK
1. What two characteristics should a servant of the Lord have?
2. What are the two rewards for being faithful to the Lord?

LEARNING GAME
Use the chalkboard to teach the verse. See page 5, "Preparation for Each Unit, Unit 2."

AWARD
Initial the tickets for those who have memorized the verse.

Guidebook

Small Things We Can Do

If desired, this drill can be visualized by showing correlating magazine pictures on a "television screen." With a knife, cut a window on one side of a carton. Cut a slit on either side. Glue the pictures to shelf paper and thread the ends through the slits. Fasten each end to a dowel stick so the paper can be rolled up as the pictures are pulled through or past the window.

Small ways we can serve the Lord:

1. By singing during music time or when alone.—Psalm 100:2 (group singing)
2. By letting our lifes show we love Jesus.—Matthew 5:16 (kindness picture)
3. By being faithful in what we do.—Luke 16:10 (child at work)
4. By having a good attitude.—Proverbs 17:22 (a happy child)
5. By learning memory verses.—Psalm 119:11 (child with Bible)
6. By making good use of our time.—Ephesians 5:16 (clock)
7. By doing good deeds for others.—Galatians 6:10 (child helping)

Front View Adventure

Little Things Count

MATERIALS:
Four sheets of shelf paper
Wide black felt marker and crayons

PROCEDURE:
On Sheet 1 write the letters of the alphabet.
On Sheet 2 write the numbers 0-9.
On Sheet 3 make the musical notes.
On Sheet 4 color the seven rainbow colors.

We have just twenty-six letters in the English alphabet. With these few letters we can write information about the whole world. *(Ask a student to use a combination of letters to write a word on Sheet 1.)* With these letters the printers are able to write books, magazines, and newspapers that tell us all sorts of things about people, nature, history, and hundreds of other things. We have our Bibles and story books because of these letters. Each one is small, but it has an important job. *(Write a word, leaving one letter out, to demonstrate)*

There are only ten numbers *(Show Sheet 2.)* But with these few we do our math, find chapters and verses in our Bibles, count our money, use the telephone, read the calendar, and tell time. Where we stand one number beside another makes a great difference in the value. We would not want to pay $9.01 for a $1.09 bag of potato chips. One incorrect number in our zip code or telephone number causes a letter or phone call not to reach us.

All songs in church and school are made up of just eight different notes. *(Show Sheet 3 and write "do, re, mi, fa, so, la, ti do.")* They are divided into half notes, quarter notes, etc., but all the music of the choirs, orchestras, and bands comes from just these notes. Each note is important. *(Demonstrate by eliminating one note of a familiar song.)*

There are seven colors of the rainbow. Can you name them? *(Red, orange, yellow, green, blue, indigo, and voilet. Write them on Sheet 4.)* The colors are different shades and tones, but there are no more than seven real colors. Yet, when combinations of these are put together, we have beautiful views, flowers, paintings, clothes, and book covers. If God had left out one of the colors, many beautiful blends and shades would be gone.

You may feel that the little things you do are not important. But they are. The Lord is ready to use the smallest service of the smallest child.

Worshiping Our Guide

Quiet music: "Submission" (page 127)
Song: "Step by Step" (page 118)
Theme chorus: "Serve, Serve, Serve the Lord."
Song: "Serve the Lord With Gladness."
  (page 131)
Bible reading: Mark 9:41
Prayer

Bible Story

Paul's Quiet Helpers

A young Christian man and his wife lived in the beautiful land of Italy. Aquila was a Jewish man who had once lived near the Black Sea. His wife's name was Priscilla. Their occupation was tentmaking.

One day Aquila must have left his work of whittling tent pegs and come to where his wife was weaving tent strips, and said, "Priscilla, we must leave this land. We must hurry because my life is in danger."

Priscilla, no doubt, laid down her weaving shuttle and listened as her husband continued to speak. "The emperor, Claudius, has commanded that all Jews leave Rome. It will not be safe for us to live here. We are being forced out of Italy. But let us not greatly fear; the Lord will protect us and show us where to go."

In a few days their simple household furnishings, clothing, and tent supplies were packed, and they were on their way. They decided to move to Greece, a country they probably had not lived in before. At the harbor they found a ship that was sailing across the Great Sea. Many other Jews were at the harbor because they, too, were forced to leave Rome.

"We will settle in Corinth," Aquila told Priscilla. "We will set up our tent business. We will be able to sell our tents to tourists who come to the capital city. Many people travel from place to place."

But Corinth was not a good city. The people who lived there were among the most evil on earth. They worshiped the god of the sea. They also worshiped at a shrine in honor of a goddess whose statue towered high above the city.

"We must do everything we can to show these idol worshipers that there is a much better way," Aquila and Priscilla must have said. "Remember Jesus said that we are to let our lights shine? We must pray for the Corinthians and tell them of the living Lord."

One day they had a pleasant surprise when they attended the Jewish synagogue. A new speaker had come. He was the apostle Paul, the great missionary for whom they had been praying while they still lived in Italy. Everyone listened as Paul taught the congregation things the Lord had taught him.

"Let us take the missionary home with us," said the couple one to another. "He can live with us as long as he stays in Corinth. His occupation is tentmaking like ours. We can make tents together when he is not preaching."

Paul lived with Aquila and Priscilla for eighteen months. Together, they made tents and sold them in the marketplace. Paul was a good tentmaker. He had learned the trade when he was a boy. As they worked, they talked about the Lord and they encouraged one another. It was not easy to be a missionary in Corinth. But coming home to friends where he felt welcome was a help to Paul.

Paul went into the synagogue to preach and talk to the Jews and others who came to worship. Some agreed that he was telling the truth that Jesus was God's Son. They became Christians. Others were rude and spoke against Christ and against Paul. When he saw that they would not listen, he shook his robe and said, "Let your sin be upon you; not upon me." He then left the synagogue.

A Christian man named Justus lived next to the synagogue. He said that Paul could take the believers to his house for meetings. Thus it was that in Justus' home the church began to meet. Aquila and Priscilla helped with the work.

Cenchrea was a town about ten miles from Corinth. Paul probably went there to teach in the church. Cenchrea was the hometown of a lady named Phoebe. She had become a dear friend of Paul's. In one of his letters Paul says she was a servant of the church at Cenchrea; that she had been a great help to many people including him. She may have taught the women. She may have prepared the Communion bread and grape juice and visited the needy families. So many Christians were asking her to do things that Paul wrote and asked the Christians to give her any help she needed.

One day Paul said, "The time has come for me to leave Corinth and continue missionary work other places."

"We will go with you," Aquila and Priscilla replied. They packed their furnishings and tent equipment and went to the harbor with Paul. They sailed to Ephesus in Asia. Paul went to the synagogue and preached. The people urged him to stay longer, but he said he wanted to go to Jerusalem. This time Aquila and Priscilla did not go along. They remained in Ephesus and served the Lord in the church there.

A very good Christian teacher and preacher named Apollos was teaching and preaching in Ephesus. He was sincere and loved the Lord, but he wasn't teaching the Word of God correctly. He was causing confusion among Christians and the unbelievers as well. Aquila and Priscilla took him home and helped him understand the Bible more clearly. How thankful they must have been that Paul had lived with them and taught them. Now they could teach others.

Bible Story Application

Once a builder gave one of his men a pattern of a leaf and asked him to carve the design on a common stone. Later he was given another leaf design to carve and also a tree branch design. All the while he worked, he wished the builder had given him some beautiful ornamental design to carve on marble instead of simple designs on ordinary stones.

A few months later, while walking through town, he saw a beautiful new building with a picture carved on the front. As he came close, he saw that part of the carving was his own. He said that if he had been careless with the simple designs, the beautiful picture would have been ruined.

Aquila and Priscilla had done the simple things, but they had done them well. They may have felt that the things they did were of little importance. But after nearly two thousand years, we still read the account of their example in the Bible. Their deeds were important to the Lord. Jesus said that if we serve Him by giving as little as a cup of cold water to someone in His name, we will be rewarded (Mark 9:41). Paul said that whatsoever we do, we should do with all of our heart (Colossians 3:23). The small things we do will count if we do them for the Lord (Colossians 3:17). When the Lord sees we are faithful in smaller things, He will give us bigger and more important things to do (Luke 16:10).

Activity Book

Refer to "Preview" in the "Learning Centers" section for information concerning Bible tents.

At the bottom of the page, the student supplies the missing letters to complete the words that describe Aquila, Priscilla, and Phoebe.

At the top of the second page, the student is to draw a line to the correct answer to complete the matching quiz.

(The answer to the coded puzzle is "God is pleased with my small deeds.")

Children will need to find the three verses in their Bibles in order to complete the sentences.

Discuss the list of small things that can be done to serve the Lord. Then ask each child to mark the ones he will do this week.

Craft Souvenir

Small Things for Giving

The goal for this unit has been to help students realize the importance of serving the Lord in small ways. To help them reach the goal during souvenir time, let them make simple items to give friends or family.

Children are creative. Have on hand materials such as construction paper, typing paper, stickers, envelopes, pattern books, pens, crayons, glue or paste. Make samples of simple crafts, such as bookmarks, folded crosses, and cardboard figures to trace around. Print a few mottos on the chalkboard.

Some children love to write or make up poems. They could write notes to missionaries, or make greeting cards to send to relatives.

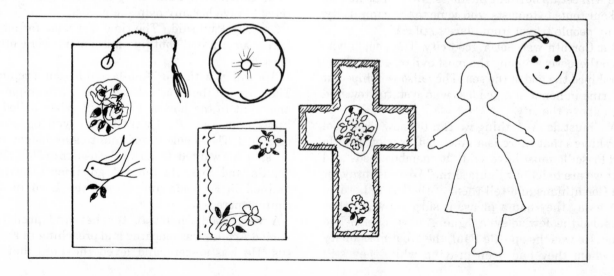

A Happy Foreigner

Ruth 1—4

Goals: That the student (1) will know that Ruth's choice resulted in lasting rewards and (2) will decide to depend upon the Lord for help when making important choices.

Student Responses: As a result of this lesson, the student should be able to do the following:

• Tell the Bible story.
• Describe Ruth.
• Tell two ways Ruth was rewarded for choosing Naomi's God.
• Tell what kinds of choices he has to make.
• Say the memory verse.

Learning Centers

Preview

MATERIALS:
Pictures of Bible-times and modern-day harvesting
Shallow pan containing grain (barley, oats, wheat, or others)
A sickle if available

PROCEDURE:

If you live on or near a farm where grain is raised, you have seen the heavy equipment that is used to harvest it.

During Bible times, the barley and other grains were gathered by hand. The only equipment was a curved knife called a sickle. Farmers used cords or long, strong blades of a plant to tie the bundles together. One person, who was called a reaper, cut the grain by the handfuls. As he worked, he laid the small bundles on the ground. Behind him came other people who tied the stalks in larger bundles. The bundles were set up in the field to dry.

When God gave the laws for the Jewish people, He had laws for the farmers. When harvesting the grain, they were to be kind to the poor and strang-ers. They were not to cut close to the edge of the field, and they were not to pick up the stalks they had missed or dropped (Leviticus 19:9, 10; 23:22). The poor people, widows, and strangers could come to the field and gather, or glean, the grain that had not been taken when harvesting.

Memory Ticket Office

"Choose you this day day whom ye will serve ... but as for me and my house, we will serve the Lord."
Joshua 24:15

THINK
1. Who said this? (Joshua)
2. Why should this verse be important to us?

LEARNING GAME

Cut the following shapes from construction paper and print on them the portions of the verse as shown. Spray with adhesive or glue on small pieces of flannelgraph paper so they will adhere to the flannelgraph board. Proceed as in Unit 1, Lesson 1.

AWARD
Initial the tickets for those who have memorized

the verse. (See page 5 for information concerning VISA on the passport)

Guidebook

Their Choices Were the Lord's

Print the following Bible references on cards and place them in a pocket chart, printed sides concealed. Let the students take turns choosing cards and reading the references. When a student finds the verse, he may ask the question.

1. Matthew 9:9 – Who chose to follow the Lord?
2. Luke 10:42 – Who chose the Lord as the good part?
3. Mark 1:16-18 – Who chose to leave their nets and follow the Lord?
4. John 21:6,7 – Who chose to swim to shore to be with the Lord?
5. Hebrews 11:8 – Who chose to leave his country to follow the Lord?
6. John 8:12 – What does the Lord promise to those who choose to follow Him?
7. Acts 26:28 – Who almost chose to become a Christian?

Front View Adventure

Review With Pantomime

Use pantomime (acting with no words) to review the Bible stories of previous units.

MATERIALS:
Puppet stage and two puppets
Twenty students for pantomime, or as many as feasible

PROCEDURE:
PUPPET A: Hear ye, hear ye! All ye students of the _____ Church. Our Bible story today is about choosing. Do you like to choose? *(Wait for response.)*
PUPPET B: Have you found that it is best to do right instead of wrong? If there was a hard thing to do and an easy thing to do, which of the two would you choose?
PUPPET A: If you knew the difficult thing would prove to be the best, which would you choose?
PUPPET B: Many people in the Bible had to make important choices. Our students are about to dramatize some of these people. You are to guess who the people are and what choices they made.

No. 1 – Noah and three sons building the ark. (Chose to believe God. Lesson 1)
No. 2 – Hezekiah receiving the letter from a soldier and then praying in the temple. (Chose to pray about the problem. Lesson 3)
No. 3 – David and Goliath. (Chose to have courage. Lesson 2)
No. 4 – Philip beside the chariot. (Chose to tell others. Lesson 17)
No. 5 – Jesus and Zacchaeus. (Chose to believe. Lesson 4)
No. 6 – Stoning of Stephen. (Chose to suffer and die. Lesson 9)
No. 7 – Rebekah prepares Jacob's hands before he goes to Isaac. (Chose not to wait for the Lord. Lesson 10)
No. 8 – Smiling worshipers depositing offerings. (Chose to give cheerfully. Lesson 16)
No. 9 – Paul and Aquila whittling pegs and Priscilla weaving. (Chose to do what they could. Lesson 18)

Worshiping Our Guide

Quiet music: "What a Friend We Have in Jesus."
Song: "What a Happy Day." (page 128)
Theme chorus: "Young Traveler" (See preparation for this unit, on page 6)
Song: "My Lord Knows the Way." (page 134)
Bible reading: John 10:9-11
Prayer
Offering and announcements
Special: Testimony of an important choice.
Song: "He Is Lord."
Song: "He's Able." (page 122)
Prayer

Bible Story

A Happy Foreigner

During a time of famine, food is scarce because there has been no rain on the crops for a long time. After a while people become very hungry. This is what happened in Bethlehem in our Bible story.

Elimelech and his sweet, pleasant wife Naomi lived in Bethlehem with their sons, Mahlon and Chilion. They may not have been rich people, but they owned land, a home, and probably other possessions.

"We must leave Bethlehem because of this terrible

famine," Elimelech told Naomi one evening. "Let us move to Moab where there is plenty of food for our family. We will come back when the famine is over."

They packed their things and traveled to the country of Moab. There they settled and there they lived for a long time. Moab was not a good place for Jewish people to live because the Moabites worshiped idols. Elimelech's family worshiped the Lord. When Mahlon and Chilion grew up, they married girls who worshiped idols. The girls' names were Orpah and Ruth.

After they had lived in the new4 land for a while, sadness came to the little Jewish family. Naomi's husband, Elimelech, died. Later both of her sons died. This was a sad experience for Naomi. Now she was all alone in a foreign country with just the two daughters-in-law. Since her family was gone, she longed to be back in Bethlehem among her relatives and old friends. She wanted to live among her God-loving people.

One day Naomi surprised her daughter-in-law by saying, "The famine in Bethlehem is over so I am going to move back."

Orpah and Ruth thought about her decision for a while. They had come to love Naomi. They said, "We are going with you."

The three of them started on their long journey together. How excited they were at first. The girls probably had never been in Israel before, and Naomi had not seen her friends for ten years.

After they had walked a way, Naomi urged the girls to return home. She didn't want them to feel that their duty was to go with her. She didn't want them to become homesick. Orpah took her advice and returned to Moab, but Ruth chose to continue the journey.

"Orpah is going home to her family and to her gods; you should go, too," Naomi said.

But Ruth had made up her mind. She said, "Do not ask me to leave you. Where you go, I am going. Where you live, I want to live. Your family shall be my family and your God, my God." When Naomi saw that Ruth had made her choice, she let her go with her to Bethlehem.

When the two women came to the streets of Bethlehem, the people gathered around and said, "Look who is back from Moab! It's Naomi!"

Naomi went to the house that had been saved for her, and Ruth went along. It was the time of barley harvest, and the farmers were cutting grain. Seeing they had no provisions in the house, Ruth asked her mother-in-law if she could go to a field and glean. Then they could have barley to grind into flour.

The girl found a nice field where workmen were cutting the grain and tying it into bundles. The field belonged to a rich Jewish man named Boaz. When he came to the field he saw Ruth. She was so lovely that he asked the workmen who she was.

"It's the woman who came back with Naomi. She asked permission to glean. She's been working for several hours," they said.

Boaz was pleased. He liked Ruth. He called her to his side and told her not to go to any other farmer's field to glean. She was to drink from the cool water the men had drawn from the well for themselves. Ruth asked, "Why do you treat me so kindly when I am a stranger?"

Boaz answered, "Because you have been good to your mother-in-law and left your home to come here with her to live among people you do not know." Then Boaz told Ruth at mealtime to eat with him and his reapers. Later he told the men to purposely leave grain for Ruth to gather.

"Boaz is a relative of my husband," said Naomi excitedly when Ruth came home with a basket of grain and told her where she had gleaned.

Boaz loved Ruth and soon they planned to be married. But there was a problem the couple had to face. Naomi needed to sell her property. According to the Jewish law she must sell it to no one else but the nearest relative of her husband's. The relative who bought it must also marry Ruth.

But there was still another problem! There was a closer relative of Naomi's husband than Boaz. Would he want to buy the property? Then he would marry Ruth. Boaz went to the city gate and waited for the man to appear. When he was asked, the relative said that he could not buy the property for himself. This meant that Boaz was free to marry Ruth.

Boaz's marriage was good, for he married a lovely lady who was not only thoughtful of him but of others as well. She showed so much kindness to her mother-in-law that people all around talked about it. Although she was pretty, Ruth was humble. She was thankful for what others did for her.

God gave Boaz and Ruth a son whom they named Obed. Many years after Obed grew up, he became the grandfather of King David.

Bible Story Application

When Ruth chose to follow the living God, she made the wisest choice of her lifetime. She must have been glad many times that she didn't return to Moab as Orpah did. Many good things happened because Ruth made the right choice. She found a good field to glean in, and was asked to return to the field time after time. She had a good mother-in-law and finally married a rich man. She had the honor of being the great grandmother of good King David.

Like Joshua, Ruth chose to serve the Lord (Joshua 24:15). She learned of the true God. We have the Bible to tell us about the Lord and how to be His followers. Ruth was rewarded, and the Lord promises to reward us when we make the right choices.

Young travelers must make some kind of choice every day. Sometimes that choice is to decide between right and wrong. Then sometimes we have a choice between two good things, and it is so hard to decide. The Lord always cares about these decisions. He helps us know what to do.

Activity Book

Refer to "Preview" for information concerning harvesting in Bible times.

At the bottom of the page, students cross out statements that are wrong and print an "R" beside those that are right.

Give help as needed as the students fill in the blanks at the top of the next page. They may need to look in the book of Ruth to find some of the answers.

Discuss the questions in "Keeping Close to My Guide," and then ask the children to write their answers in the blanks.

Craft Souvenir

Good News Swimmer

MATERIALS:
Construction paper and pattern from pattern page
Pen or pencil and scissors
Shallow pans with water

PROCEDURE:
Using the pattern, trace the swimmer on the paper. On his chest print "I choose Christ" or "Jesus' way brings happiness." Cut out.

Fold the head forward first. Then fold arms across the chest and legs up. Press firmly.

Lay the folded swimmer on the water. The moisture will cause the paper to unfold revealing the message. Because paper dries nicely, the swimmer can be used over and over. Each child can make an extra swimmer to give to a friend.

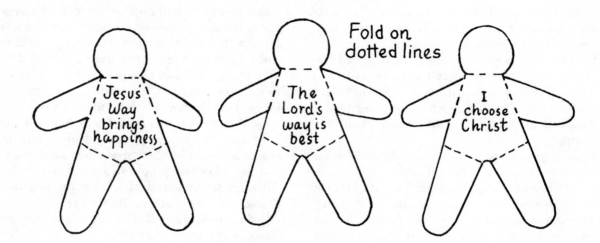

A Princely Friend

1 Samuel 17:57—18:9; 19:1-7; 20

Goals: (1) That the student will have a better understanding of Jonathan and David's friendship. (2) That the student will know that Christ is the best Friend he can have and the closest friends are those who love the Lord.

Student Responses: As a result of this lesson, the student should be able to do the following:
- Describe David.
- Describe Jonathan.
- Tell how Jonathan showed his love for David.
- Tell who is his very best friend.
- Tell why we should choose our friends carefully.

Learning Centers

Preview

Bible-times Clothing

MATERIALS:
Dress a student in Bible-times clothes.
Alternative: Pictures and samples of clothing and fabrics.

PROCEDURE:
What was the first piece of clothing mentioned in the Bible? It was fig leaves fastened together and worn by Adam and Eve. Later God made them coats from skins of animals (Genesis 3:21).

The clothing for a man in Bible times was very simple. He wore a garment something like a shirt that reached to his knees. It had short sleeves or no sleeves at all. Around his waist he wore a cloth or leather belt called a girdle. Part of it was sewed together to make a place to keep coins.

Over this he wore a loosely fitted coat, something like our bathrobes. Another belt or sash held the coat closed or partly open. In the fold, the man could carry his lunch, a lamb, or even grain.

Then there was the cloak, sometimes called a robe or mantle. It had no sleeves, was loose, and was usually made of heavier material than the other garments. It could be used as a blanket for keeping warm at night.

The headpiece could be one of several kinds, but the most simple was a cloth held on by a band.

The clothing of the woman was similar to the man's except it came to the ankles and was decorated with embroidery and colorful threads.

Rich men and kings wore clothing of finer fabrics. Sometimes a gold thread or fine wire was woven into the fabric.

Memory Ticket Office

"A man that hath friends must shew (show) himself friendly: and there is a friend that sticketh closer than a brother."   Proverbs 18:24

THINK
1. Who is the Friend who sticks closer than a brother?
2. What is one way you can prove you are friendly?

LEARNING GAME
See page 5 for the use of the pocket chart.

AWARD
Initial the tickets for those who have memorized the verse. (See page 6 for information for using the "visa" on the "passport.")

Guidebook

Find the Clue

The following verses contain clues for making or keeping friends. The clues may be put on cards, sprayed with adhesive spray or having added pieces of flannelgraph paper, scattered on a flannelgraph board. When a student finds the verses, he may choose the proper clue card and place it on one side of the board. (All clues in the Bible verses do not start with "be.")

1. Be kind. – – – – –Ephesians 4:23
2. Be an example. – – – – –1 Timothy 4:12
3. Be friendly. – – – – –Proverbs 18:24
4. Be content. – – – – –Hebrews 13:5
5. Be gentle. – – – – –2 Timothy 2:24
6. Be humble. – – – – –James 4:10
7. Be honest. – – – – –Romans 13:13
8. Be loving. – – – – –Proverbs 17:17

Front View Adventure

Poor-Company Pete

MATERIALS:
Three puppets and Howie's clubhouse (puppet stage)
A medal or badge
A sign that reads "Two weeks later" attached to a stick

(Howie and Mindy enter.)

HOWIE: Hey, it sure is great to get back to the clubhouse. I've missed it.

MINDY: Me, too! But I've had gobs of homework. Mr. Sanders gives us long lists of spelling words. No way do I like spelling. Mike says he hates it.

HOWIE: Say, I haven't seen Mike around lately. Was he in school yesterday?

MINDY: Nope! He was goofing around with that new kid all day. He made me promise not to tell our parents he was skipping school.

HOWIE: Pete's not good company for your brother. The kids say he's rough and mean.

MINDY: Right! Mike acts different around home, too. He didn't used to be sassy. Wow! Does he ever talk smart now. He's careful what he says when Dad's around, but he gets smart to Mom.

HOWIE: Your brother is a Christian, but bad company can sure spoil a fellow.

MINDY: He doesn't even want to go to Sunday school lately. My folks have to make him. Shh! Here he comes!

(Mike enters in a hurry, nervous and out of breath.)

MIKE: Hi! I thought you'd be here. You're supposed to go home and sweep the porch and walks.

MINDY: Why me? I helped Mom all morning. What are you going to do?

MIKE: It's none of your business, Mindy. I got a date with Pete.

HOWIE: That's a neat hat you're wearing. Where did you get it?

MIKE: Oh, my hat? Ah—well—hmmmm. Oh, I found it. I found it by the river.

MINDY: Mike, you have Dad's honor badge on your shirt. You can't wear that; you'll lose it. He didn't tell you that you could wear it.

MIKE: Don't worry. I'll not lose it. Just see that you don't tell him.

HOWIE: I just memorized a Bible verse in class Sunday. "Be not wise in your own eyes. Fear the Lord and depart from evil."

MIKE: Don't worry about me. I can take care of myself.

(Mike leaves)

HOWIE: It's okay to be friendly, but Mike shouldn't choose Pete as a close friend. He should try to help Pete. I think we should pray for both of them.
(Both leave. Lift the sign to stage and lower it again.)
(Mindy and Mike enter.)
MIKE: Mindy, you told Dad and Mom that I skipped school yesterday.
MINDY: Nope! I didn't tell on you. Dad saw you on the street.
MIKE: Oh. I wondered how he knew. I have a problem! I lost his honor badge. I've looked everywhere for it.
MINDY: How come you wanted to wear it in the first place.
MIKE: Pete thinks his dad is so smart. He's always bragging. I wanted to show him that Dad got honors, too.
MINDY: I have a surprise for you. Mom found it still pinned on your shirt when she washed it.
MIKE: Some of the kids say Pete's not very good company for me. Maybe they're right.
(Howie enters.)
HOWIE: Did you hear the news?
MIKE AND MINDY: What happened?
HOWIE: Your friend Pete and another guy got caught shoplifting this morning. Pete had a transistor radio under his sweater.
MIKE: Wow! He wanted me to steal but I wouldn't. I'd better take my hat back. I didn't steal it, but Pete did and gave it to me. Ooooh, I guess I'm in trouble, too. How will I return the hat?
HOWIE: You better ask your dad. You might have to see the police. Or maybe the merchant. It's better not to take things from people we are not sure we can trust.
(All leave.)

Worshiping Our Guide

Quiet music: "I Would Be True."
Song: "Oh, How He Loves You and Me."
Theme chorus: "Young Traveler" (See page 6.)
Song: "Jesus Is My Answer." (page 125)
Bible reading: John 15:12-14
Prayer
Offering and Announcements
Special music: "What a Friend We Have in Jesus."
Song: "Like a Shepherd" (page 121)
Song: "My God Is a Great God" (page 117)
Prayer

Bible Story

A Princely Friend

Everyone was thrilled when David killed Israel's terrible enemy, the giant Goliath.

"What a hero that young fellow is," Jonathan may have said to those who stood around him. Jonathan and David met and became very close friends.

Jonathan did something very special to show how great his love was. Because he was a prince, he wore princely clothes. He took off his beautiful robe and put it around David's shoulders. He even gave him his sword and bow and his belt.

Saul was pleased with David at first. He brought him to the palace to live and to be his musician. And he gave him a high rank in the army. When the soldiers returned home after defeating the Philistines, the women came out from the towns and cities to meet King Saul. They danced, played tambourines, and sang joyful songs. They sang, "Saul has slain his thousands, and David his ten thousands." This made Saul very jealous. From that time on, there was much trouble for David. Many times the king tried to kill him, or have him killed.

One day Saul called Jonathan and all the servants to the throne room and said, "I demand that you kill David!"

Jonathan loved David. He could never slay his dear friend—even at the command of the king.

"David, go and hide," he said. "I will talk to my father. Then I will come and tell you what he said."

The young prince said very kind things to the king about his friend. He told him that David was there to serve the king and to do him good. To kill him would be a sin against God. He reminded his father how David had risked his own life when he dared to defy Goliath's challenge.

Saul promised not to do David any harm, and Jonathan brought David back from the hiding place. But Saul still had a terrible sinful, jealous feeling toward David. He knew the boy had been chosen to be king. Before long he made more attempts to slay him, and again David had to hide.

One day David asked Jonathan, "What am I doing that your father wants to kill me?"

"You haven't done anything," said Jonathan. "You shall not die, David. I shall once again ask my father why he is angry. He tells me everything."

"Your father knows we are friends," said David. "He won't tell you. And I know he is going to kill me!"

"Whatever you want me to do, I'll do for you, David," said Jonathan.

So the two young men worked out a plan. David

always ate at the king's table on the day of the new moon. If he was absent, the king would miss him. Jonathan would tell his father that he had given David permission to go to Bethlehem to offer sacrifices with his family. David was to hide behind rocks in a field and wait. If the king agreed that it was all right, then David was safe. If the king was angry, then David needed to stay away. Jonathan would go to the place where David was hiding. If it was safe, Jonathan would shoot arrows close by and ask an errand boy to go and get them. If his father was angry, he would shoot the arrows beyond the rock where David was hiding and tell the boy to run and get them.

When King Saul and Jonathan sat down to eat, Saul asked where David was. He had missed two meals at the king's table. The king was angry. He said, "Don't you know you will not be king as long as David lives? Bring him here, for he shall die."

Jonathan went to the field with the errand boy. He shot the arrow far beyond the rock. "Isn't the arrow beyond you?" he called to the boy. David got the message. He must escape for his life.

Jonathan sent the boy back to town with his bow and arrows. David came out of his hiding place, and the two friends cried as they told each other good-bye.

Jonathan was admired by all who knew him. He was strong and he was quick in action. He was an expert with his bow and arrow. He was brave and he wasn't afraid to speak the truth. He was a famous warrior, yet he was tender-hearted. He was a faithful friend, especially to David. And he loved the Lord.

Bible Story Application

Jonathan did not choose David as a close friend without considering what he was like. He knew that any fellow who would risk his life to save his country would be a worthy friend. What David had shouted to Goliath assured Jonathan that David was a true believer in God. The two of them would agree on much of what they talked about and did together.

When we love the Lord, we ought to choose our friends carefully. This does not mean that we should snub others. We can be friendly and helpful without doing what they do.

Proverbs 22:24, 25 says we are not to make friends with those who are always angry or we may become like them.

Paul said that we are not to tie our close friendship with people who do not believe in the Lord (2 Corinthians 6:14).

Our best friend is Jesus. There's no one like Jesus. He will stand by us. His love is far better than Jonathan's love for David because He gave his life for us and His love is everlasting.

Activity Book

Discuss clothing of Bible times as the children color the picture. (See "Preview.")

At the bottom of the page, the students list some of the characteristics of Jonathan that would make him a good close friend.

Allow plenty of time for students to complete the crossword puzzle at the top of the second page.

Scripture verses supply the words that go in the blanks in "Keeping Close to My Guide."

Craft Souvenir

Friendship Notes

MATERIALS:
Good quality typing paper
Crayons, scissors, ball-point pen or pencil
Used greeting cards
Bible verses and short poems to copy

PROCEDURE:
Fold typing paper twice to form a French-folded note paper.

Use crayons to decorate the front of the folder, drawing and coloring a scene, flower, or design.

Alternative: Flowers, birds, scenes, or little animals may be cut from greeting cards and glued to the front of the folder.

Write a poem, message, or greeting, and a Bible verse to a friend.

French fold

A King's First Look in the Book

2 Chronicles 34

Goals: That the student (1) will see how effective God's Word was in the lives of Josiah and his people and (2) will be determined to faithfully read the Bible and obey it.

Student Responses: As a result of this lesson, the student should be able to do the following:

• Tell the Bible story
• Describe Josiah.
• Tell the forms in which the Bible was written. (See "Preview" and Activity Book)
• Tell why reading the Bible is important.

Learning Centers

Preview

The Bible

MATERIALS:
Bibles and a scroll
Picture of the Gutenberg press if available

PROCEDURE:

Please hold your Bible and look at it. Do you have more than one Bible? What kind of cover is on your Bible? Look at the thin, white pages and the neat rows of printing. Notice that the chapters and verses are numbered. Why? Did you know the Bible did not always look like this?

When Jesus lived on the earth, every Jewish town had a part of our Bible called the Old Testament. It was handwritten on scrolls and unrolled as it was read. *(Demonstrate.)*

The first time we read that God's words were written down was when Moses was on the mountain and God himself wrote on two tablets of stone. What were those laws called?

At first, clay tablets were used to write on. While the clay was soft, words were written with a sharp tool, and the tablets were dried in the sun. Animal

skins were also dried, made smooth, and used to write on. Later papyrus was used. The Bible was copied by hand on scrolls. Later the book form was used, paged, and bound very much like our books today.

Then more than five hundred years ago Mr. Gutenberg invented the printing press. After that, Bibles were produced much easier, faster, and with less expense. Today almost everyone can own a Bible.

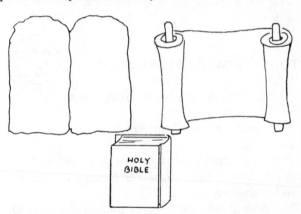

Jan and Johnny's father went to Africa on a long business trip. He couldn't talk to them on the telephone, so he wrote to them. Almost every day they received a letter from him, and they could hardly wait until they opened and read it. The letter contained words of encouragement and rules they were to follow. He said that he loved them very much and promised to come back to them soon.

God's Word is a letter to us. We should read it every day and obey it.

Memory Ticket Office

"Blessed are they that hear the word of God, and keep it."   Luke 11:28

THINK
1. What is another word for "blessed"? (Happy)
2. What does the word "keep" mean?

LEARNING GAME

Use the chalkboard. (See instructions for Unit 2.)

AWARD

Initial the tickets for those who have memorized the verse.

Guidebook

"Mystery Seat" Bible Drill

On a card write, "You have been chosen to be the leader for today's Bible drill," and tape it under a chair. The student who finds the card under his chair may lead the drill until one person locates two verses. Then that student is the leader.

1. The Bible is forever.－－－－－1 Peter 1:23
2. The Bible is powerful.－－－－－Hebrews 4:12
3. The Bible shows the way.－－－－－Psalm 119:105
4. The Bible is to be studied.－－－－－Timothy 2:15
5. The Bible is to be obeyed.－－－－－James 1:22
6. The Bible helps us keep from sinning.－Psalm 119:11

Front View Adventure

Van Anh Finds Happiness

"Why was I named Van Anh?" asked the young girl.

"When you were a tiny baby you were soft and nice to hold. Your name means 'Beautiful Cloud,'" her grandmother answered.

Van Anh lived with her grandmother in a big house with bamboo walls and thatched roof.

Along one of the walls was a piece of furniture holding an altar. Every day Van Anh stood before it and prayed. Her mother and father were dead, so she prayed to the spirits of her parents and ancestors. In her hand she held rice and sometimes a banana. Before she went away she burned an incense stick and watched the smoke rise. "The smoke will take my gift to the spirits," she thought.

"Grandmother, what can I do to be happy? I pray to the altar and give my gifts, but I have no peace," she said.

"Go to the temple on top of Mt. Tay Nink. When people want very much to please the gods, they make the journey and pray to the great altar. It is a dangerous trip. Wildcats, tigers, and many wild jungle animals are on the long, high trail," her grandmother warned.

Van Anh was not very brave, but she decided to go.

Carrying a basket of food, she made her way up the mountain. Jungle birds flew among the trees, and frightening sounds came from behind bushes, but she continued on.

Finally she reached the top where the temple stood. Oh, how pleased the spirits must be that she had made the dangerous journey. She went straight to the altar. The priest taught her little prayers to say, and how to beat the gong. She burned incense and it rose high. She looked at the motionless idol and waited. Finally she turned away, sad and unhappy. Slowly, sadly, she returned home.

The days went by, and Van Anh could find no happiness. Then one day a man and woman came to the village. They told about one true God. They told about His Son—One called Jesus. The missionaries gave Van Anh a book to read. It was a New Testament.

Van Anh read the book. She read of a Man called Jesus who did wonderful things, who died on a cross, and came alive again. She didn't understand it all, but someone had underlined John 3:16. "None of my gods loved me like that," she thought.

Van Anh read parts of the book over and over to her grandmother. Especially she read John 3:16.

She and her grandmother went to the meetings the missionary had. They became Christians. At long last Van Anh was happy!

Worshiping Our Guide

Quiet music: "Wonderful Words of Life"
Song: "The Bible Is God's Word."
Theme chorus: "Young Traveler"
Song: "Loving and Kind" (page 119)
Bible reading: John 1:1-4
Prayer
Offering and announcements
Special: Say the books of the Bible.
Song: "The B-I-B-L-E"
Song: "Thy Word Have I Hid in My Heart." (page 126)
Prayer

Bible Story

A King's First Look at the Book

The Bible tells of two persons who became kings when they were little boys. Both of them ruled over the kingdom of Judah and both of them had the temple repaired. Even their names were similar: Joash and Josiah.

Josiah was eight years old when the crown was put on his head and he began to reign. Before him, the nobles and captains bowed low. No person was greater than their little king. The Bible says that "while he was yet young, he began to seek after God."

But how could Josiah learn what the Lord wanted him to do? The old scroll (a part of the Bible) he could have learned from was lost. The people in the kingdom had forgotten God and were worshiping idols. They didn't read God's Word or take care of it, and finally it was gone. What Josiah knew about the Lord may have been taught to him by his mother or the priest, Helkiah.

When Josiah was twenty years old, he gave orders that wherever the false gods were found, they were to be destroyed. To make sure the job was done right, he stood and watched as the workmen hacked them to pieces.

"Now we must do something about the temple," Josiah said. "The building is no longer beautiful. It needs to be repaired. " It was true! The walls and floors needed to be mended, and the building needed to be thoroughly cleaned. It had been terribly neglected. The leaders at the temple went about collecting money so that workers could be hired and materials could be purchased.

One day while the men were gathering up a pile of rubbish from a dark corner of the temple, Helkiah the priest saw something that looked like a scroll. When he brushed off the dust from the parchment, he saw that it was a very special book.

"Look! I have found a book," Helkiah told Shaphan the scribe as he held the scroll in his trembling hand. "It is the Book! The Book of the Law of the Lord, given through Moses!"

Shaphan took the valuable scroll to Josiah. As he stood before the king, he gave a report that the money given by the people had been used to pay the workmen. Then he said "Helkiah the priest gave me this Book." As he spoke, he unrolled the scroll and read some of the words to the king.

King Josiah leaned forward as he listened to words he had never heard before. It was indeed the message from God. The words of the Holy Book caused him to tremble with fright. The message was that the Lord was angry about the sin of the people. They had not kept His commandments.

Josiah believed every word of the Book. He tore his royal clothes to show how sorry he was for the evil ways the people had been living. He ordered everyone in the kingdom to come to the temple to hear for themselves what God had to say.

People came from every corner of the kingdom of Judah. As Josiah looked out over the crowd, he saw standing before him captains, nobles, prophets, workmen, men, women, children, rich and poor. God's message was for all. As they waited, he unrolled the scroll and read the Word of the Lord to them. How quiet they were as they listened. And how frightened they must have been. They were thinking how foolish and how evil they had been for bowing to gods of stone.

Josiah stood beside a pillar of the temple and made a promise to God that he would follow Him and keep His commandments. He also made the great crowd promise to keep the commandments and to follow the Lord as he had promised to follow the Lord.

Josiah ruled over Judah for thirty-one years. As long as he lived, the people continued to worship the true God and obey His Word. Josiah was a good king and a good leader. He had respect for God's house. When he heard God's Word read for the first time, he believed it. He read the Word and obeyed it.

Bible Story Application

When God gave the laws to the Jewish people in the wilderness. He told them that they were to continually remind their boys and girls that His Word was very important. They were to have it in their hearts (memorize it). They were to teach it to their children, talk about it as they traveled and while they ate their meals. They were to talk about the Word when they went to bed at night and when they got up in the morning (Deuteronomy 6:6, 7).

God's Word is pure. This means that there are no flaws or mistakes. This is because God himself caused it to be written and took care of it down through the years.

We must not only read the Bible, but obey it. God has promised that those who do obey it will have real peace and happiness. Reading the Bible and obeying it is very important for young travelers (2 Timothy 3:15).

Activity Book

Discuss the pictures in "Our Bible and How We Got It" as the children fill in the blanks.

Students fill in the blanks and then the squares of the simple crossword puzzle.

Students may need to look in 2 Chronicles 34 to find some of the answers to write in the blanks at the top of the second page.

In "Keeping Close to My Guide," students can find the verses and fill in the blanks before the group discusses each verse and its meaning. Help students to make using the Bible a vital part of their lives.

Craft Souvenir

Bookmark

MATERIALS:
Lightweight posterboard and construction paper
Bible seal, yarn or string
Ball-point pen and felt-tip pen
Scissors, stapler, paper punch and ruler.

PROCEDURE:
For bookmark, punch a hole in one end of a 2 by 6 inch piece of posterboard. Stick on a Bible seal. With felt pen print "Be ye doers of the word" (James 1:22).

Make a tiny booklet by folding three pieces of 1¼" by 2" paper in half. Assemble the pages. Staple the lower edge with one staple and punch a hole in the upper lefthand corner. Print "The Bible" on the cover. Open the book and write on the pages, "Read it. Believe it. Obey it. Tell others."

Fasten the book to the bookmark in this way: Fold a twelve-inch piece of yarn in half and tie a knot on the end. Draw the loop end through the hole in the bookmark. Spread apart and draw the knot end through. Pull the yarn firm. Thread the knotted end of the yarn through the hole in the book. Spread yarn apart and pull the bookmark through. Pull the yarn firm against the book.

A Wealthy Farmer on an Ash Heap

Job 1; 2; 42:10-17

Goals: That the student (1) will remember that Job is an example of faithfulness to the Lord; (2) will know that God allows Satan to go just so far; and (3) will promise the Lord that he will be more faithful.

Student Responses: As a result of this lesson, the student should be able to do the following:

• Pretend he was a cub reporter in the land of Oz and tell what he saw and heard. (See Activity Book.)
• Tell how Job was rewarded for his faithfulness.
• State the one thing that God expects of us. (Faithfulness)
• Ask God to help him to be faithful.

Learning Centers

Preview

God's Wonderful Work

MATERIALS:
One picture each of a night sky, clouds, snow scene, and an ocean.

You may have heard of the seven wonders of the world. The book of Job tells us of several wonders of God's creation. If we were to see all of these wonders, we would need a powerful telescope, ride a cloud, make a snowball, and do some deep-sea fishing.

Job said he knew the Lord could do everything (Job 42:2). Here are four things:

1. Job 26:7. Job said the Lord stretched out the north over the empty places. Astronomers have discovered a space in the north that is completely without a star.

2. Job 37:16. Job was asked if he knew about the balancing of the clouds. We watch clouds float along quietly. Even when they are full of water, they do not tumble down.

3. Job 38:16. The Lord asked Job if he had ever walked or entered into the springs of the sea. Many years ago it was discovered that seas and oceans have springs of water.

4. Job 38:22. The Lord asked Job if he knew about the treasures in the snow and hail. For thousands of years people have thought that snow was a nuisance. It wasn't worth much more than to look pretty, play in, and hold moisture. Now we know that snow is valuable because of the nitrogen it puts into the soil.

Memory Ticket Office

"Moreover it is required in stewards, that a man be found faithful." 1 Corinthians 4:2

THINK
1. What was a steward in Bible times? (A caretaker)
2. We are caretakers for the Lord. What is required of us?

LEARNING GAME
Print the verse and reference on the chalkboard. Read the verse together. Erase the verse, leaving just the first letter of each word as a clue. Continue to erase the clue letters as the verse is being memorized.

AWARD
Initial the tickets for those who have memorized the verse.

Guidebook

"Helps on Being Faithful" Drill

1. God is faithful to us. – – – – –1 Corinthians 1:9
2. Be faithful to Christ because of what He did for us. – Galatians 2:20

3. Pray about our faithfulness. – – – – – Isaiah 40:31

4. God cares that we remain faithful. – 1 Corinthians 10:13

5. Christ will help us be strong in our faithfulness. – Philippians 4:13

6. Satan will try to stop us from being faithful. – 1 Peter 5:8

7. We will be rewarded for our faithfulness. – 1 Corinthians 15:58

Front View Adventure

Stump the Experts

Give a copy of each of the following clues to individual or group speakers. Choose two "experts" to face the audience. The speakers read each clue and wait for the experts to answer. If their answer is correct, give the experts 100 points. If the audience must answer the clue, give them the 100 points.

You may wish to put more value on the answers given by the audience depending upon the Bible knowledge of the experts.

Experts	Class
100	100
100	100
100	100
100	100
100	
100	
_____	_____
600	400

1. I was a young Jewish girl who was captured and taken to Syria. Although I was a slave and away from home, I remained faithful to God. My master had leprosy, and I suggested that he go to the prophet where God would heal him. What was my master's name? (Naaman. 2 Kings 5)

2. I was the faithful deacon who preached in the Jewish synagogue. I was martyred because I preached that Jesus is God's beloved Son. Who was I? (Stephen. Acts 7)

3. We were Hebrew boys who were taken to Babylon. We remained faithful to our God when everyone else bowed to Nebuchadnezzar's golden idol. Who were we? (Shadrach, Meshach, and Abednego. Daniel 3)

4. I was the faithful evangelist who was ready to preach wherever the Holy Spirit led me. I helped an Ethiopian understand the Scripture. Who was I? (Philip. Acts 8)

5. I faithfully built a boat on dry land even though people mocked and said I was foolish. I believed God would do what He said He would do. Who was I? (Noah. Genesis 6)

6. I was an unfaithful slave until I became a follower of Christ. Then I became faithful and profitable. Who was I? (Onesimus. Philemon)

7. God asked me to leave my country and my people and move to another land that He would show me. I faithfully obeyed. Who was I? (Abraham. Genesis 12)

8. When I first heard the scroll read, I listened. I believed it, and later I read it to the people of my kingdom. Who was I? (Josiah. 2 Kings 22)

9. We were a man and wife who kept the apostle Paul in our home. We faithfully helped him in his missionary work. Who were we? (Aquila and Priscilla. Acts 18:1-3)

10. I lived in Cenchrea and attended church there. I faithfully helped many Christians. I helped the apostle Paul. Who was I? (Phoebe. Romans 16:1)

Worshiping Our Guide

Quiet music: "Great Is Thy Faithfulness."
Song: "He Is Lord."
Theme chorus: "Young Traveler"
Song: "Jesus, the Son of God" (page 135)
Bible reading: Psalm 92:1, 2
Prayer
Offering and announcements
Special music: "My God Is a Great God."
Song: "If God Be for Us" (page 117)
Song: "The Bible Is God's Word."
Prayer

Bible Story

A Wealthy Farmer on an Ash Heap

In the land of Uz lived a man named Job. He was a good man who loved and obeyed the Lord, and prayed to Him every day. He had seven sons and three daughters. And he wanted his children to love and obey the Lord. Job was rich. He owned thousands of sheep, camels, oxen, and donkeys. He also had many servants.

One time, when the angels stood before the Lord, Satan stood among them. When the Lord asked from where he had come, he said that he had been walking back and forth on the earth.

The Lord's next question was, "Have you noticed my servant, Job? There is not another man upon the earth like him. He is a good man who serves Me and does no evil."

"Does he not serve You for rewards?" asked Satan. "You have put a protecting hedge around him and his family. You have favored him so that now he is wealthy. If all that he has is destroyed, he will curse You to Your face."

God gave Satan permission to do whatever he wished to Job's family and flocks, and all that he possessed. But he was not to kill Job. Satan left the presence of God, and before long, great trouble began for the faithful man, Job.

First, a servant ran to Job with a message. Wild people from the desert had come to the field where servants were plowing. They had taken away all the donkeys and oxen, and killed every workman but the messenger.

Before he left, another servant rushed in to report that a great fire had come down and burned the sheep and shepherd boys. He said that he was the only one who escaped.

While he was talking, the third servant dashed in to tell Job that all those who cared for his camels had been slain. The Chaldeans had taken the three thousand camels back to their country.

Most tragic of all was the messenger who came to say that a high wind had caused Job's oldest son's house to collapse and all ten of his children had been killed while feasting.

Poor, poverty-stricken Job! He was so grieved that he tore his mantle, shaved his beard, bowed to the ground, and worshiped the Lord. The Bible says that in all of his troubles, he sinned not, nor blamed God.

But still Satan was not satisfied. When the angels stood before God, he again came and stood among them.

"Have you noticed Job?" God asked. "There is none as perfect as he. He serves Me and hates evil. You have caused him much sorrow, but still he remains faithful to Me."

"Just let me hurt his body," replied the devil. "A man will do anything to keep from suffering."

God gave Satan permission to do what he wanted to with Job's body, but he was not to kill him. Soon

Job was covered with boils—from the top of his head to the bottom of his feet! He hurt so badly with the painful sores that he sat down among the ashes.

When Job was rich and wealthy, he did many things for his friends and neighbors. Surely they would come to comfort him while he was suffering. But they didn't. Even Mrs. Job looked on her husband sitting on the ashes and said there was no use for him to serve God. She said that he might just as well blame God and die.

"You talk foolishly! We take good things from God. Shall we not take the difficult things?" Job asked.

His three best friends came, but their long speeches were not helpful. Job called them miserable comforters. They tried to persuade him that his troubles were the result of sin. They wanted him to confess his wickedness. But he knew of no way he had sinned against God. He had kept God's ways, and he said that when the testing time was over, he would come forth as pure gold.

God rewarded Job for his faithfulness. He healed his boils and gave him twice as many of each kind of animal as he had had before. His relatives and friends came to a dinner and presented him with gifts of money and gold earrings. Best of all, he was given seven sons and three daughters. The Lord also gave him one hundred and forty more years to live and faithfully serve Him.

Job was patient and faithful. He trusted God no matter what happened to him.

Bible Story Application

Satan must have laughed when he could destroy Job's wealth and children and finally hurt him. Imagine living near a man who has lost his family, hired men, and thousands of animals within two hours, and then finding him sitting on an ash heap suffering with stinging boils!

Job told his best friend, "Though he slay me, yet will I trust in him" (Job 13:15). He was strong in faithfulness because he put his trust in God. God will also help today's young travelers to be faithful. In Philippians 4:13 we read (read from your Bible), "I can do all things through Christ which strengtheneth me."

The Lord does not require His followers to be wise, rich, or talented. The important part is to be faithful.

Satan is a rascal! He hasn't changed a bit since Job's time. He is a deceiver and a liar. And he still tries to get Christians to disappoint the Lord. But the Lord has not changed, either. He is much more powerful than the devil. Young travelers will be rewarded for their faithfulness.

(Have a prayer time during which the children ask God to help them to be faithful.)

Activity Book

Students write the rhyming words in the blanks to complete the poem about questions God asked Job. You may want to read, or have students read, some of the verses from Job 38. *(The answers are you; sea; live; Me; snow; found; gold.)*

Have students find Job 37:14 in their Bibles and fill in the blanks to complete the verse. Read the verse together. Help your students to appreciate the beauty of these words.

This word-search puzzle is a bit different. It contains nine words that describe Job and five words that do not belong in the puzzle. Students are to circle the words that describe Job and draw a red line through the words that do not belong.

Give help as needed as students fill in the blanks on the second page. Call attention to the "quote" and information in "Keeping Close to My Guide."

Craft Souvenir

Circle Plaque

MATERIALS:
One six-inch plastic lid (Smaller lids may be used.)
Pastel shades of quality construction paper
Cardboard or heavy paper (for easel)
Magic markers or crayons
Pencil, scissors, and white glue
Pattern of easel from pattern page

PROCEDURE:
Cut a paper circle to fit the inside of the lid. With a marker, color an attractive design around the outside edge. Use a dark felt pen to print "Lord, help me to be faithful" on the paper circle. Glue the circle to the inside of the lid.

Trace and cut out the easel, fold on the dotted line and place the motto on it.

NOTE: It is advisable to precut the circles to fit the various sizes of lids, and hand them out as kits.

A Man with Determination

Daniel 1, 6

Goals: That the student (1) will realize that Daniel's God-honoring habits were formed while he was young and (2) will be challenged to form good habits and to correct those that could hinder his spiritual growth.

Student Responses: As a result of this lesson, the student should be able to do the following:

- Tell the story of Daniel and his three friends.
- Describe Daniel.
- In the activity book, write down a good habit he has that pleases the Lord and a habit that the Lord can help him to overcome.

Learning Centers

Preview

A View of Babylon

(Use a map to locate Babylon and Jerusalem.) When Daniel was a teenager, he was captured and taken from his home in Jerusalem. He and his friends were marched hundreds of miles to the great city of Babylon. There he lived for the rest of his life.

Babylon was destroyed long before Christ was born, but archaeologists tell us that it was the most beautiful city in the world. It was a huge city where about one million people lived.

Surrounding the city was a high wall so wide that six horse-drawn chariots could travel side by side. There were 250 towers on the wall.

Around the outside of one wall was a wide moat filled with water from the River Euphrates. Draw bridges crossed the moat at the main entrances. The river flowed through the center of the city and the people crossed it on ferryboats.

The houses, made of bricks, were three or four stories high. The streets were straight. The cross streets had bronze gates at the river.

Within the city limits were parks and two palaces. If we could have been there, we would have seen a tower seven stories high. Beside the tower stood a temple where people worshiped a false god named Marduk.

A famous garden called the Hanging Gardens was built of slabs of stone on stone arches. On these slabs were planted trees and shrubs. From the top of the wall, the garden looked like a green mountain.

Memory Ticket Office

"Let no man despise thy youth; but be thou an example of the believers, in word, in conversation, in charity, in spirit, in faith, in purity."

1 Timothy 4:12

THINK

1. What is the meaning of the word "conversation"? (Manner of life)

2. What is the meaning of the word "charity" (Love)

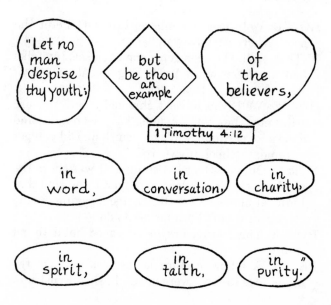

95

3. Paul said that Timothy was to be an example of the believers. How many ways are listed?

LEARNING GAME

(See "Introduction," "Preparation for Each Unit: Unit 2" for information concerning making and using the symbols.

AWARD

Initial the tickets for those who memorized the verse.

Guidebook

How To

What to do when you have the bad habit of
1. Staying home from church.─ ─ ─ ─ ─Psalm 100:4
2. Swearing.─ ─ ─ ─ ─Exodus 20:7
3. Being angry.─ ─ ─ ─ ─Proverbs 15:1
4. Being selfish.─ ─ ─ ─ ─Philippians 2:4
5. Thinking bad thoughts.─ ─ ─ ─ ─Psalm 19:14
6. Lying.─ ─ ─ ─ ─Proverbs 19:5
7. Gossiping.─ ─ ─ ─ ─Proverbs 11:13
8. Stealing or cheating.─ ─ ─ ─ ─Exodus 20:15
9. Choosing bad company.─ ─ ─ ─ ─Proverbs 24:1

Front View Adventure

Peter the Poet

MATERIALS:
Two puppets: Howie and Peter.
Howie's clubhouse stage

(If a new puppet is not available, dress Mike differently. Use a different puppeteer.)

HOWIE: Well, look who's here! If it isn't Peter the poet! Wherever have you been?
PETER: Well, I've been gone, don't you see. My folks took me to Germany. And to England also we flew. We went over to Israel, too.
HOWIE: Well, you haven't changed a bit! You are still Peter the poet. You must have seen a lot, and done a lot of things while on your trip. Did you get to Sunday school anywhere?
PETER: Oh, yes! Over in Scotland. It was there the teacher asked me to lead in prayer. I was glad that I pray at home, and at church, too. Praying among strangers wasn't hard for me to do.
HOWIE: That's true. Prayer is a good habit to get into.
PETER: A fellow in Europe—he was so nice; the other boys in town were mean. I asked Ernst how

he could remain so kind, be friendly, and keep his thoughts so clean.
HOWIE: What did he say?
PETER: He said, "I'm a Christian. I love the Lord. I pray. I read my Bible. It's my sword."
HOWIE: I'd sure like to know Ernst. Reading God's Word helps me, too.
PETER: You should have seen what happened to me: two girls got me to climb a big, tall tree. A great big bird had her nest up there. She got so angry, she flew in my hair.
HOWIE: *(Laughs)* That's funny! Tell me what happened.
PETER: Well, the girls laughed and laughed, and made much fun, and then away home both of them did run.
HOWIE: Did anyone scold the girls. How did it turn out?
PETER: Well, it turned out for the best for me; for over my anger, the Lord gave victory. I treated the girls kind, and helped them do their chores. I even taught them how to make smores.
HOWIE: Did you get to tell them about Jesus and how He loves them? Did they know that Christ died on the cross for them?
PETER: Oh yes, I did, and they listened good. They said I acted as a Christian should. I wasn't trying to show off in any way; it's God who helps me be careful what I do and say.
HOWIE: I sure hope that I can be a Christian example in our town. It's so important.
PETER: It's important while young to form good habits. But now I must run home and take care of my rabbits. I'm glad I came to say Hi! Now, I'll say to all—good-bye!
(Both leave.)

Worshiping Our Guide

Quiet music: "Day by Day"
Song: "Evening and Morning" (page 124)
Theme chorus: "Young Traveler"
Song: "Serve the Lord With Gladness." (page 131)
Bible reading: 1 Thessalonians 5:15-22
Prayer
Offering and announcements
Special music: "My Lord Knows the Way Through the Wilderness." (page 134)
Song: "Thy Word Have I Hid in My Heart." (page 126)
Song "Whisper a Prayer." (page 124)
Prayer

Bible Story

A Man with Determination

Babylon was a great and powerful nation. Their king was Nebuchadnezzar. Every country his army fought against had to surrender. Finally the army came to Judah and marched to Jerusalem, and surrounded it. After two years, the wall of the city was broken and the Babylonian soldiers poured into the streets to kill, capture, and destroy.

King Nebuchadnezzar had commanded Ashpenaz, the master of his servants, saying "Capture the best young men in Jerusalem. Take only those who are intelligent, strong, and healthy. I want those who are of the royal family of Judah."

Among the fellows captured and brought to Babylon were Daniel and his three friends, Hananiah, Mishael, and Azariah. Later their names were changed to Belteshazzar, Shadrach, Meshach and Abednego.

"These Jews must have the very best education we can give them," ordered the king. "They must have the best food so they will be in good health and be wise."

Melzar, the king's steward, told the boys that they were to have the same meals that were served to the royal family. They were to drink the king's wine. After three years of the rich diet, they would be nourished and they would be wise.

But the orders didn't please Daniel. Though he was still young, he remembered the laws of God regarding clean and unclean foods (Leviticus 17:10-12). Daniel knew that sometimes the meat served to the king would first be offered to idols. This also was against God's law for the Jewish people.

Daniel went to his three friends and told them that he could not eat the meals or drink the strong drinks served at the king's table. "Let us ask to have vegetables and water for our meals," he said. "I will go to Melzar and tell him of our decision."

Melzar loved Daniel and wanted to favor him, but he was afraid. He knew that at the end of three years of study and training, the Jews were to appear before the king to be tested. Just suppose that after a vegetable diet, they became pale and sickly. Then King Nebuchadnezzar would surely punish Melzar. He would probably have his head taken off.

"Just let us try our own diet for ten days," Daniel asked Melzar, and he agreed. At the end of that time, the four fellows came for inspection. They were healthier and fairer than all the others who had been eating the king's food and drinking the king's wine. Because of this the fellows were permitted to continue the vegetable and water diet.

God gave the four young men knowledge and skill in all learning.

Three years passed and the training time was over. Every Jewish fellow prepared himself to appear in the throne room. This was indeed a fearful time. The king talked to them and asked them many questions. Every fellow was expected to answer wisely and mannerly, speaking in the Babylonian language. At the end of the interview, Daniel, Shadrach, Meshach, and Abednego were found to be the most intelligent, gave the wisest answers, and spoke the best Babylonian language. The Bible says that they were ten times better than all the rest. They were even ten times wiser that the wise men of the land.

Time went by and Daniel became an old man. King Nebuchadnezzar died, and other kings came into power. While Darius was king, he divided the nation into many parts and set a prince over each part. Over these, he appointed three presidents, and Daniel was one of them. He was chosen for this job because he was a very wise and trusted man.

Daniel did such a good job that the king planned to give him the highest position in the kingdom. This made the presidents and princes jealous of Daniel. They decided to do what they could to have him destroyed. Do you remember what they caught him doing three times a day? They trapped Darius into signing a law. The law said that anyone caught asking a favor of any other person or god than the king for the next thirty days would be put in with the lions. The king sealed the law with his ring, which meant that it could not be changed.

The presidents and princes caught Daniel praying to God. He had the good habit of praying three times a day. For this, he was put in the lions' den. But he was not torn to pieces. God's angel came and stood in the den and protected Daniel. He shut the mouths of the lions and made them tame for the hours that Daniel had to spend in their den.

Daniel was faithful, courteous, and wise. When he was sure something was God's will, he never gave up. He had formed good habits when he was a young boy. These helped him throughout his whole life.

Bible Story Application

Daniel, like David, behaved himself wisely. While still in Jerusalem, he formed good habits of eating, of obedience, and of prayer. He also must have been obedient to his parents. These good habits helped him to be strong when he was so far away from home among evil people.

Good habits will help us obey our Lord and serve

Him better. Paul told Timothy to continue in the things he had learned and to be a good example of the believers (2 Timothy 3:14). Good habits are important for the Lord's service.

Daniel stuck to what he knew was right. He "purposed" or stayed with it. Anything we do for the Lord is the work for the Lord. Paul said we should be steadfast; we should stay with the work.

Habits are formed by doing things over and over—by staying with them and by purposing in our hearts to continue to do them. The Lord has promised to help us, for we can't stay with good habits without His help.

Activity Book

For the first activity, refer to "Preview" for information concerning Babylon.

For decoding the puzzle, 1 is A, 2 is B, etc. Write the letters of the alphabet and the numbers on the chalkboard, or each child may write them on a piece of paper to refer to as he does the puzzle. (The answers are 1. prayed; 2. formed, habits; 3. faithful, God; 4. obedient; 5. courage; 6. honest.)

The students should be able to do "Choose the Word" without looking up the verses. However, they can find those they need to in order to mark through the wrong words.

Discuss "Keeping Close to My Guide," and then ask the students to fill in the blanks.

Craft Souvenir

Sticker Book

MATERIALS:
Sample wallpaper book or construction paper
Heavy paper, scissors, glue or tape
Paper fasteners
Appropriate seals

PROCEDURE:

From wallpaper cut a 9″ by 12″ piece. Fold in half to make a cover. Cut a label from construction paper and on it print "Stick to good habits." Tape the label to the cover. Cut five sheets of paper and insert between the covers. Fasten with paper fasteners or staple.

In one corner of each page write the following:

1. I will pray for children of the world.
2. I listen to Bible lessons.
3. I will be good to animals.
4. I will read my Bible.
5. I will eat good foods and treats.
6. Bees and butterflies want to live.
7. I will protect birds' nests. (Birds)
8. I like flowers.
9. I will honor Jesus at Christmas and Easter.
10. I love my country.

Add appropriate stickers or pictures to each page.

The Mother of the Heavenly King

Luke 1:26-56; 2

Goals: That the student (1) will have a better understanding of Mary and (2) will want to live a pure and useful life.

Student Responses: As a result of this lesson, the pupil should be able to do the following:
- Answer questions about the Bible story.
- Describe Mary.
- Say and explain the memory verse.
- List two ways of being pure. (Thoughts and words.)

Learning Centers

Preview

Angels Are Real

MATERIALS:
Pictures of angels
A recording of Christmas music (played softly)

PROCEDURE:
Have you ever seen an angel? Do you know of anyone who has? No, but people in Bible times saw them.

We know God created angels because He made everything in heaven and on earth (Colossians 1:16). The Bible says there are a great host of angels, so many that they could not be numbered except by God (Hebrews 12:22).

Angels are real, but they are different from us. They are spirits (Hebrews 1:14). They took on the form of bodies and appeared before people. We do not know exactly what they looked like when people saw them. Sometimes they had a glow or were brilliant. Sometimes artists draw wings on angels, but we are not sure they have wings.

Angels are messengers. They brought information and warnings from the Lord. Angels have names.

The Bible tells us of only two: Michael and Gabriel.

Although we can't see angels or talk to them, they are around us all the time. God has appointed them to help protect us.

Memory Ticket Office

"Wherewithal shall a young man cleanse his way? by taking heed thereto according to thy word."

Psalm 119:9

THINK
1. What is another word for "wherewithal"? (How, or with what.)
2. How can we have our ways cleansed?

LEARNING GAME
Make the heart and open-Bible symbols of heavy paper. Print the verse on them as shown. Spray with adhesive spray or glue on small pieces of flannelgraph paper so they will adhere to the flannelgraph board.

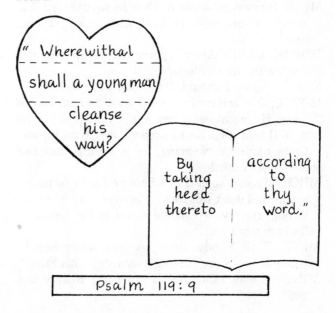

Guidebook

The Lord's Desires for Young Travelers

1. The Lord desires that we say clean words. Psalm 19:14
2. The Lord desires that we think clean thoughts. Philippians 4:8
3. The Lord promises to bless those who hear and obey the Word. Luke 11:28
4. The Lord blesses those who have pure (clean) hearts. Matthew 5:8
5. The Lord knows if our hearts are clean. 1 Samuel 16:7
6. The Lord wants us to pray about His desire for us. Philippians 4:6

Front View Adventure

Mindy's Overnighter

MATERIALS:
Three puppets and stage.

(Howie and Mike enter.)

MIKE: Guess what? My dad says we can enter our pony at the fair this summer.

HOWIE: Hey! That sounds like fun. Maybe Moonlight will get the blue ribbon. Do you need me to help you at the fairgrounds?

MIKE: No, thanks. Mindy is going to help. Rusty offered to help, too, but I sure wouldn't want him around.

HOWIE: Oh, no? Why not?

MIKE: He swears so much. Then he says things that aren't—a—er—well, he tells dirty jokes. I hate that!

HOWIE: Me, too. Are you going to tell him why you don't want him to help?

MIKE: I 'spose I should. What can I say to him?

HOWIE: Just tell him you don't want to hear his old jokes. He might get angry, but he'll respect you for it. Tell him it's a sin to swear. Every time he uses God's name in swearing, he is saying that God isn't worth much.

MIKE: My dad says that when we listen to people swear and don't tell them it is wrong, then we are wrong. He says we should stand up for Jesus.

(Mindy enters.)

MIKE: Well, Mindy, what are you doing here? I thought you were staying overnight with Susie?

MINDY: I was. I did. Well, I was going to stay, but, well–.

MIKE: But what happened?

MINDY: Susie's a lot of fun to be with when we are alone. She invited Abby to stay, too, and all Abby wants to do is watch TV.

HOWIE: I bet they were watching junk shows.

MINDY: Yes, and they were terrible! Really weird! Mom and Dad don't want us to watch stuff like that. I don't want to, either.

MIKE: So then you came home. It wasn't very nice just to walk out on them, was it?

MINDY: But I didn't just walk out. I did what my Sunday-school teacher suggested.

HOWIE: What is that?

MINDY: She said that when we know the Lord isn't pleased about what other kids ask us to do, we should think of something better.

MIKE: So what better thing did you suggest?

MINDY: I invited Susie and Abby to come and stay at my house all night. I said we could make malts. I was quite sure that Dad would take us out to get pizzas. I told them that I didn't think the Lord wanted me to fill my mind with junky shows.

MIKE: Good for you, Sis. What did they say?

MINDY: Susie liked the idea, but Abby wouldn't leave the TV. They said they might come over in an hour. I'd better go home just in case they decide to come.

HOWIE: Let's pray for these kids and for each other that the Lord will help us give them the right answers.

(All leave.)

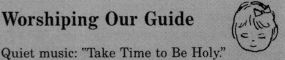

Worshiping Our Guide

Quiet music: "Take Time to Be Holy."
Song: "We Worship You." (page 130)
Theme chorus: "Young Traveler"
Song: "Oh How He Loves You and Me."
Bible reading: Philippians 4:8, 9
Prayer
Offering and announcements
Special music: "Who Is on the Lord's Side?"
Song: "What a Happy Day" (page 128)
Song: "Whisper a Prayer." (page 124)
Prayer

Bible Story

The Mother of the Heavenly King

Open your Bibles to the first chapter of Matthew. In most Bibles there is a plain page with the words

"New Testament" printed at the top. This divides the Old Testament from the New Testament. On this page we could write the words "About 400 years," for it had been that long since God had said His last words to Israel.

God had promised many times throughout the Old Testament that some day He would send His wonderful Son to the earth to live among people, and then die a cruel death. He would die so that He could save us from our sins. The Lord told Isaiah that His beloved Son would be born like any other new baby is born, but He would not have a human father (Isaiah 7:14).

For hundreds of years every Jewish mother wondered if her baby would be a boy. "Maybe I will be chosen by God to be the mother of the promised Messiah," they must have often said to one another.

Mary was a lovely young woman who lived in Nazareth. She was engaged to a nice man named Joseph. Soon the two would be married, and they would start a home of their own in the town. There would be things Mary would need to start housekeeping. She must have been busy every spare minute weaving and sewing.

One day while she was working alone, an angel appeared before her. He said, "Greetings. You are highly favored. The Lord is with you."

Mary had not heard anyone enter the room. She was startled to see an angel standing before her! And what did he mean when he said that she was highly favored?

The angel Gabriel spoke gently. He told Mary not to be afraid. He said she was favored by God, for she was chosen to be the mother of the promised Messiah.

"You shall call His name Jesus," Gabriel said. "He will be great, and He will be called the Son of the Most High. He will sit on the throne of David and reign forever, and his kingdom will never end."

"How can this be? I am not married yet," Mary exclaimed.

The angel told her that her little Son would not need an earthly father because He was the Son of God. Gabriel told her that her cousin, Elizabeth, was also to have baby.

Mary was filled with so much joy that she could hardly contain it. In her sweet voice, she answered, "I am the Lord's servant. May it happen as you have said." Then Gabriel left.

"I must go to visit Elizabeth," Mary said to herself. "I must tell her the wonderful news that the Messiah will soon be born."

Elizabeth was excited. When Mary came in to her presence, Elizabeth spoke with a loud voice saying, "You are a blessed woman. I am honored that the mother of our Lord should come to me." Mary spent three months with her cousin and then returned home.

Joseph was extremely worried. He had not seen the angel that had come to Mary. Just when he was considering breaking their engagement, the angel came to him in a dream. The angel said he should become Mary's husband. "You shall call the baby's name Jesus," said the angel. "He will save His people from their sins." After this, Joseph obeyed the Lord and took Mary as his bride.

One day, several months later, Joseph came home and said, "The Roman Emperor has made a law that all people in his kingdom must go to the town where their ancestors were born and register. We must go to Bethlehem."

It was close to the time when Mary's little Son would be born. She may have known that the Bible said that He was to be born in the city of Bethlehem. Could this be God's plan to get her to Bethlehem? Did she think about this as she packed a few things for the trip?

When they came to Bethlehem, there was no room in the inn. "We must sleep in the stable behind the inn," Joseph said. "So many travelers have come back here to register that all the available places are filled."

So it was that Jesus was born in a stable where the animals stayed. Mary tenderly washed Him and wrapped Him in strips of cloth and laid Him in a manger.

"Someone is outside! I hear voices," said Joseph as he started toward the entrance.

They were shepherds, and they were extremely excited as they entered. They explained that an angel had visited them while they were watching sheep on the hillside. The angel had said that Christ, the Messiah, had been born. Then the shepherds probably held a light high above where Jesus was sleeping. He was lying in a manger and was wrapped in strips of cloth just as the angel had said they would find Him. They fell to the ground and worshiped Him.

A few months after Jesus' birth, several richly dressed men came riding into Bethlehem on camels. They were the Wise-men who had followed His special star. They had come to worship Him. They brought Him costly gifts.

After the Wise-men had left, an angel came and spoke to Joseph in a dream. He said, "Herod has made plans to have Jesus destroyed. You must flee with the young child and Mary. Go to Egypt. Remain there until I bring you word that it is safe to return." For a time they lived in Egypt, and finally the little family moved to their house in Nazareth.

Mary was a kind, loving, and tender Jewish woman. She cheerfully obeyed the Lord and humbly accepted the great honor God gave her. She would not have been chosen to be the mother of God's Son if she had not tried to keep her life and thoughts as pure as possible. But she was not perfect. She is not to be worshiped. She had to ask to have her sins forgiven just as we do.

Bible Story Application

We want our bodies and clothes to be clean. This is important. But most important is to be clean on the inside. We need to know that the Lord has forgiven us of our sins and made us clean by His blood when He died on Calvary.

Keeping our thoughts clean is a good way of being pure. Being careful of what we say is important. Proverbs 15:26 says, "The words of the pure are pleasant." Good, clean words and deeds will build young travelers' characters. The Lord loves us very much and is eager to help us stay away from evil and live beautiful lives.

Activity Book

Discuss angels (see "Preview") before the children fill in the blanks on the first page of today's activity.

For the puzzle, explain the code to any who have difficulty with it. (The answer is "Angels are living spirits.")

At the bottom of the page, the student lists four words that describe Mary. Discuss the questions at the bottom of the page.

Give help as needed as students do "Matching Review" on the top of the second page.

Have students find the verses and fill in the blanks in "Keeping Close to My Guide." Discuss the statements.

Craft Souvenir

Standing Angel

MATERIALS:
Heavy yellow construction paper
Felt-tip pen and ball-point pen
Scissors, tracing paper
Angel from pattern page

PROCEDURE:
Trace the angel onto construction paper. Cut on the black lines. Decorate the robe with the felt-tip pens. Make a book and print on it the words, "He shall be great and shall be called the Son of the Highest." Crease the book slightly.

Assemble by pulling the wings back to form the body and placing one wing slot into the other. Tape at the bottom to hold the wings in place. Bend the arms forward and place one wrist slot into the other. Place the book in the angel's hands and stand the angel up.

A Lady Who Made News

John 12:1-8; Matthew 26:6-13; Mark 14:3-9

Goals: That the student (1) will know that Mary of Bethany gave to the Lord to show her love and (2) will be determined to do his best for the Lord.

Student Responses: As a result of this lesson, the student should be able to do the following:
• Describe Mary of Bethany.
• Tell what Mary did to show her love and give her best to Jesus.
• Tell what Jesus said.
• Say and explain the memory verse.
• Tell one way in which he can give Jesus his best.

Learning Centers

Preview

Fragrant Spikenard

Spikenard is a plant that grows in India. Its flowers grow on top of long stalks, and they are very fragrant. The spikenard ointment was made from the substance gathered after crushing the roots of the plant. It was kept in sealed alabaster jars to preserve the perfume. The very fragrant ointment in Bible times was expensive and was used mostly by the rich people.

Alabaster bottles and boxes were made from a whitish stone or crystals. Alabaster is usually white and translucent. This stone is named from the town of Alabastron, Egypt, where there are quarries.

Alabaster can be polished to a beautiful shine. People in Bible times thought that spikenard ointment kept best in bottles and jars made from alabaster.

Memory Ticket Office

"And whatsover ye do, do it heartily, as to the Lord, and not unto men."   Colossians 3:23

THINK
1. How could you memorize this verse heartily?
2. What are some of the things we should do heartily as to the Lord and not to please men?

LEARNING GAME
Make a large heart pattern and divide it into four sections (as shown). Draw the pieces onto construction paper and cut them out. Print the verse on the pieces and the reference on a card. Spray all pieces with adhesive spray or glue bits of flannelgraph paper on them. Let the students assemble the puzzle as they quote the verse.

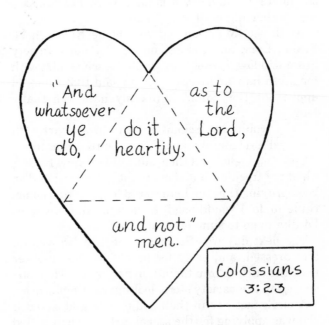

AWARD
Initial the tickets for those who have memorized the verse. (See page 6 for information concerning the "visa" on the "passport," and for the final award.)

Guidebook

"Our Best" Bible Drill

Choose one of the favorite methods of keeping score from a previous Bible drill. Or try this:

Using the memory-verse idea from this unit, cut two identical heart puzzles and the card. The first team completing the puzzle is the winner.

1. Christ's best for us.– – – – –John 15:13, 14
2. Our best gift to God.– – – – –Luke 10:27
3. Our best protection from sin.– –Ephesians 6:11
4. Our best service.– – – – –Psalm 100:2
5. Our best giving.– – – – –2 Corinthians 9:7
6. Our best work.– – – – –Colossians 3:23
7. Our best studying.– – – – –2 Timothy 2:15
8. Our best reward.– – – – –John 14:2, 3

Front View Adventure

Just Enough Freckles

"Mom, look at my hair. Is it long enough to be called long hair?" Cozette asked, as she dashed into the living room.

"Well–yes. Your hair is quite a bit below your shoulders. I would say it is long. Why do you ask?" her mother inquired with a smile.

"Well, see, Mom, on the way home from school, Frank, Dory, and I saw a notice in Peter's Variety Store window. It said they wanted a school girl with long, red hair and freckles. Fran said that I should apply, but Dory didn't think my hair was really long."

"Why would a merchant want to hire a girl with long red hair and freckles?" Mrs. Dutton mused.

Cozette giggled and then said, "It is funny. I never liked my freckles, but they might get me a job. I've been praying that the Lord would help me find something to do. I would use it toward my flute lessons. I'd like to go to summer camp, too."

The next day was Saturday, and Cozette was up and dressed, and early for breakfast. Her mother used the curling iron to fluff up her bangs. Then she was off to the variety store, looking neat but scared.

A clerk met her in the middle aisle and asked if she was applying for the school-girl job. She was led to an outer office where six girls were waiting. They all had red hair and freckles. One by one, they were led to the manager's office. Soon they returned to the waiting room again. One said her freckles were only on her nose, another had too few, and still another was told that her red hair was too curly.

"I wonder what this is all about," Cozette thought as she waited for her turn. She was rather amused, but still she was getting more frightened.

"There's the girl," said a lady with a smile when Cozette entered the office. "She has bangs and lots of freckles, and hair of just the right length."

"You are hired if you want the job," said the manager.

"I am Mrs. Davis, and the manager is my brother," the lady explained. "You are the girl who helped me through the hall at the school and to my car. I had my baby and my little blind boy with me that day. You didn't wait for me to get your name or to pay you."

Looking very surprised, Cozette replied, "Oh, that's okay. I saw that you were trying to manage your children, your music case, and your music."

"Cozette, I need a girl to play with Danny for a little while after school. You were so thoughtful that I felt I could trust my blind son with you. Will you consider helping me?"

Cozette took the job and loved it. She did her work faithfully, and even did little extra things around the house. She did her very best to entertain Danny. And Mrs. Davis gave her free flute lessons on Saturdays so she could save her money to go to camp.

Worshiping Our Guide

Quiet music: "Take My Life and Let It Be."
Song: "We Can Reach Around the World."
  (page 133)
Theme chorus: "Young Traveler"
Song: "He Is Lord."
Bible reading: 1 Corinthians 6:19, 20
Prayer
Offering and announcements
Special music: "Give of Your Best to the Master."
Song: "Serve the Lord With Gladness."
  (page 131)
Song: "The B-I-B-L-E"
Prayer

Bible Story

A Lady Who Made News

"Master, where are we going today?" Jesus' disciples may have asked.

"We are going to Bethany this morning," could

very well have been the Lord's answer many times. He often visited the tiny town which was located at the edge of the Mount of Olives. Jesus' friends, Martha, Mary, and their brother Lazarus, lived in Bethany. Jesus always felt welcome and comfortable when He was in their home.

The two women and Lazarus loved Jesus very much. They were His true followers. Martha was a good cook, and the two women liked to entertain Jesus and His disciples when they stopped in Bethany. They tried to do all they could to make their honored Guest feel comfortable.

One day the two sisters became very concerned about their brother because he had become seriously ill. They sent a messenger to find Jesus and ask Him to come to the bedside of Lazarus. They knew that He performed miracles of healing. They were sure that He would do something to restore their suffering loved one.

But Jesus didn't go to Bethany right away. When He finally arrived, He was told that Lazarus had died four days before, and that he was buried in a tomb. Jesus went to the tomb and spoke to the dead man. Lazarus came out of the tomb, alive and well!

Later, one springtime afternoon, Jesus said to His twelve disciples, "Let us go to Bethany." It was just six days before the great Passover feast when all Jewish people would be going to Jerusalem to celebrate the religious event. Jesus knew that soon He would be taken by His enemies and crucified on a cross. He must have wanted to visit Mary, Martha, and Lazarus one more time.

A dinner was given in Jesus' honor. How happy His friends were to see Him once again. Martha prepared a good meal for the guests. Lazarus probably was busy telling the disciples more about his experience of being raised from the dead. Surely He thanked the Lord over and over again for the miracle.

Finally the men were notified that their meal was ready. In Bible times people didn't sit at a table as we do. They reclined on couches around a low table with their feet extended behind them.

Mary listened as Jesus asked the blessing on the food, and then as they talked with one another. Oh how much she loved the Lord. She had listened to His teaching and must have realized that He was soon to die. She wanted to honor Him before His death. She wanted to show Jesus that she was giving the very best of herself because she loved Him. She had a secret plan, and she had saved up for it for a long time.

"This is my moment," she must have whispered, her lips scarcely moving. "I will give my very best now."

From the folds of her robe, she took a small alabaster box and held it gently in her hand. Then she walked around the circle to where Jesus was reclining, and stood. Firmly she pressed the thin box with her fingers and broke the seal. She could smell the fragrant spikenard ointment. How glad she was that she had saved her money so that she could purchase the spikenard.

She annointed the head of Jesus. Then seeing His travel-worn feet, she stooped low and poured the ointment over Jesus' feet. Every drop of the costly perfume was used until His feet were wet. Then she let her long hair fall over her shoulder and wiped off the excess moisture with it. The fragrance filled the whole room.

"Why the waste?" shouted Judas Iscariot. "Why wasn't this costly ointment sold and the money used to help poor people?"

It was Judas, the disciple who was soon to betray Jesus, and sell Him for thirty pieces of silver. He didn't really care about the poor. He was the treasurer for the disciples and carried the money bag. He was a thief. He was looking for ways to put more money into his bag. He was only pretending to be concerned about the poor people.

"Let her alone," Jesus said. "She has done a beautiful thing to me. You will always have the poor around to help. But you will not always have me."

Jesus explained to those who stood around that Mary had done this because of her love. He was soon going to die and be buried. By annointing Him, she was preparing His body for the burial. He said that wherever this story is told, the whole world would hear how Mary gave her best because of her love for Him.

Mary is remembered for her sincere love for the Lord. She was a good listener. She put the things of the Lord first. She was unselfish and kind.

Bible Story Application

Mary could have saved a little of the ointment in the bottom of the box for herself. She could have felt that just a little would not be missed. But instead, she gave it all. She gave it heartily, as our memory verse says.

When you are a Christian, you love the Lord with all your heart. With this kind of love in your heart, you want to read the Bible, and you have a special desire to please Jesus. This does not mean that you will not sin. The devil will always try to get you to do wrong (1 Peter 5:8), and sometimes he wins. But there is a "want-to" inside of you that gives you the desire to come closer to Jesus.

We want to love Jesus as Mary of Bethany did and give Him our best. Can you think of some ways you can give Jesus your best?

Activity Book

Review the lesson as the children color the picture. Refer to "Preview" for information concerning spikenard.

At the bottom of the page, the students fill in the pyramid puzzle with words that tell something about Mary of Bethany.

After everyone has completed the True or False Quiz at the top of the second page, check the answers together.

Discuss each statement in "Keeping Close to My Guide," and then have the students find the verses in their Bibles and fill in the blanks.

Craft Souvenir

Rocket Motto

MATERIALS:
One waxed paper tube
Blue, red, and pastel shades of construction paper
Scissors, glue, and a black felt-tip pen
Pins and rocket nose from pattern page

PROCEDURE:

Cut one end from the tube, leaving 9 inches.

Cut a 6″ by 9″ pastel shade of construction paper and on it print "DOING MY BEST FOR THE LORD IS MY GOAL." Wrap it around the tube, glue the edge, and hold until it adheres.

Cut two blue fins. Assemble, and ease the cone into the four slashed areas so that it will stand erect. (The slashes may need to be trimmed.)

Cut the half circle from red paper, shape into a rocket nose, and glue the edge. Set it on top of the rocket.

A Young Preacher

Acts 16:1-5; 1 Timothy 1:1-7; 2 Timothy 3:15

Goals: That the student (1) will understand that Timothy's early training helped him during his whole life and (2) will want to be like Timothy.

Student Responses: As a result of this lesson, the student should be able to do the following:

- Tell how Timothy's early life prepared him for the future.
- List some of the things Timothy did to serve the Lord.
- Tell why the memory verse is important to him and to his family.
- List three things he is doing now that will help him obey God in the future.

Learning Centers

Preview

The Bible-Times Child

If you had been a child in Bible times, what do you think it would have been like? What are a few of the things you have or do that a Jewish boy or girl knew nothing about? *(Discuss.)*

Jewish people loved children. When a baby was born, it was washed in a basin of water and salt was rubbed on its little body. Then the baby was wrapped in long strips of cloth called swaddling cloths. The parents loved both the boys and girls, but the boys were considered more important.

In New Testament times baby boys were taken to the temple on the eighth day, and it was there they were given their names. In forty days the mother went back and offered a sacrifice for her cleansing. When the baby was a girl, the mother waited nearly three months to offer a sacrifice.

Each of the boys was given a part of the father's inheritance. The oldest son received a double portion and was given more responsibilities.

Jewish children had fun. Some of the games were similar to those children play today. They played tag and running races. They didn't have marbles, but they did different things with pebbles. They had toys such as rattlers, whistles, and dolls. They walked on fallen logs and on straight lines. They practiced archery and the use of sling shots. They practiced music on harps, lyres, and other musical instruments.

Jewish children were educated. At first, they were taught at home, first by the mother and then by the father. Later schools were established. In Christ's time every synagogue had a school. Parents were required to teach their children a trade. They had a saying: "He who does not teach his son a useful trade is bringing him up to be a thief." Parents taught their children the laws of God. They told them Bible stories that we now have written down. The children memorized many Bible verses.

Memory Ticket Office

"Children, obey your parents in all things: for this is well pleasing unto the Lord." Colossians 3:20

THINK
1. What is the most important reason given for obeying parents?
2. Why should this verse be important to you and your family?

LEARNING GAME
MATERIALS:
Paper, felt marker, adhesive spray, and flannelgraph board
Picture of parents and a picture of Jesus
PROCEDURE:
Cut squatty letters "OBEY," and on them print parts of the verse.
Use the pictures instead of the words "your parents" and "the Lord."

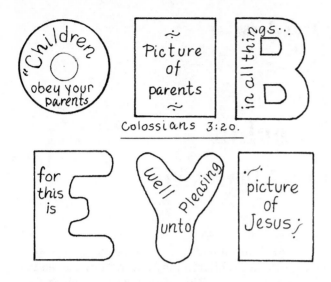

Colossians 3:20.

AWARD

Initial the tickets for those who have memorized the verse.

Guidebook

"The Child" Bible Drill

To keep score for this drill, draw two children's heads on the chalkboard. The team finding the verse first may draw a facial feature. Give points for eyes, ears, nose, mouth, hair, and either a boy's tie or a girl's bow under the chin. The team with the most complete head is the winner.

1. What does a child mean to the Lord? Matthew 18:10
2. What are children to parents? Psalm 127:3
3. Why should children obey their parents? Ephesians 6:1-3
4. Why do parents punish their children? Proverbs 13:24
5. A child who was quick to obey. 1 Samuel 3:8
6. A command from the Lord. Proverbs 4:1

Front View Adventure

The Forbidden Field

"Run to the house and ask your mother to send my dinner to the field," Mr. Kurtis said when the twins came near the big tractor. It was October, and their father wanted to get the crop of winter wheat planted before the ground froze.

That night at the supper table, he said, "Tomorrow the pheasant hunting season opens. There will be a lot of hunters out here with their guns. They must not walk all over my new wheat field."

"But we will not be able to keep them out," said Mother. "Every year a lot of hunters tramp across our fields to get to the hunting grounds. We can't stop them."

"Oh, but we must stop them this year," said the twins' father. "We will put up 'No Trespassing' signs, and we will shut the gate at the head of the driveway. Then, Ken and Kory, you must stay along the edge of the field and see that the hunters do not come through. They can go through our woods."

That night the twins prayed that they would be brave but kind. They wanted to do a good job for their dad, but it would be hard.

All afternoon the hunters stopped their cars and came to the gate. Each time Ken and Kory explained the reason for not letting them through. Some hunters were kind, but others were angry.

Two men came on horseback. One man insisted that Ken must open the gate so they could ride along the edge of the field. They insisted that they would be very careful not to walk on the seeding.

Finally the other man said, "Now children, I know your daddy. I am the vice-president of your dad's bank where your parents keep their money. Now will you let us through?"

"No!" said Ken and Kory. "Our father said we must not let anyone through the gate."

The banker got off his horse and stood beside the gate. He reached his hand through the bars and shook hands with Ken and Kory.

"Children, I admire you," he said. "You are faithfully doing what you are told. I am going to give each of you a twenty-five dollar gift certificate. And, Kenneth, when you are out of high school, we will train you to work in our bank if you want to. A boy who is faithful to his parents will be a faithful banker."

Worshiping Our Guide

Quiet music: "Praise Him! Praise Him!"
Song: "Jesus Is My Answer." (page 125)
Theme chorus: "Young Traveler"
Song: "Jesus the Son of God" (page 135)
Bible reading: Deuteronomy 5:16
Prayer
Offering and Announcements
Special music: Instrumental number
Song: "Thy Word Have I Hid in My Heart."
  (page 126)
Song: "Serve, Serve, Serve the Lord."

Bible Story

A Young Preacher

Introduction

"What can you tell me about Jerusalem?" a teacher asked her class. Hands went up all over the room because everyone had good answers. The children knew much about the famous old city. One of the girls found it on a modern map.

Many places mentioned in the Bible can no longer be found because they have completely disappeared. Derbe and Lystra are two of the towns. They were near the foothills of a mountain range northwest of Jerusalem. When Paul was on his missionary journeys, he preached in both towns.

In Lystra lived a dear Jewish grandmother named Lois. At the time of our story her husband was dead.

Lois had a daughter named Eunice. Eunice was married to a man who was not a Jew. The Bible says that he was a Greek.

The couple were thrilled when a baby boy was born. "I will name him Timotheous," Eunice said. "The name means 'Honoring God.' I will honor God because He has given us such a fine boy."

Timothy's father may have died when Timothy was very young; we do not know. We do know that his grandmother and his mother brought him up in the way of the Lord.

"I will help you teach Timothy about God and help him learn the Scripture," said Grandmother Lois.

"I want my son to obey us," his mother probably exclaimed. "I believe the Lord has some special work for him to do. If we teach him to obey while he is young, he will find it easier when he is grown."

Eunice and Lois told Timothy the Old Testament Bible stories. They told him of Abraham and Moses and David. They taught Him of God and God's love for His people.

Eunice and Lois had not yet heard of Jesus, God's Son. They did not know that He had come to earth, done many miracles, taught about God and His love. They did not know that He had died on the cross for the sins of all people, and then risen from the dead.

Then one day the missionary Paul came to their town. Paul preached about Jesus. Probably this was the time when Eunice, Lois, and the boy Timothy heard about Jesus. They believed Paul's words and they were baptized.

As Timothy grew to be a young man, his mother and grandmother continued to teach him. He obeyed them. He was well liked by everyone who knew him in the town of Lystra.

When Paul was traveling on his second missionary journey, he again visited the churches in Lystra and Derbe. Timothy had grown to be a young man. Paul was impressed with him.

"I believe that young Timothy would be a good helper to travel with me," he said. "I will check with the church people and ask how he is doing in his Christian life."

To Paul's delight, everyone of whom he inquired said that Timothy was a fine Christian young man in every way. Their reports were very good.

Timothy was ready to accept the challenge and travel with Paul. He wanted to serve the Lord. From that time on, Timothy had many experiences as he traveled with Paul on much of his second and third missionary journeys.

Paul also sent the young man to different churches to encourage them and teach them. Once he went to Corinth with a message from Paul (1 Corinthians 4:17), and also to Thessalonica (1 Thessalonians 3:1-7).

Paul left Timothy to work in the church in Ephesus for a while. Later he sent a letter to him there, encouraging him, guiding him, and warning him against false teaching.

When Paul was in Rome and knew he would undergo hardship, he wrote and asked Timothy to come and be with him.

Timothy was glad to serve the Lord. He admired Paul and was glad to travel and work with him. He was not afraid of the dangers and difficulties they often faced. Timothy was a good preacher. He was always faithful to God and His Word.

Bible Story Application

The training Timothy had when he was young helped him to be a useful and faithful follower of the Lord. Studying the Bible, listening to parents, teachers, and the preacher, and obeying your parents are important now. But they will also help you when you are older. You will be a happier person and you will be a better follower of Christ.

Why is obeying parents important? *(Discuss.)*

You may be a preacher or a missionary like Timothy some day. Whatever you do, you can have some of his qualities and be a useful servant of the Lord. God is pleased with young travelers today who love Him and want to travel in His way.

Activity Book

Naming four children mentioned in the Bible should not be difficult for your students. They may include Joseph, Moses, Samuel, David, Timothy, Jairus' daughter.

Refer to "Preview" for information concerning games children played in Bible times, toys, and activities.

Students will need to find and read Deuteronomy 6:6, 7 in order to fill in the blanks.

Read together and discuss the Timothy pictures at the bottom of the page.

Students will need their Bibles for finding some of the answers needed to fill in the blanks at the top of the second page.

After the children have found the Scripture verses and filled in the blanks under "Keeping Close to My Guide," discuss the statements and the question at the bottom of the page.

Craft Souvenir

Mounted Photo

MATERIALS:
One picture of child or family
One small, clean tuna fish can
Wallpaper or construction paper
Cardboard, scissors, pencil, and glue
Chenille wire and package wrapping tape.

PROCEDURE:
Prepare a wallpaper band about 1⅜" by 11". Wrap it around the outside of the can, leaving the tiny rim exposed. (Removing the label is not necessary.) Glue the overlapping end and hold it until it adheres.

Cut a cardboard circle that will fit the bottom of the can, but leave the outside bottom rim showing to serve as a frame for the picture. The circle should be slightly less than 3 inches in diameter.

Cut the picture into a circle and glue it to the cardboard. Glue the cardboard to the outside bottom of the can.

For a hanger, shape a piece of wire into a loop and bend the ends toward the inside of the can. Tape.

Lesson 1

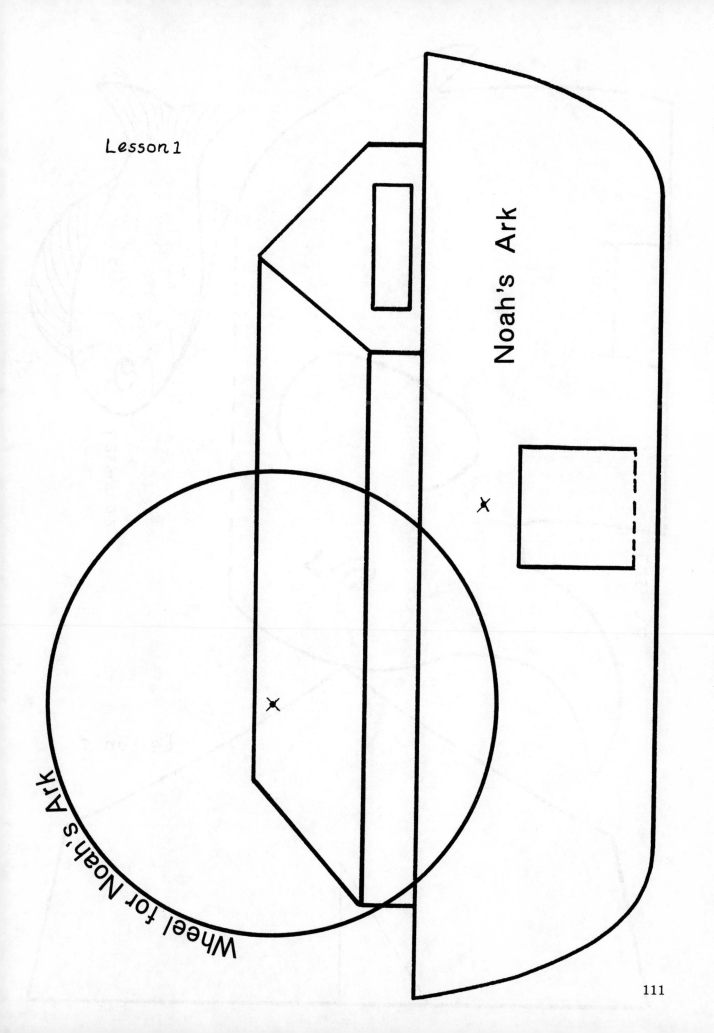

Noah's Ark

Wheel for Noah's Ark

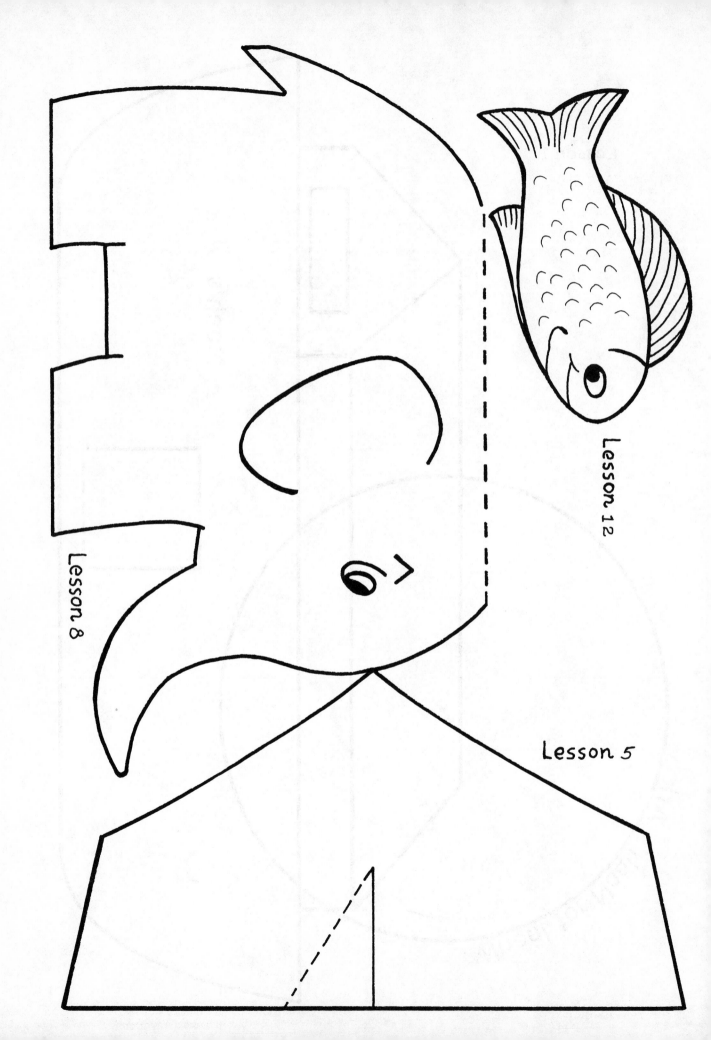

Lesson 12

Lesson 8

Lesson 5

Lesson 11

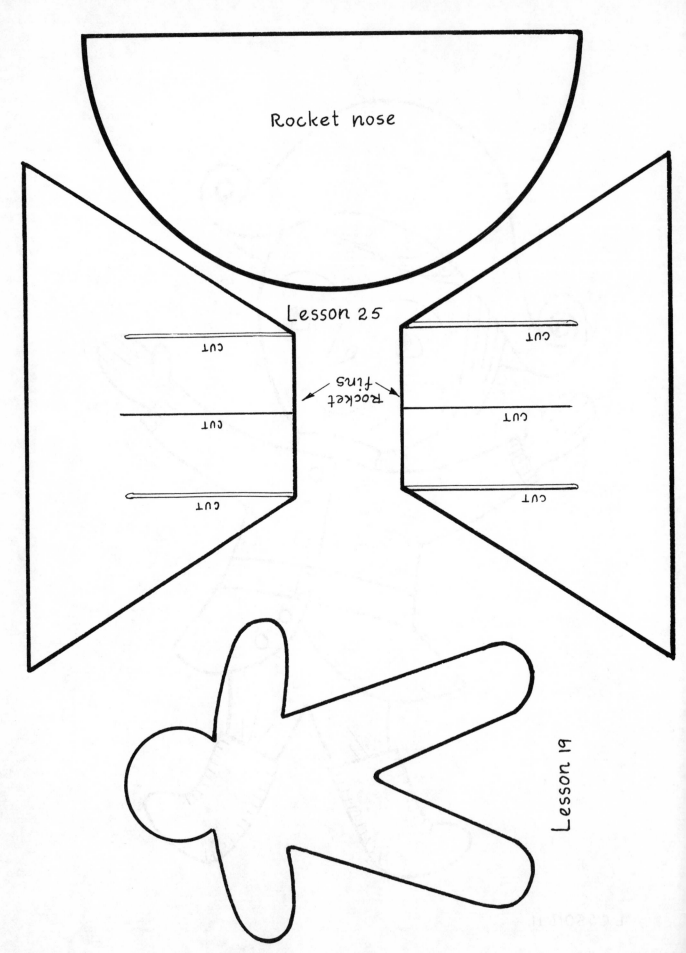

Rocket nose

Lesson 25

Rocket fins

CUT

CUT

CUT

CUT

CUT

CUT

Lesson 19

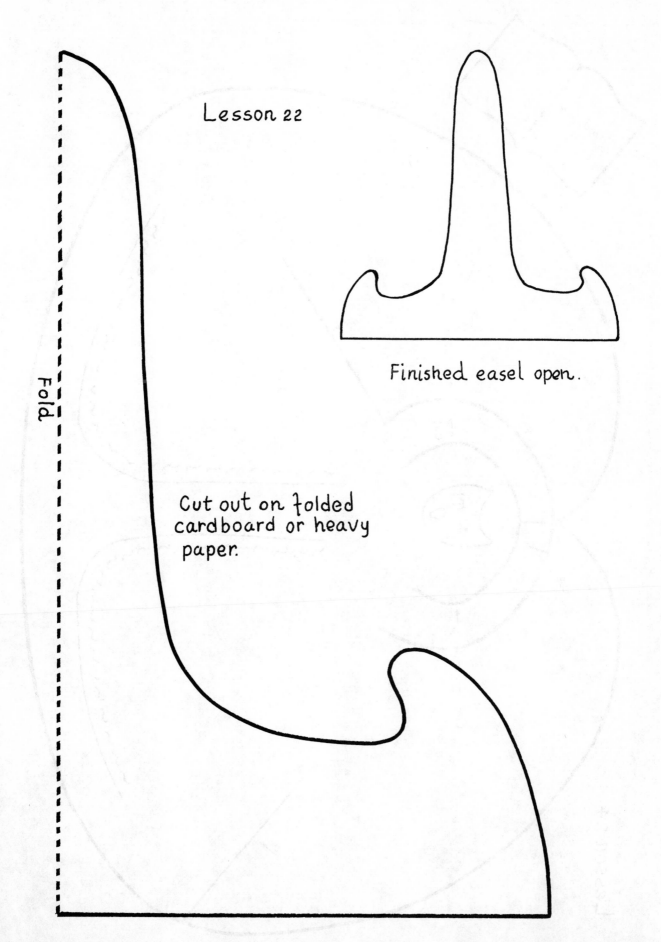

Lesson 22

Finished easel open.

Cut out on folded cardboard or heavy paper.

Fold

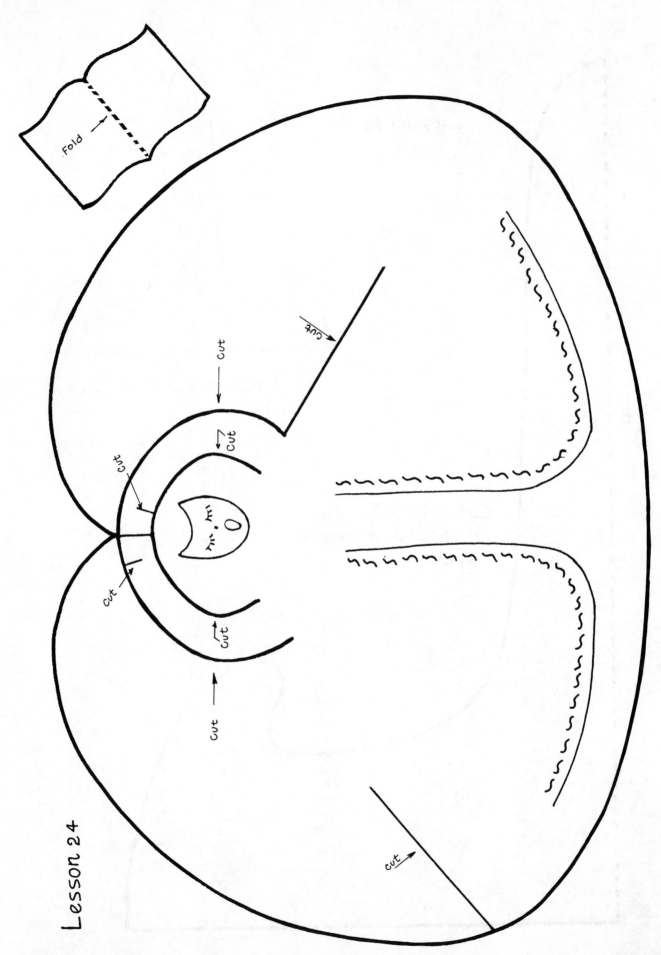

Lesson 24

116

My God Is a Great God

S. B. S.

Stella B. Stack

great God,   A   great God   is   He.

He's Got the Whole World in His Hands

SPIRITUAL

Arr. by R. J. HUGHES

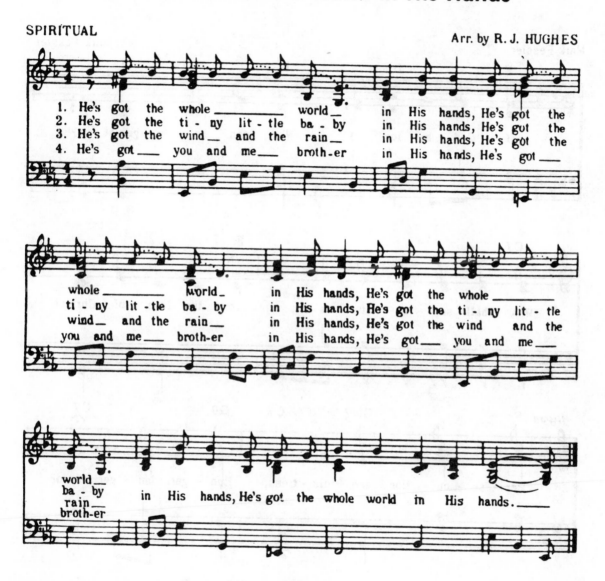

If God Be for Us

Mark Fessler

Mark Fessler

120

Step by Step

BUD METZGER

MAXINE ANDERSON

Step by step I'll fol-low Je-sus, Hour by hour I'm in His care

Day by day He walks be - side me, Thru the years I'll know He's there,

He can still the might-y tem-pest, He can calm the trou-bled sea,

He the wa-ters trod, He's the Son of God, He's the One who al-ways walks with me.

Loving and Kind

M. W.

Margie Watson

Lov - ing and kind — to oth - ers I'll be. I want the world to see
Lord, help me fol - low His Word and His way, Help me to share His love

Je - sus in me. day af - ter day. Lord, as I read my Bi - ble and pray

Give un - der - stand - ing and show me the way To be fill'd with love,

from a - bove, This now I pray. Je - sus, Your Word lives in me. —

There Is Power in Christ

P. H.

Patricia Hetrick

There is pow - er in Christ! ____ And, when Christ is with - in, ____ There's
pow - er in me ____ To live vic - to - ri - ous - ly! ____ There is

Pow'r in ____ Christ means ____
Pow - er in Christ ____ and when Christ is with - in ____ There's

Pow'r to ____ live vic - to - ri - ous - ly! ____ to - ri - ous - ly! ____
Pow - er in me ____ to live vic - to - ri - ous - ly! ____ There is

What a Happy Day

M. K. B.

Mary Kay Bottens

Jesus, the Son of God

D.W.

DON WHITMAN

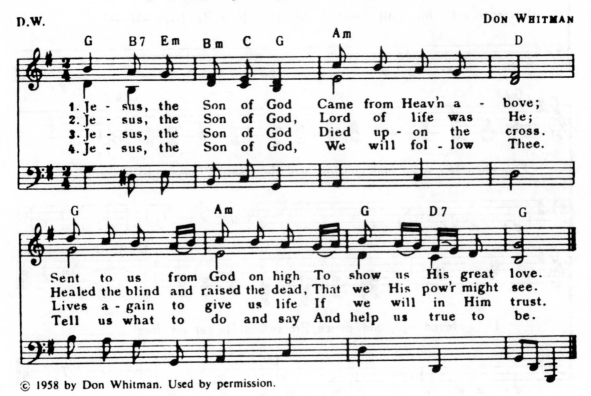

1. Je - sus, the Son of God Came from Heav'n a - bove;
2. Je - sus, the Son of God, Lord of life was He;
3. Je - sus, the Son of God Died up - on the cross.
4. Je - sus, the Son of God, We will fol - low Thee.

Sent to us from God on high To show us His great love.
Healed the blind and raised the dead, That we His pow'r might see.
Lives a - gain to give us life If we will in Him trust.
Tell us what to do and say And help us true to be.

Oh How He Loves You and Me

Words and Music by
KURT KAISER

37710

He's Able

P. E. P.

Paul E. Paino
Arr. by John W. Peterson

He's a-ble, He's a-ble, I know He's a-ble, I know my Lord is a-ble to car-ry me thru. He's a-ble, He's a-ble, I know He's a-ble, I know my Lord is a-ble to car-ry me thru; He healed the bro-ken-heart-ed and set the cap-tive free, He made the lame to walk a-gain and caused the blind to see. He's

Jesus, I Believe in You

N. L. S.

Norman L. Starks

Jesus Is My Answer

Mary Kay Bottens

So I will come to Him, And learn of Him, And fol-low in His way;

Grow in Him, and give my life In ser-vice ev'-ry day;

Walk with Him, and talk with Him, And faith-ful-ly o-bey;

Use my tal-ents for Him, Read His Word and pray. For I know

Evening and Morning

Based on Psalm 55:17

Doris J. Owens

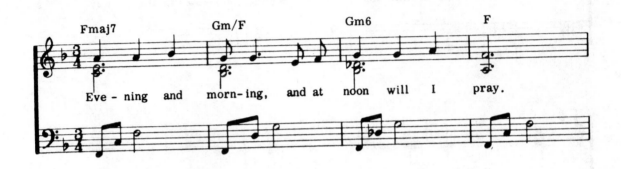

Eve-ning and morn-ing, and at noon will I pray.

Pray with-out ceas-ing, _____ pray ev-'ry day.

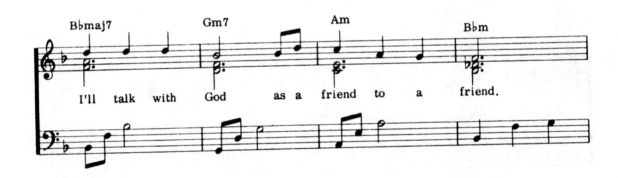

I'll talk with God as a friend to a friend.

My walk with Him shall nev-er, nev-er end!

Submission

J. L.

John Leinbaugh

Dear Je - sus, I long to give to You My life, my heart, my all._____ I pray that I will sur - ren - der, Lord, To ser - vice, great or small._____ You know all things; You hear each prayer, And sure - ly You must see_____ Not on - ly what I am and seem, But what I long to be._____

Whisper a Prayer

Arr. Herbert G. Tovey

1. Whis-per a pray'r in the morn-ing, Whis-per a pray'r at noon;
2. God an-swers pray'r in the morn-ing, God an-swers pray'r at noon;

Whis-per a pray'r in the eve-ning, 'Twill keep your heart in tune.
God an-swers pray'r in the eve-ning, He'll keep your heart in tune.

Forgive One Another

N. L. S.

NORMAN L. STARKS

Slowly

For - give one an - oth - er, For - give one an - oth - er; Do as you'd

have done to you. For - give one an - oth - er, And love one an-

oth - er; And He will for - give you too!

We Worship You

L. K.

LaVern Karns

Serve the Lord With Gladness

Text: Psalms 100:2, 3

Mark Fessler

Giving to Jesus

E. P.

Eleanor Pankow

Giv - ing to Je - sus, my priv' - lege shall be,

When I con - sid - er His great love for me -

Dy - ing on Cal - v'ry to show me His love.

I'll give my all for the Sav - ior I love.

We Can Reach Around the World

Ruth Gibbs Zwall

Evelyn F. Tarner

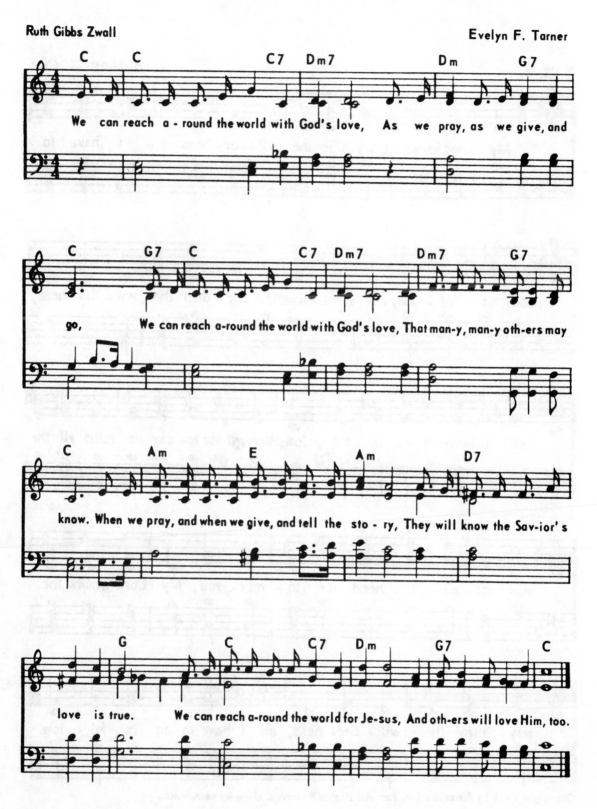

We can reach a-round the world with God's love, As we pray, as we give, and go, We can reach a-round the world with God's love, That man-y, man-y oth-ers may know. When we pray, and when we give, and tell the sto-ry, They will know the Sav-ior's love is true. We can reach a-round the world for Je-sus, And oth-ers will love Him, too.

My Lord Knows the Way

S. E. C.

Sidney E. Cox

My Lord knows the way thro' the wil-der-ness, all I have to do is fol-low, My Lord knows the way thro' the wil-der-ness, all I have to do is fol-low; Strength for to-day is mine all the way and all I need for to-mor-row, My Lord knows the way thro' the wil-der-ness, all I have to do is fol-low.

He Is Lord

Philippians 2:10-11

Unknown

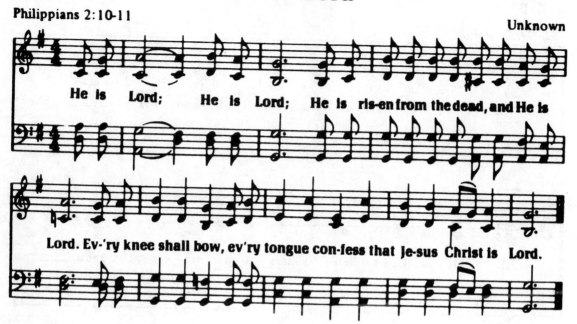

He is   Lord;   He is Lord;   He is ris-en from the dead, and He is Lord. Ev-'ry knee shall bow, ev'ry tongue con-fess that Je-sus Christ is Lord.

The Bible Is God's Word

M. K. B.

Mary Kay Bottens

Like a Shepherd

L. K.

LaVern Karns

Like a shep-herd, _ lov-ing, kind, Je-sus _ leads this
In green pas-tures, _ rich and sweet, He will _ rest my

life of mine. In the paths of _ right-eous-ness,
wea-ry feet. By still wa-ters _ I will lie,

I _ will _ fol - low _ Je - sus.
When _ I _ fol - low _ Je - sus.

THY WORD HAVE I HID IN MY HEART

Psalm 119:11

Adapted by E.O.S.

E. O. SELLERS

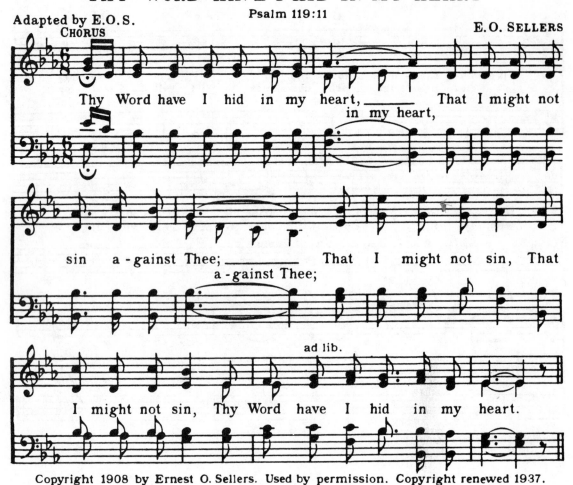

Thy Word have I hid in my heart, _____ That I might not
in my heart,

sin a-gainst Thee; _____ That I might not sin, That
a-gainst Thee;

I might not sin, Thy Word have I hid in my heart.

Fourth Edition

bju **press**®

Greenville, South Carolina

SCIENCE 3
Fourth Edition

Writers
Peggy S. Alier
Debra Harrold White

Contributing Writers
Sandra Bircher
Betty Doeppers
Joyce Garland
Janet E. Snow
Nancy Wilkison

Bible Integration
Wesley Barley

Project Editor
Kristin McClanahan

Page Layout
Peggy Hargis
Northstar

Concept Designer
Drew Fields

Designer
Joshua Frederick

Project Coordinator
Gina Stewart

Consultants
Brad Batdorf
Charlene McCall
Michelle Rosier

Cover Design
Craig Oesterling

Permissions
Sylvia Gass
Kathleen Thompson
Carrie Walker

Illustrators
Preston Gravely
Amber Cheadle Lindsey
Dave Schuppert
Lynda Slattery
Heather Propst Stanley
Del Thompson
Courtney Godbey Wise

Photograph credits appear on pages 247–49.

© 2016 BJU Press
Greenville, South Carolina 29609
First Edition © 1976 BJU Press
Second Edition © 1989, 1996, 2003 BJU Press
Third Edition © 2009 BJU Press

ISBN 978-1-60682-882-3

15 14 13 12 11 10 9 8 7 6 5

Contents

Let's Explore God's World

When you travel, you see many amazing things in nature. God created the world and all that is in it! You are studying science to learn about God's world. Christians should use science to worship God and to work in His world. How people think about the world is called their worldview. To help you understand a Christian worldview, remember the following points as you study science.

1. God is the Creator.

God created all things in just six days! God made everything perfect and called it "very good" (Genesis 1:31). He created all things for His own glory. When you observe and study the world, you see many things. You see God's power, His goodness, and His wisdom. Learning about God's creation makes us want to praise Him.

1

2. Sin changed God's world at the Fall.

God's world is no longer perfect. Adam disobeyed God. Because of Adam's sin, the world changed (Genesis 3:17). Thorns grow from the ground. Work is hard. Living things die. But using science helps people live and work in this imperfect world.

3. God has provided redemption.

God judged the world because of sin. But God loves and cares for all people. He sent His own Son, Jesus, into the world to save all who repent of their sin and believe the gospel. One day God will make the world perfect again. Until then, Christians should live to obey and glorify God.

4. People are important.

God created all people in His own image (Genesis 1:26). You are made in God's image. Your neighbor is made in God's image. And God wants you to show His love to other people (Matthew 22:39). Science can be used in helpful or harmful ways. You should use science to honor God and show love to other people.

5. God put people in this world to work.

Because work is part of God's creation, work is good too. God gave people the job of managing the plants and animals. God wants people to use the world and work to make it better (Genesis 1:28). This means that you should learn about things like plants and animals. You should know about gravity and friction. Learning about these things can help you honor God in your work.

These points can help you serve God with the science you are learning. Keep them in mind as you read!

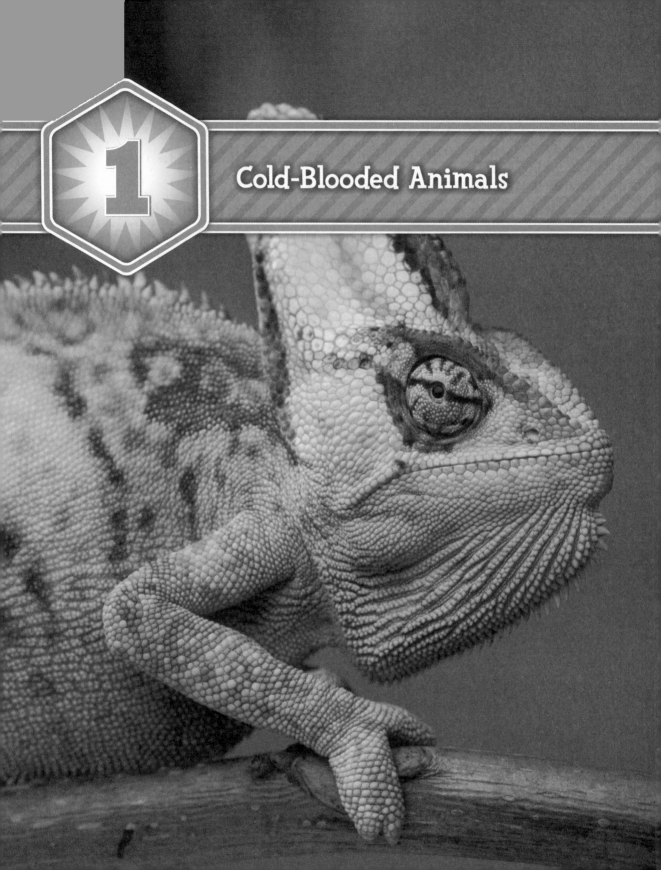

1

Cold-Blooded Animals

Worldview Focus

What do I need to know
to take care of a
cold-blooded animal?

God made our world and all that is in it (Genesis 1).
He made the land and the water. He made a wide variety
of plants and animals. Last of all, God made people. He
named the first man Adam.

God gave Adam the job of naming the animals.
What a big job that was! Genesis 2:19–20 tells us that
Adam named the cattle, the birds, and the
other animals. Have you ever
named a pet?

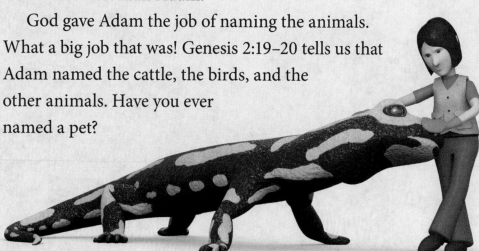

5

Classifying Animals

Adam named the different kinds of animals. But we do not have a list of all the names he used. So other people have given names to the animals too. Some of the names come from scientists. They look at the special features that animals have. These features are called **characteristics**. Scientists group animals that have the same kinds of characteristics. Grouping things that are alike is called classifying. As scientists classify animals, they give the groups and animals names.

Scientists have put all animals into two main categories. The animals in one category have backbones. The animals in the other category do not have backbones.

Giraffes, zebras, and gazelles have backbones.

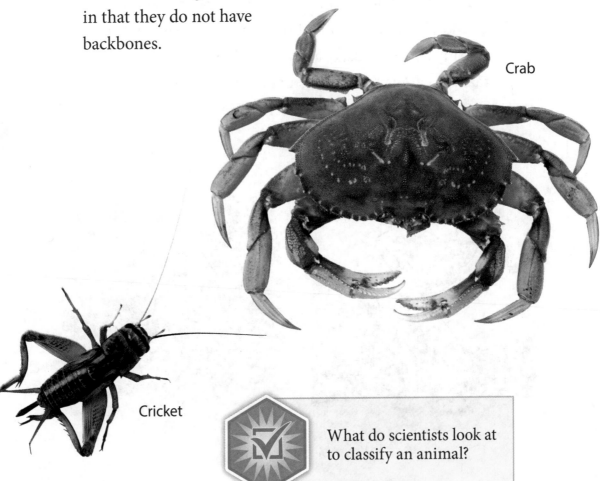

Invertebrates

Have you ever seen a worm on a sidewalk after a rainstorm? Did you pick it up? A worm is soft and wiggly. It does not have a backbone. Worms and other animals without backbones are called **invertebrates**.

There are millions of invertebrates around the world. Large octopuses and smaller crabs live in the water. Tiny crickets and slugs live on land. All these animals are alike in that they do not have backbones.

Worm

Crab

Cricket

What do scientists look at to classify an animal?

Vertebrates

What do a fish, a bird, a cat, and a lizard have in common? All these animals have backbones. Animals with backbones are called **vertebrates**. These animals can be as big as a cow, or as small as a frog. They might walk, fly, or swim. There are thousands of animals in this category.

Scientists separate vertebrates into groups. One way they are classified is by how their bodies stay warm. Some vertebrates are warm-blooded. Others are cold-blooded.

Any animal that has fur or feathers is **warm-blooded**. This kind of animal has about the same body temperature all the time. Cats, birds, bears, and seals are warm-blooded animals. A cat may sit in the sun for a while. Later it might take a nap in the shade. No matter where a cat is, its body temperature stays about the same.

Warm-blooded animal

Lizards, turtles, and fish are cold-blooded animals. Cold-blooded animals do not have fur or feathers. Instead they have scales or smooth skin.

A **cold-blooded** animal has a body temperature that changes depending on its surroundings. For example, when a lizard sits in the sun, its body gets warmer. The heat from the sun warms it, and its body temperature rises. Cold-blooded animals move around more when they are warm. But if they get too warm, they look for places to cool off. If a lizard is too hot, it might crawl into the shade under a plant or lie in some cool mud.

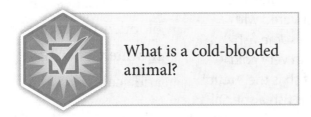

What is a cold-blooded animal?

Cold-blooded animal

Cold-Blooded Animals

There are thousands of cold-blooded animals. Most live in their natural habitats. Some live in zoos or are pets. We need to learn all we can about cold-blooded animals so that we can care for them properly. These animals can be classified into smaller groups. Three groups are fish, amphibians, and reptiles.

Fish

What makes a fish a fish? All fish have some of the same characteristics. **Fish** are cold-blooded vertebrates that live in water. They have gills, fins, and scales.

Characteristics of Fish

A fish lives its entire life in water. It may live in the ocean, in a river, in a pond, or in a stream. But a fish cannot live on land. It does not breathe with lungs like you do. It has gills, which allow it to breathe in the water.

A fish has fins that help it move in the water. It has fins on top, underneath, and on its sides. A fish's tail is also a fin. Each fin has a purpose. The tail fin helps the fish move. Its other fins mainly help the fish stop and rest without rolling over.

Fish Features

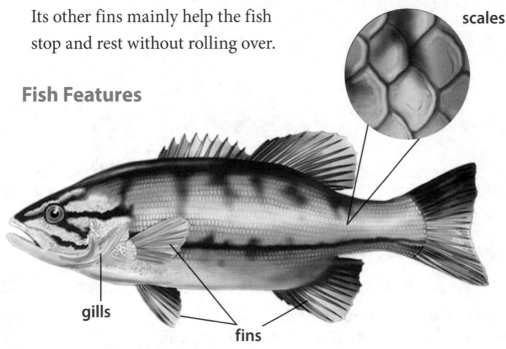

scales

gills

fins

Fish have scales covering their bodies. God designed the scales to be lightweight and strong. The scales overlap each other and help protect the fish. A fish's body is also covered with a clear slime. This slime helps the fish move through the water easily. It also helps protect its skin from pests and infections.

Fish Characteristics
Fish are cold-blooded vertebrates.
Fish live in the water.
Fish breathe with gills.
Fish have fins.
Fish have scales and slime covering their bodies.

What are five characteristics of fish?

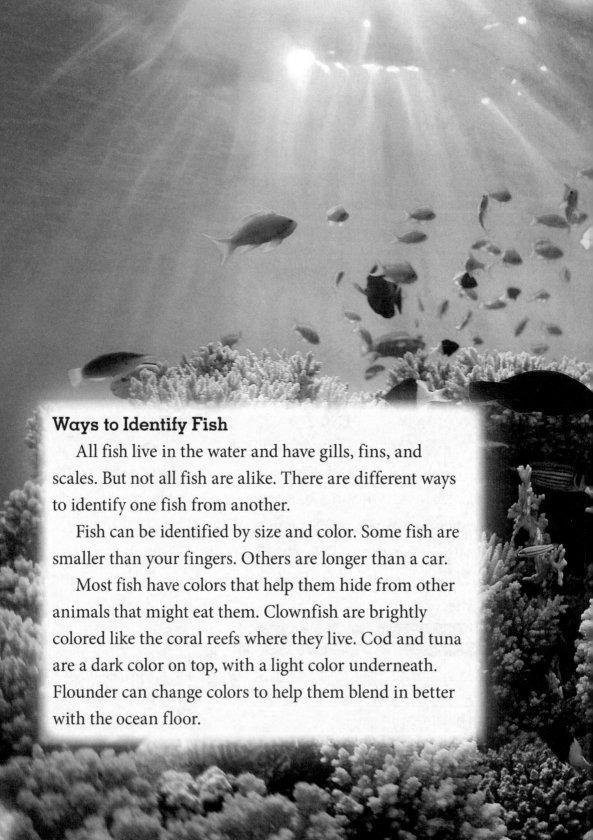

Ways to Identify Fish

All fish live in the water and have gills, fins, and scales. But not all fish are alike. There are different ways to identify one fish from another.

Fish can be identified by size and color. Some fish are smaller than your fingers. Others are longer than a car.

Most fish have colors that help them hide from other animals that might eat them. Clownfish are brightly colored like the coral reefs where they live. Cod and tuna are a dark color on top, with a light color underneath. Flounder can change colors to help them blend in better with the ocean floor.

Another way to identify fish is by where they live. Many fish live in the salty ocean. Some live in warm, shallow waters near the shore. Others, such as anglerfish, live deep in the ocean where it is very cold and dark.

Fish also live in lakes and rivers. The water in these places is called fresh because it is not salty. Maybe you have fished for perch or bass. They are freshwater fish. Each type of fish lives in the kind of water that is best for it.

Some kinds of fish are born live. But most fish hatch from eggs that are laid in the water. The eggs are like soft balls of jelly that stick together. A fish can lay thousands of eggs or more at one time.

Science and the Bible

Luke 5:1–11 tells about a miracle that involved many fish! Some fishermen had fished all night and had not caught anything. Jesus told them to cast their nets one more time. This time they caught so many fish that their boats began to sink!

Do you know what kinds of fish they caught? The men were fishing in the Sea of Galilee. It is a large freshwater lake. The people caught and ate sardines, barbels, and musht. These three kinds of fish are still caught there and eaten today.

What are the two kinds of water that fish can live in?

Amphibians

What is the difference between a frog and a toad? Frogs are thinner than toads. They also have longer legs. Though different in these ways, frogs and toads are alike in most other ways.

Tree frog

Both frogs and toads belong to the same group of cold-blooded animals. Salamanders also belong to this group. They are all amphibians. **Amphibians** are cold-blooded vertebrates that live part of their lives in water and part of their lives on land.

Salamander

Characteristics of Amphibians

Amphibians have thin, smooth, moist skin. Because their skin is thin, they do not have to drink. They absorb, or soak up, water through their skin.

Amphibians live in many places. Most adult amphibians live near water or in damp places. Others live on trees or under rocks and leaves.

Amphibian Characteristics
Amphibians are cold-blooded vertebrates.
Amphibians live in water and on land.
Amphibians have thin, smooth, moist skin.
Young amphibians breathe with gills.
Adult amphibians breathe with lungs.

Toad

Life Cycle of Amphibians

The name *amphibian* means "double life." This name describes how these animals begin life in water then move to land as adults.

Most amphibians lay eggs in water. For example, an adult frog looks for a safe place in the water to lay its eggs. Soon a tiny tadpole hatches from each egg. A tadpole must be able to breathe and swim in the water, so it has gills and a tail. As the tadpole grows, it changes. It loses its gills and forms lungs. It also loses its tail and grows legs. Then the adult frog is finally ready to move onto land.

God designed frogs and other amphibians to grow in this special way. They change form as they grow. When an animal changes form as it grows, scientists call the process **metamorphosis**.

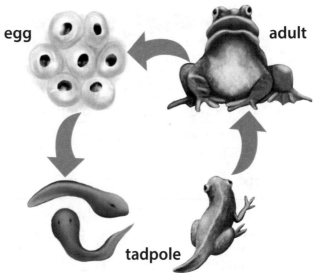

Stages of Frog Metamorphosis

egg

adult

tadpole

What do scientists call it when an animal changes form as it grows?

Reptiles

How are turtles, lizards, and snakes alike? All these animals are reptiles. **Reptiles** are cold-blooded vertebrates with tough, dry, scaly skin.

Snake

Characteristics of Reptiles

Reptiles live on land their entire lives. This means that they always breathe using lungs.

A reptile's tough, dry, scaly skin provides good protection. It helps protect the reptile from other animals that might want to eat it. The skin also protects the reptile as it moves across the ground.

Turtle

Reptile Characteristics
Reptiles are cold-blooded vertebrates.
Reptiles live on land all their lives.
Reptiles breathe air through lungs.
Reptiles have tough, dry, scaly skin.

Alligator

Ways to Identify Reptiles

Many reptiles shed their skin several times a year. New scales grow under the old scales. This causes the old skin to loosen. Some reptiles, such as snakes, shed all their skin in one piece. Lizards and some other reptiles shed their skin in many pieces.

The tiniest reptile is a Jaragua lizard. This lizard is so tiny that when it curls up it can fit on a dime. It can stretch out to its full length on a quarter. Scientists discovered these tiny lizards on a small island in the Caribbean Sea in 2001.

Snake shedding skin

Reptiles include animals of many sizes. Some are very small. There are types of lizards that could fit on your finger. But other reptiles, such as crocodiles and alligators, grow to be very large.

Reptiles live in different kinds of places, such as deserts or forests. They may also live in swamps or in oceans. Reptiles that live in water still breathe with lungs. Some, such as turtles, can stay underwater for more than an hour at a time. But they all must come to the surface to breathe air.

Lizard

What are four characteristics of reptiles?

Life Cycles of Reptiles

Fish and most amphibians lay their eggs in water. Reptiles lay their eggs on land. Some reptiles dig a hole in sand or soil and bury their eggs. Others make a nest in grasses or hide their eggs in rotting logs. A sea turtle might swim thousands of miles to lay its eggs on the same beach every year.

Most reptiles lay several eggs at one time. Some lay 20 or 30 eggs in their nests. Others lay more than 100 eggs at a time.

Baby reptiles hatch from eggs. They look like adult reptiles but are smaller. They do not have gills. They breathe with lungs as soon as they are born.

Reptiles can live a long time. Some live as long as most people do. Giant tortoises and alligators can live more than 80 years.

Turtle's nest

God's Power

Genesis 1 records God's power at Creation. God made the birds and the water animals on the fifth day of Creation. The next day He made the land animals. He did this just by the power of His words. He simply spoke, and all the animals were made.

God made a great variety of animals. No two are exactly the same. Even within the groups of fish, amphibians, and reptiles there are many differences. God planned and provided for each animal. He gave each animal the right body parts for breathing and protection.

God gave people the job of having authority over the earth. This includes authority over cold-blooded animals (Genesis 1:28). We need to learn about and understand cold-blooded animals in order to take care of them properly.

What job did God give people?

MEASURE UP

You have learned that some animals are cold-blooded. They have body temperatures that change depending on their surroundings. Scientists who study cold-blooded animals need tools to measure temperature. These scientists use thermometers. A **thermometer** is a tool used to measure temperature.

But scientists are not the only people who measure temperature. Cooks use thermometers to measure how hot foods are. A nurse might use one to tell whether you have a fever. Your parents might use a thermometer to measure how hot or cold it is outside. You need to know how to use a thermometer in order to measure temperature.

One kind of thermometer has numbers along the side. The red liquid in the thermometer's thin tube rises when warm and lowers when cool. The numbers along the side tell how hot or cold it is.

The set of numbers on the side of a thermometer is called a scale. Some thermometers measure temperature with the Fahrenheit scale. Others use the Celsius scale. Some thermometers have both scales written on them. Scientists usually use the Celsius scale to measure temperature.

Look at the number next to where the red liquid stops. That number will tell you the measurement of how hot or cold something is. Look at the thermometer pictured in the cup of water. The red liquid stopped at the number 30. You would read this temperature as thirty degrees Celsius. You would write it as 30 °C.

If you were using a Fahrenheit thermometer, you would read the same temperature as eighty-six degrees Fahrenheit. You would write it as 86 °F.

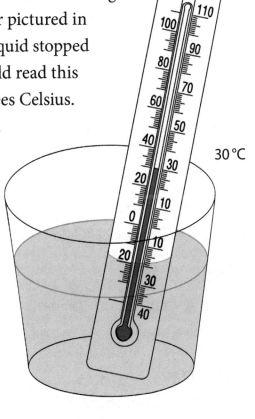

30 °C

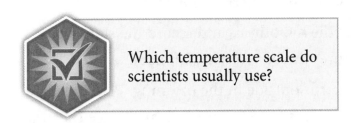

Which temperature scale do scientists usually use?

Leaping Lizards

Like all cold-blooded animals, reptiles can change their body temperature by changing their surroundings. For a reptile to be active, it must be warm. If you had a pet reptile, you would need to give it warm and cool places to live. One thing you would need to know in order to take care of your pet is how to measure temperature.

In this activity you will measure different temperatures. You need to find a place where your "lizard" would be active. These "lizards" are active when their body temperatures are about 21 °C–31 °C (70 °F–88 °F).

Problem

Where would your "lizard" be more active during the daytime?

Materials
2 paper lizards
crayons
scissors
tape
2 thermometers
Activity Manual

Procedure

1. Color and cut out the paper lizards.

2. Attach the thermometers to the lizards.

3. Complete the hypothesis and record the starting temperatures in your Activity Manual.

4. Put the lizards outside in the morning. Place one in a sunny spot. This is your Sunny Lizard. Place the other in a shady spot. This is your Shady Lizard.

5. Wait 10 minutes. Read both thermometers. Record the temperatures in your Activity Manual.

6. Leave the lizards in their places for at least two hours. Then read the thermometers again. Record the temperatures.

Conclusions

- Did the temperature change in the shady spot?

- Would your Shady Lizard have to move to a warmer area to be active?

Follow-up

- Check and record the temperatures every hour throughout a day.

- If you had a pet lizard, how might you apply what you learned? Find ways that owners provide warm and cool places for pet lizards.

2

Warm-Blooded Animals

Suppose you take your temperature while you stand outside in the hot sun. Then you go inside a cool building and take it again. Do you think the temperatures would be different or about the same?

You may feel hot outside and cool inside. But your body temperature would not change much. Because you are warm-blooded, your body temperature stays about the same no matter where you are.

25

God has given your body different ways to keep the same body temperature. When you are hot, you sweat to cool off. When you are cold, you shiver to warm up.

Many vertebrate animals are warm-blooded. Birds and mammals are warm-blooded animals. They have ways to keep their body temperature the same. Some mammals and birds shiver as we do. Dogs pant to keep cool. Birds fluff up their feathers to keep warm.

Bird fluffing its feathers

What are some ways that God gave you to keep the same body temperature?

Dog panting

26

You can learn about other people by talking with them. Most birds cannot talk to you. But you can learn about birds by watching them.

In this exploration you will make a bird feeder. After hanging your feeder, observe the birds that visit it.

What to Do

1. Your teacher will give you directions to make a bird feeder.

2. Fill the feeder with food. Place the feeder near a window or in another place where you can easily observe the birds.

3. Observe the birds that come to the feeder. Record your observations on the *Bird Watching* page.

Birds

A **bird** is a warm-blooded vertebrate that has feathers and wings. Most birds can fly. All birds breathe air through lungs.

Characteristics of Birds

Feathers

Feathers help a bird stay warm. A bird's body makes a kind of oil that the bird spreads on its feathers. This oil helps make the feathers waterproof. Feathers can also help birds to fly.

Wings

Another characteristic God gave birds is their two wings, but they need more than feathers and wings to fly. God gave birds a special bone structure. Many of their bones are hollow and lightweight. These hollow bones make the birds lighter.

Hawk

Some birds do not fly. The ostrich is the largest bird in the world. It cannot fly, but it can run fast. It uses its wings to help it change direction when running. The penguin cannot fly either, but it uses its wings to swim.

Bird Characteristics
Birds are warm-blooded vertebrates.
Birds breathe air through lungs.
Birds have feathers.
Birds have two wings.
Most birds fly.

Ways to Identify

If you watch a bird feeder, you will see birds with different colors, sizes, and sounds. Your observations can help you identify the kinds of birds you are seeing.

Nests and Eggs

Birds lay eggs with hard shells. Most birds lay their eggs in nests. The eggs are different colors. Some are blue, brown, white, or gray. Others are speckled.

A nest of leaves and twigs might have speckled brown eggs in it. The eggs are often camouflaged in their surroundings. **Camouflage** is the color or pattern that allows something to blend in with its surroundings. This blending helps hide the eggs. Animals that want to eat the eggs might not see them. Some birds' nests are camouflaged in trees or in tall grasses. Other birds hide their nests in the cracks of rocks.

What are some characteristics of birds?

29

Size and Color

Birds are different sizes. The ostrich and emu are both very large birds. The adult ostrich is taller and heavier than most adult men. Hummingbirds, however, are very small birds. They are so small that they can fit in the palm of your hand.

Birds also have different colors. The male and female birds may look different. A male cardinal has bright red feathers, but the female cardinal is a plain reddish brown.

God designed some birds to be camouflaged. But other birds, such as bluebirds, have bright feathers. Birds may also have markings on their wings. A bird's coloring and markings can help you identify what kind of bird it is.

Ostrich

Hummingbird

Female cardinal

Male cardinal

Sounds

Some people enjoy sitting in a quiet place outside and listening to the birds. The chirping and tweeting of some birds are like songs. God has given each kind of bird its own sound.

The bobwhite quail gets its name from the sound that it makes. It sounds like it is saying "bob white." In the evening you might hear the hoot of an owl or the screech of a hawk. The mockingbird sings the songs of many other birds. It can even mock other sounds, such as the bark of a dog or the squeaking of a rusty hinge.

What are some ways you can identify birds?

Bighorn sheep

Mammals

If asked to name an animal, you would most likely name some kind of mammal. Most pets are mammals. So are most farm animals. A **mammal** is a warm-blooded vertebrate that has hair or fur and feeds milk to its babies.

Characteristics of Mammals

Many mammals have hair or fur all over their bodies. Other mammals, such as elephants or whales, have only small amounts of hair.

Lioness with cub

All mammals breathe with lungs. Mammals that live in the water can stay underwater longer than we can, but they still breathe with lungs. They must come to the surface to breathe.

Seal

Instead of laying eggs, almost all mammals give birth to live babies. The mothers feed them with milk. The babies need their mother's milk until they can eat other foods.

Many mammal babies are small and helpless at birth. Kittens and puppies are born with their eyes closed. They need their mothers for everything. Some mammals, such as mice, are ready to be on their

Mother cat with kittens

own in just a few weeks. Other mammals, such as gorillas, stay with their mothers for years.

Some mammal babies, though, are not small or helpless. Baby giraffes can be as tall as an adult man! They can stand and run soon after they are born.

Mammal Characteristics
Mammals are warm-blooded vertebrates.
Mammals breathe air through lungs.
Mammals have fur or hair.
Mammals give birth to live babies.
Mammals feed milk to their babies.

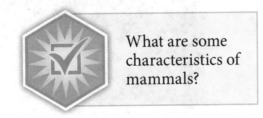

What are some characteristics of mammals?

Ways to Identify

Mammals can live in many different places. They can live in wooded areas, mountains, deserts, and water. Most mammals have four legs. Some have fins or flippers.

All mammals have hair or fur and breathe with lungs. Even so, they can be very different from each other.

Hoofed Mammals

Some mammals have hooves. The hoof is the hard part of the mammal's foot that touches the ground. It helps protect the animal's feet. Horses, deer, and giraffes are a few examples of hoofed mammals.

Yak

Pig

Zebra

Flying Mammals

Bats are the only mammals that can fly. Some bats fly during the daytime. But most bats sleep during the day and are active at night. Bats live in dark places. They usually make their homes in caves, rocks, and trees. They often hang upside down when they are resting.

Bat

Marine Mammals

Some mammals spend most of their time in **marine** surroundings. The word *marine* is used to describe something that lives in salt water or the ocean. Mammals that live in the ocean are called marine mammals. Dolphins, whales, and seals are examples of marine mammals.

Sea otter

Manatee

Where do marine mammals live?

Upright Mammals

Lemur

Upright mammals spend much of their lives in trees. Monkeys, gorillas, and lemurs are examples of upright mammals. They have four legs. These animals usually use their front legs as hands that can grasp and hold on to things. Many of them have long tails. Monkeys often use their tails like an extra arm or hand.

Gnawing Mammals

Some mammals have large front teeth. Look at the beaver's teeth. Its teeth never stop growing! Gnawing mammals have to gnaw, or chew, on things to keep their teeth worn down and sharp. Squirrels, mice, and porcupines are gnawing mammals.

Beaver

Hunting Mammals

Hunting mammals chase and eat other animals. Big cats, such as lions and tigers, are hunting mammals, but so are pet cats. You may have seen a pet cat chasing a mouse or bird. Dogs are also hunters. Wolves and coyotes are types of dogs.

Wolf

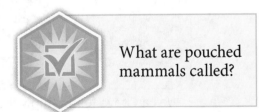
Kangaroo with baby in pouch

Pouched Mammals

Some mammals have pouches outside their bodies. Their babies grow and develop inside these pouches. Mammals with pouches are called **marsupials**. Kangaroos, opossums, and koalas all have pouches.

What are pouched mammals called?

37

Humans

Humans have the same characteristics as mammals. Humans are warm-blooded vertebrates. They breathe air through lungs and have hair. They feed milk to their babies after giving birth. But humans are not animals. The Bible tells us that God made people in His own image. This means that people are like God in certain ways and can have fellowship with Him.

God gave people the job of managing the earth. This includes warm-blooded animals. We need to understand these animals in order to take care of them properly.

Why are people not animals?

We can have fellowship with God through our prayers.

Behaviors

Perhaps you have seen a dog shake hands or do other tricks. You may have seen a service dog do tasks for its owner. Those are all examples of learned behaviors. Someone taught the dogs to do those things. A **learned behavior** is something that an animal learns to do.

Many animals learn new behaviors. Birds learn to come to a feeder for seeds and nuts. Dolphins learn to search for objects in the water. A chimpanzee might learn to crack nuts by seeing another chimpanzee smash a nut with a rock.

This dolphin was taught to do tricks.

This dog was trained to help its owner.

There are other behaviors, though, that animals do not have to learn. Birds are born knowing how to build a nest. Dolphins and whales are born knowing how to swim. These are instincts. **Instincts** are the basic knowledge and skills that an animal is born with. Animals need instincts to survive.

People can teach animals many things. Animals also teach each other and learn by experience. Instincts, though, cannot be taught.

This Asian golden weaver was born with the instinct to build a nest.

Herd of elephants protecting their young

God gave each animal certain instincts. Many animals have shared instincts, like hunting or seeking shelter. But others have special instincts. When hunting, a cat may pounce on its prey. A spider may inject poison. God provided the exact instincts that each animal needs to live.

How are learned behaviors different from instincts?

Science and the Bible

Daniel 6 tells of a time when God kept some lions from following their instincts. A law was made commanding people to pray only to the king. Daniel was a servant of God and refused to stop praying to Him. Because of this, Daniel was thrown into a lions' den, but God kept the lions from following their instincts. They did not eat Daniel. The king took Daniel out of the lions' den. The men who had told the king about Daniel's praying were then thrown into the den. The hungry lions attacked the men before they even fell to the bottom. When God causes something to happen outside of nature, we call that a miracle.

Animal Books

You probably are familiar with many mammals. But there are other animals that you might not know much about. In this activity you will research, or look up facts about, a few animals of your choice.

Process Skills
- Communicating
- Classifying

Problem

Research and classify vertebrates.

Procedure

Materials
Animal pages
resources about animals

1. Choose three vertebrates that you would like to know more about.

2. Write the name of each animal on one of the *Animal* pages.

3. Look up information about each animal. Find out where the animal lives and what it eats. Record that information on the animal's page.

4. Decide which vertebrate group each animal belongs to and identify the group.

   amphibians   reptiles   fish   birds   mammals

5. Add a picture of each animal to its page.

6. Find two interesting facts about each animal. Record those facts.

7. Share your *Animal* pages with your classmates.

8. Organize all the pages by the groups the animals belong to. Put each group of *Animal* pages into a different folder. Write the name of the animal group on the front of each folder.

9. Display your animal books.

Conclusions

- How did you know which animals belong to each group?

3 Plants

If you take a walk in a forest, you might see animals that live there. Birds fly from tree to tree. Squirrels chase each other up and down tree trunks. Spiders spin webs between plants. Rabbits nibble on low bushes. All around these animals are plants. When God created the world, He filled it with many kinds of plants. People use plants in different ways as they work in God's world.

People and animals use energy to grow, move, and work. **Energy** is what is needed to cause change or to do work. But people and animals are not the only living things using energy. Trees and other plants also need energy to grow and to make food.

Plants

A plant is a living thing that makes its own food. A rabbit can hop from one place to another to get food, but a plant cannot get up and move to find food. It must be able to get what it needs without moving from place to place.

Food is important because it contains nutrients. **Nutrients** are substances that help plants and animals live and grow. Plants get nutrients from the soil. Animals get nutrients from the food that they eat.

Plants have different parts that help them get what they need to grow and make food.

Parts of a Plant

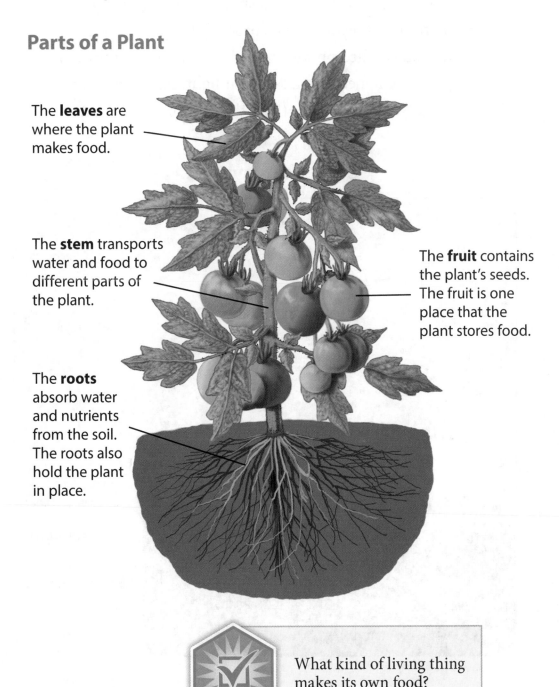

The **leaves** are where the plant makes food.

The **stem** transports water and food to different parts of the plant.

The **fruit** contains the plant's seeds. The fruit is one place that the plant stores food.

The **roots** absorb water and nutrients from the soil. The roots also hold the plant in place.

What kind of living thing makes its own food?

Photosynthesis

God designed plants with a special process, or way, to make the food they need. The process that plants use to make food is called **photosynthesis**. For photosynthesis to happen, a plant needs to take in sunlight, carbon dioxide, and water. Plants then use these things to produce food and oxygen.

Basic Photosynthesis

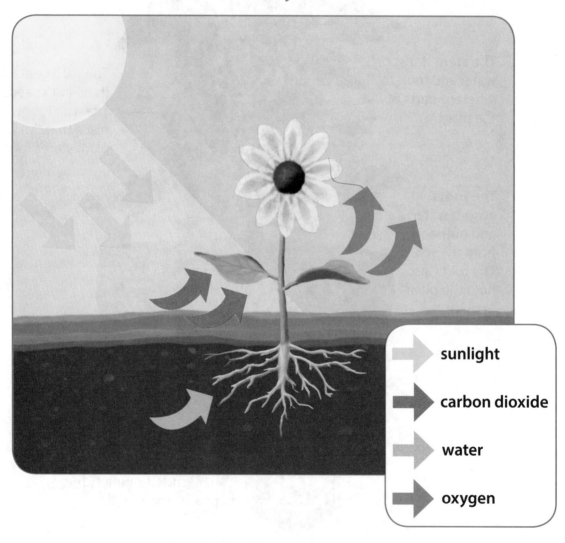

sunlight

carbon dioxide

water

oxygen

What a Plant Needs

Photosynthesis takes place in the leaves of a plant. Leaves help the plant absorb, or take in, sunlight. The sunlight is the energy that the plant needs for photosynthesis to happen.

The leaves of most plants are green. Plants get their green coloring from **chlorophyll**. The chlorophyll helps the leaves use the energy from sunlight.

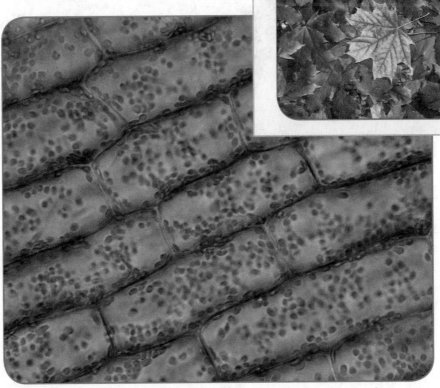

Tiny dots of chlorophyll, called chloroplasts, are seen in this magnified view of a leaf.

49

A plant also needs carbon dioxide for photosynthesis. Carbon dioxide is a gas that is part of the air. To take in the air that you need, you breathe with lungs. But a plant does not have lungs to get carbon dioxide. God gave it tiny openings on the underside of its leaves. They open and close to allow carbon dioxide into the plant.

The third thing a plant needs for photosynthesis is water. The roots of a plant absorb water from the soil. Then small tubes carry the water through the stems to the leaves. There the water can help the plant make food.

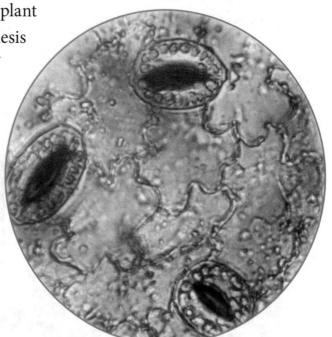

Openings on the underside of a leaf are called stomata.

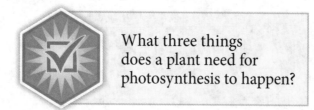

What three things does a plant need for photosynthesis to happen?

What a Plant Produces

Once a plant has what it needs, it continues the process of photosynthesis to produce food and oxygen. The chlorophyll in the plant uses energy from the sunlight to produce food. The food that the plant makes is a type of sugar. More tiny tubes carry the sugar to all parts of the plant. The sugar becomes food for the plant and gives it energy to grow.

Plants make food to supply their own energy. They use this energy to grow. But sometimes plants make more food than they need. That extra food is stored in the plants for later use.

The oxygen that plants produce is a gas. Like carbon dioxide, oxygen is a part of the air. It is a gas that animals and humans need to survive. Carbon dioxide enters a plant through tiny holes in the leaves. The same tiny holes release oxygen into the air. By doing this, plants help provide oxygen for other living things.

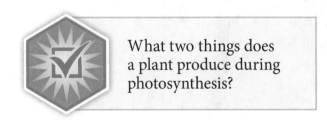

What two things does a plant produce during photosynthesis?

Length

Scientists use metric units of measurement. The **meter** is the standard metric unit used to measure length and distance.

A meter stick is a tool used to measure length. It has marks that show smaller units of measurement. The numbers on a meter stick show units called *centimeters*. There are 100 centimeters (cm) in 1 meter (m).

A centimeter ruler is shorter than a meter stick. It is easier to measure small lengths with this ruler. You will use a centimeter ruler in many of your science activities.

A centimeter ruler has centimeters and millimeters marked on it. *Millimeters* are smaller than centimeters. There are 10 millimeters (mm) in a centimeter. Some rulers have centimeters marked on one side and inches marked on the other side.

When you measure, find the centimeter side of the ruler. Place the ruler next to the object you are measuring. Line up the first mark on the ruler with the end of the object. Look at the centimeter number closest to the other end of the object. If the object ends between two centimeter marks, choose the mark beyond the end of the object.

For example, the length of the pen shown below is 14 centimeters. The length of the pencil is between 14 and 15 centimeters. So you would say that the pencil is about 15 centimeters long.

The pen is 14 centimeters long.

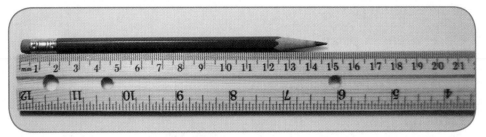

The pencil is about 15 centimeters long.

What standard metric unit do scientists use to measure length and distance?

A Place to Grow

Plants need light to make food. But will they grow without light? In this activity you will compare two plants to find out whether the amount of light they receive affects their growth.

Process Skills
- Measuring
- Observing

Problem

How does the amount of light affect plant growth?

Procedure

1. Prepare both cups the same way. Label one cup *Light* and the other cup *Dark*. Put the same amount of potting soil in each cup. Plant two of the same kind of seed in each cup. Carefully water the seeds in each cup with the same amount of water.

2. Observe the cups and record in your Activity Manual the date you see each plant poke out of the soil. Water the plants as needed with the same amount of water in each cup.

3. Place the Light cup where it will get sunlight. Place the Dark cup in a dark place. A box can be used as a dark place. Try to find places that are about the same temperature.

Materials
2 plastic cups, 9 oz
potting soil
seeds
water
centimeter ruler
Activity Manual

4. Measure each plant every day. Carefully place the end of the ruler on top of the soil. Measure the height of the plant. Be careful that you do not pull the plant out as you measure it.

5. Observe the color and leaves of each plant.

6. Record your measurements and observations in your Activity Manual.

Conclusions

- Which plant grew taller?

- In what other ways are the plants different? What caused the difference?

- How would your results affect where you plant a garden?

Follow-up

- Repeat the activity with a different type of plant and compare the results.

Uses of Plants

Food

One of the main uses of plants is food.
All living things need energy and nutrients.
Plants make food for their own energy needs.
They store the extra food and nutrients. In
this way they provide energy and nutrients
for other living things. Photosynthesis is
important to both people and animals
for oxygen and food. When people
and animals eat plants, they receive
the stored energy and nutrients.

Roots

God made many wonderful plants for us
to eat. But we don't always eat the same part
of every plant. Some plants have tasty roots.
Carrots, turnips, and sweet potatoes are roots
that we eat.

Stems

A stalk of celery is a stem that we eat. We can eat the
stem of the broccoli plant, but we also eat its flowers. The
ends of broccoli stems have florets, or unopened flowers,
that we eat.

Stems
and
flowers

Try It Yourself

Trim the bottom end from
a stem of fresh broccoli. Place
the stem in a container of water.
Observe the tiny flowers as the
florets open.

We eat the leaves of some plants. Lettuce, cabbage, and spinach are all plant leaves.

Seeds are another part of the plant that is eaten. Nuts, beans, and peas are seeds. Wheat, oats, corn, and other grains are also seeds that we eat.

The part of the plant that we most often eat is the fruit. You can probably think of many kinds of fruit, such as apples, oranges, and pineapples. But squashes, cucumbers, and tomatoes are also fruits. A fruit is the part of a plant that contains the seeds.

God has given us many wonderful plants to eat. He designed plants not only to make their own food but also to store food for other living things to use.

Leaves

Seeds

Seeds and fruit

Fruit

How do humans and animals get energy and nutrients from plants?

Other Uses

Plants have many other purposes besides food. Animals use plants to construct their homes. Birds and squirrels build nests in trees. The nests are made of leaves, twigs, and other parts of plants. Beavers build their homes in the water with parts of trees.

Animal home

People use trees in many ways. We make wooden furniture and houses. Most of our paper is also made from trees.

Aloe plant

Some medicines are made from plants. A common heart medicine comes from a plant called foxglove. Aloe is a plant that is helpful to treat minor burns or scrapes. People sometimes treat small skin cuts with liquid from the witch hazel plant. Some plants can also calm upset stomachs.

Paper

• Meet the Scientist • George Washington Carver

George Washington Carver was born in the 1860s. From an early age, he was interested in plants. Carver wanted to learn. He worked hard to get schooling wherever he could.

In the 1890s insects were destroying cotton, the South's main crop. Carver suggested planting peanuts instead of cotton. He became famous for finding hundreds of uses for the peanut plant. In all his work, he gave glory to God as the Creator of all things.

Many of our clothes are made of fibers that come from plants. Cotton fibers are used to make cotton fabric. You can find clothing, sheets, and towels made of cotton.

Scientists continue to find new purposes for plants. They use plants to make plastics that can break down after they are used. This causes less pollution than regular plastics. Scientists have even found ways to make fuel for cars from some plant crops.

God gave us the job of managing plants. He gave us plants to use and even enjoy. We can relax in the shade of a tree. We can smell the fragrance of a flower. We can see the beautiful colors of the plants around us. Plants are a wonderful gift from God.

Ethanol is a fuel made from plants.

What are some uses of plants?

4 Ecosystems

**How has the Fall affected
life on the earth?**

How can you tell if something is alive? Maybe you can see it breathing. Perhaps you notice it move. There are different ways to know whether something is alive. All living things have some of the same characteristics.

Living things grow and develop, reproduce, and interact with things around them. To *reproduce* means to make more living things. For example, a tiny puppy grows quickly. Soon the puppy becomes an adult dog. Later this dog might have puppies of its own. Plants are another example. Plants make seeds, and new plants grow from these seeds.

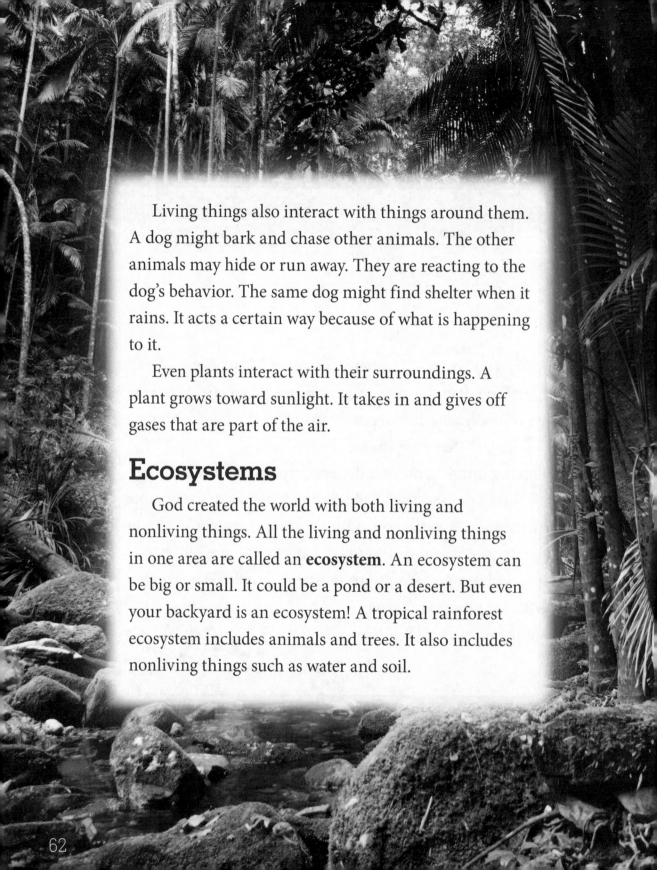

Living things also interact with things around them. A dog might bark and chase other animals. The other animals may hide or run away. They are reacting to the dog's behavior. The same dog might find shelter when it rains. It acts a certain way because of what is happening to it.

Even plants interact with their surroundings. A plant grows toward sunlight. It takes in and gives off gases that are part of the air.

Ecosystems

God created the world with both living and nonliving things. All the living and nonliving things in one area are called an **ecosystem**. An ecosystem can be big or small. It could be a pond or a desert. But even your backyard is an ecosystem! A tropical rainforest ecosystem includes animals and trees. It also includes nonliving things such as water and soil.

A subdivision ecosystem includes living things and their environment.

Living things need things that are not alive. Both animals and plants need air and water, and many living things need sunlight. All the nonliving things that surround a living thing are called its **environment**. The weather, air, and sunlight are part of an environment. Rocks, soil, and water and even buildings, sidewalks, and roads are also part of an environment.

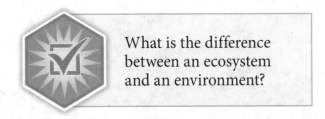

What is the difference between an ecosystem and an environment?

Living Together

An ecosystem usually has many kinds of plants and animals. A swamp ecosystem could include grasses and cypress trees. The swamp could also be a home for catfish, wood ducks, and alligators. Deer and foxes might live in parts of the swamp. These plants and animals are part of the swamp ecosystem.

All the living things of one kind that live in one area are called a **population**. All the catfish in the swamp ecosystem make up the catfish population. A wood duck is not part of the catfish population. It is part of the wood duck population.

Populations can be different sizes. Hundreds of catfish may live in the waters of a swamp. The catfish population of that swamp ecosystem is quite large. The same swamp ecosystem may have only a small herd of deer. The deer population is much smaller.

Each population has a habitat in the ecosystem. A **habitat** is a place where a living thing has the food, water, and shelter that it needs to live. An alligator spends most of its time in the water. The alligator's habitat is the water of the swamp. Since the water is also a habitat for cypress trees, the alligators and trees share a habitat. Many populations can share a habitat.

Deer live in the woods of the swamp. Their habitat is the woods. Foxes also live in the woods. The foxes share their habitat with the deer population.

All the different populations make up a community. A **community** includes all the living things in one area. For a swamp ecosystem, the community includes the cypress trees and other plants. It also includes the catfish population, the wood duck population, and the deer population.

What is the difference between a population and a community?

Eating for Energy

Living things need energy to live. Plants get energy from sunlight. They use that energy to make their own food during photosynthesis.

Plants use some of the food for their own needs. They store the rest of the food. Animals and people eat plants and get energy from that stored food.

Living things can be put into three main groups: producers, consumers, and decomposers. A **producer** makes its own food and gets its energy directly from the sun. Plants are producers.

Producers

However, many living things cannot get their energy directly from the sun. A living thing that gets its energy by eating other living things as food is called a **consumer**. Animals and people are consumers. They depend on producers for food. Consumers must eat plants or animals to get energy.

Consumers

The last main group is called decomposers. A **decomposer** helps break down dead things and wastes. Breaking down dead things and wastes adds nutrients to the soil. Plants then use the nutrients to grow and produce more food.

There are many kinds of decomposers. Some are very small. Bacteria are so small that they cannot be seen without a microscope. Other decomposers include mold, mushrooms, and earthworms.

What do decomposers do?

67

Types of Consumers

Animals eat a variety of things. Some consumers, such as squirrels and elephants, eat only plants. Consumers that eat only plants are called **herbivores**. When God first created the world, all animals were herbivores.

Herbivores eat different parts of plants. Some herbivores, such as gophers, eat the roots of plants. Giraffes and koalas eat leaves. Zebras and sheep eat the stems of grasses.

Herbivore

Sparrows eat the seeds and fruit of plants. Butterflies drink nectar from flowers. God designed each herbivore to get the energy it needs from the parts of plants that it eats.

Some consumers eat both plants and animals. These consumers are called **omnivores**. Bears, skunks, and robins are omnivores. Bears eat other animals, such as fish, insects, and small mammals. But they also eat grass, berries, roots, and nuts.

Fantastic Facts

Not all carnivores are animals. Plants such as butterworts and Venus flytraps "eat" insects and spiders. These plants still get energy from the sun, but they grow in places where the soil has few nutrients. The insects and spiders provide some of the nutrients the plants need.

Omnivore

Many omnivores change their eating habits when the seasons change. For example, a skunk eats whatever is available in its habitat. Skunks often eat rats and small mammals in the winter months. During spring and summer, they eat plants and insects. In the fall skunks add fruits and berries to their diet.

Other consumers eat only other animals. They are called **carnivores**, or meat eaters. Carnivores get their energy by eating other consumers. Wolves, weasels, tigers, and some large birds are carnivores.

Carnivore

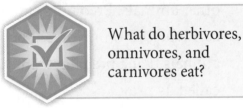

What do herbivores, omnivores, and carnivores eat?

Food Chains

A blade of grass produces its own food through photosynthesis. A grasshopper gets food as it nibbles on the blade of grass. Later a garter snake catches and eats the grasshopper.

The sun provided energy for the grass. That energy then passed from the grass to the grasshopper to the snake. The movement of energy from one living thing to another living thing is called a **food chain**.

A food chain begins with the sun. The first living thing in a food chain is always a producer. A producer uses sunlight to provide energy for itself. The next link in a food chain is usually a herbivore. The animals that make up the other links of a food chain are predators. A **predator** is any animal that hunts and eats other animals. Predators can be carnivores or omnivores. The animals that a predator hunts are called its **prey**.

Food Chain

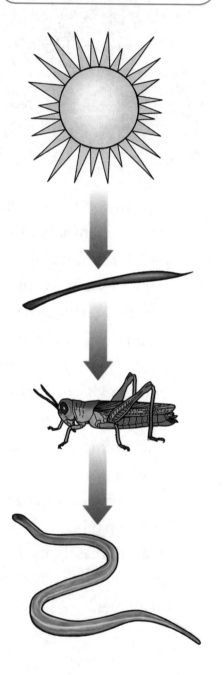

= movement of energy

Predator and prey

A food chain is only a few links. Each living thing in each link uses some of the energy and stores the rest. The grass receives energy from the sun and uses most of that energy to grow. Only some of the energy is stored.

The grasshopper ate the grass and gained the stored energy. The grasshopper used most of that energy for its own needs. Some of the energy was stored in the grasshopper's body. The garter snake then came along and ate the grasshopper. When it did, the garter snake received the grasshopper's stored energy.

Each living thing uses most of the energy it gets for its own needs. That is why a grasshopper has to eat more than just one blade of grass. It needs the energy from many plants. Likewise, a garter snake needs to eat more food than just one grasshopper.

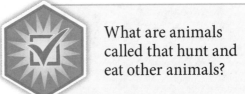
What are animals called that hunt and eat other animals?

Food Webs

A food chain shows only one source of food for each animal. Most animals, though, eat more than one kind of food. To show this, we use a food web. A **food web** is several food chains linked together.

For example, a grasshopper eats plants, and a garter snake might eat the grasshopper. That is one food chain. In the same community, another food chain might also start out with plants and a grasshopper. But in that food chain, a frog might eat the grasshopper. The frog might then be eaten by a fox. The grasshopper is prey for both frogs and snakes. It is part of more than one food chain.

The fox is a predator for frogs. But it is also a predator for snakes and grasshoppers. It will even eat plants. The fox is part of a different food chain for each food it eats. A food web shows many prey and predator links.

When one part of a food web changes, it affects the entire web. Frogs eat grasshoppers. If there were fewer frogs, fewer grasshoppers would be eaten. The grasshopper population would increase. More grasshoppers means more plants would be eaten. If there were fewer frogs, it would also mean that some of the frog's predators would not have enough to eat.

Food Web

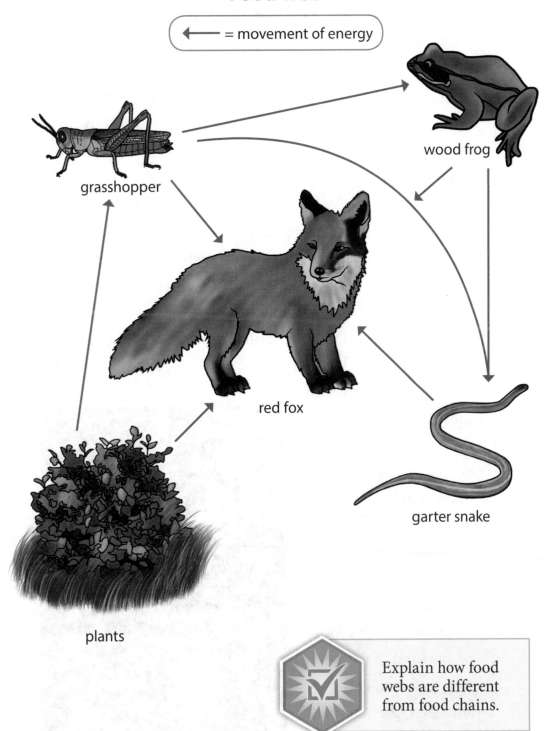

= movement of energy

wood frog

grasshopper

red fox

plants

garter snake

Explain how food webs are different from food chains.

Changes in an Ecosystem

The different parts of ecosystems are always changing. The biggest change to any ecosystem took place a long time ago. At the Fall, Adam disobeyed God. Adam's sin brought death into the world for the animals and all people (Genesis 2:17; 3:17–19). Some herbivores became carnivores. Other changes at that time were smaller.

Ecosystems today continue to change. A disease may destroy a certain plant population. Animals that eat that plant may not have enough food. They then might move to another ecosystem. The increase in animals would affect that ecosystem.

Sometimes it is the environment that causes change. Heavy rains can flood an ecosystem. The extra water might destroy plants and cause animals to move to another place. Not enough rain can cause dry soil and keep plants from growing.

Sometimes people can change an ecosystem. If fishermen catch a lot of one kind of fish, its population gets smaller. Other animals that depend on that

Long-tailed weasels are usually brown, but some weasels that live in northern areas grow white fur during the winter.

fish for food will not have enough to eat. They may have to move to another area. In some places fishing laws set limits on the amount of fish that can be caught. The limits help keep the ecosystem from being changed too much.

Sometimes animals cause ecosystems to change. Beavers build dams across streams. The dam stops the flow of the water and turns the stream into a pond. After a while, the pond dries out and becomes a meadow.

God created living things with the ability to adjust. Their characteristics help them survive in different environments. Animals might move to find more food or water. Certain animals, like deer, grow thicker coats of fur when the temperature gets colder. Trees and shrubs that live in dry areas usually have long roots. The long roots help the plants get water from deep in the ground.

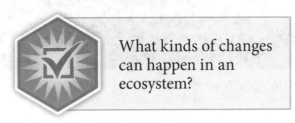

What kinds of changes can happen in an ecosystem?

Balance in an Ecosystem

Changes happen to the environment and to living things. Even a small change can cause many other changes. But God is a wise Creator. He designed ecosystems to change and to balance each other.

Lightning can start a fire that burns a forest. Many habitats are destroyed in the fire. Plants and animals might be killed. Changes like this are sad and even scary, but they also show God's amazing design. Out of the ashes of a forest fire a new ecosystem comes to life. Soon new plants start to grow. Animals that left may return to the ecosystem. Other animals also come to live in the new ecosystem. Over time another forest grows. It is somewhat like the forest it replaced, but it is also different.

A fire causes changes in an ecosystem.

God uses predators to keep an ecosystem in balance. Predators help control population sizes. The number of living things that an ecosystem can support depends on the needs of the plants and animals being met. Animals that cannot have all their needs met either move to a new place or die.

The Bible tells us that when God reveals His new heaven and new earth, there will be no more death. God promises us that He will make all things new and perfect. If we turn away from our sins and trust Jesus as our Lord, God will make us part of that new and perfect world.

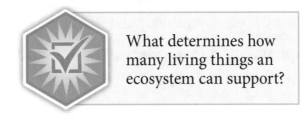

What determines how many living things an ecosystem can support?

Ecosystem Tag

Animals in a community interact with each other. Some are the prey. Others are the predators. But all are important to the balance of an ecosystem.

In this activity you will represent different animals that interact in an ecosystem.

Purpose

Model animal interactions in an ecosystem.

Materials
identity badge
life cards

Procedure

1. Get your identity badge and the correct number of life cards for your animal.

2. Chipmunks and snakes need to avoid being "eaten," or tagged. Snakes can eat chipmunks. Owls can eat snakes and chipmunks.

3. Chipmunks are safe from their predators only when they are in a "den." Only one chipmunk can be in a den at a time, and he can be there for only 10 seconds.

4. When a chipmunk or snake is tagged, he must give up one of his life cards to the predator who tagged him.

5. If a chipmunk or a snake loses all his life cards, he must sit out the rest of the round.

6. Play until your teacher tells you to stop. As a class, form three groups—one for each kind of animal.

7. Count your group's life cards. Tell that number to your teacher and turn in your identity and life cards.

8. Play the game again.

9. Your teacher will make changes to the identity badges. Infer in what ways the changes will affect the ecosystem.

10. Play the game two more times.

Conclusions

- Did each kind of animal have the same number of life cards left each time you played? Explain your answer.

- How would the ecosystem be affected if the entire population of snakes died?

Follow-up

- Add a "disease" player who can tag any animal, including owls.

5

Matter

You live in a world full of objects. Think about your bedroom. You have a bed and clothes. Maybe you keep toys, books, or even a pet fish or hamster there. Your room has many things in it.

Each thing has characteristics that you can observe and describe. The yellowed pages of an old book might smell musty. A blanket might be bright red. A fishbowl is smooth and the water inside is cool. Each object has a color, size, and shape that make it different from other things.

Physical Properties

Everything around you has certain characteristics, or properties. You can observe those properties and use them to describe objects. For example, baseballs are round and hard, and pillows are rectangular and soft. Shape and hardness are two physical properties. A **physical property** is anything about an object that can be observed with our senses. Color, size, mass, and volume are physical properties.

Mass is one physical property. **Mass** is the amount of material that any object has. Some objects have more mass than others do. Often a larger object will have more mass than a smaller one, but mass does not depend on size. A baseball is much smaller than a beach ball, but the baseball has more mass.

Volume is another physical property. **Volume** is the amount of space that an object takes up. A large object, such as a moving truck, takes up a lot of space. The volume of a moving truck is quite a large amount! Other objects, such as a toy truck, take up only a little space.

Both the trucks and the things in your room are matter. **Matter** is anything that has mass and takes up space. All matter has physical properties including mass and volume.

What is matter?

Mass

One physical property of matter is that it can be measured. A way we measure matter is by measuring its mass. Mass is a physical property that does not change unless matter is added or removed.

Think about a lump of clay. You can change the shape of a lump of clay. You can roll it into a ball or smash it flat. You can shape it into a long rope. The clay's shape can change, but you still have the same amount of clay. Its mass does not change.

Scientists use a tool called a **balance** to measure mass. There are different types of balances. But all balances work by comparing an unknown mass with a known mass. The object you are measuring has the unknown mass. The known mass on a balance is either sliding weights or a set of loose individual weights.

A double-pan balance has a set of loose weights and two pans or flat surfaces. The object you are measuring is placed on one pan. The known weights are added to or removed from the other pan until the two pans balance evenly. The mass of the object is the total mass of the known weights.

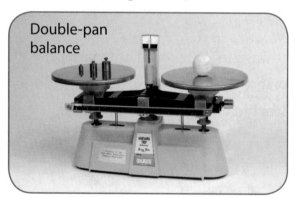
Double-pan balance

A triple-beam balance has sliding weights. The object is placed on a pan on one side. The weights are slid along the beam. When the beam is balanced, the positions of the weights show the mass of the object.

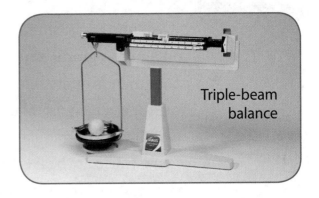

Triple-beam balance

The gram (g) is a commonly used metric unit of mass measurement. The white ball of clay pictured on both balances has a mass of 45 grams. The clay has a small amount of mass, but some things have much more mass. The mass of the cow pictured below is measured in kilograms (kg). One kilogram equals 1000 grams.

What tool is used to measure mass?

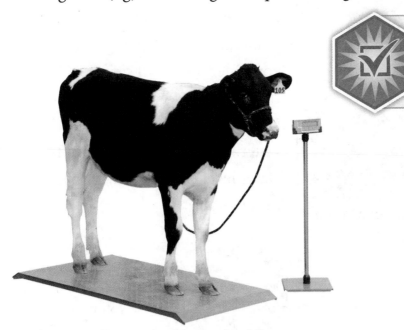

This animal's mass is measured in kilograms.

Volume

Volume is measured with a graduated container. A **graduated container** has lines and numbers on its side. The numbers tell how much space a liquid takes up.

Some of the graduated containers that scientists use are beakers and graduated cylinders. The lines and numbers on these containers are marked with milliliters. It takes 1000 milliliters (mL) to equal 1 liter (L). The liter is the metric unit of measurement for volume. However, milliliters are used to measure small amounts more accurately.

Graduated cylinder

The boys are using beakers to measure water.

To measure 400 milliliters of water, start by setting an empty beaker or other graduated container on a level surface. Find the line for 400 milliliters on the side of the beaker. Then pour water into the container until the water level is at the line for 400 milliliters.

What metric units are used to measure volume?

Which Kind of Matter?

Matter is found in different forms. The food you eat, the juice you drink, and the air you breathe are types of matter. But if you list their properties, you will find each type is different.

Process Skills
- Observing
- Inferring

Purpose

Compare properties of different kinds of matter.

Procedure

Observe Objects

Materials
2 objects of different shapes and sizes
balance
clear container
beaker or metric measuring cup
water
inflated balloon
Activity Manual

1. Measure and record the mass of the first object in the chart in your Activity Manual.

2. Observe whether your object takes up space. Mark the chart with an *X* if it does.

3. Place the object in the container to see if the volume changes to fill the entire container. Mark whether the volume stays the same or changes to fill the entire container.

4. Look to see if the object keeps its shape or takes the shape of the container. Mark your observation.

5. Repeat steps 1–3 with the second object.

Observe Water

6. Measure the mass of the empty container. Add 200 mL of water and measure the mass again. Record the difference between the two measurements.

7. Observe whether the water takes up space. Mark the chart if it does.

8. Pour the water back into the beaker to see whether the volume stays at 200 mL or changes to fill the beaker. Mark your observation.

9. Look at the shape of the water in the beaker. Pour the water into the container and look at its shape. Mark your observation for its shape.

Observe a Balloon

10. Squeeze the balloon and then press it into the container. Mark whether the shape of the air in the balloon stays the same or takes the shape of the container.

11. Observe whether the air in the balloon takes up space. Mark the chart if it does.

12. Press on the balloon and observe whether the air continues to fill the entire balloon. Mark whether the volume stays the same or changes.

13. Measure the mass of the filled balloon. Open the clip and measure the mass of the clip and the empty balloon. Record the difference between the measurements.

Conclusions

- Are all types of matter the same?
- What can you infer about each type of matter from your observations?

Follow-up

- Test other solids, liquids, and gases to see if they have the same results.

States of Matter

Matter can be a solid, a liquid, or a gas. These are called the states of matter. Each state of matter has certain properties. Matter is grouped into states by these properties.

Solids

Blocks, books, and baseballs are solids. A **solid** has a definite shape and volume. You can put an apple inside a box, but the apple is still round. It does not change its shape to fit the shape of the box. It keeps its own shape.

A solid has a definite shape and volume.

The volume of a solid also stays the same. Even when you cut the apple into pieces, all the pieces together have the same volume as the whole apple did. The apple's volume does not change.

Some solids, such as glass and tables, are hard, but solids do not have to feel hard. A blanket and the fur of a cat or dog are also solids.

Solid
Keeps its shape
Keeps its volume

Liquids

Water, milk, and oil are types of liquids. A **liquid** has a definite volume but not a definite shape. A liquid takes the shape of whatever container it is in.

Milk in a tall, thin glass takes the shape of the glass. But if the milk is poured into a short, wide bowl, it changes  shape. It takes the shape of the bowl. The volume of the milk does not change, but the shape of the milk does. A definite volume of a liquid can have different shapes.

A liquid has a definite volume but not a definite shape.

Solid	Liquid
Keeps its shape	Takes the shape of its container
Keeps its volume	Keeps its volume

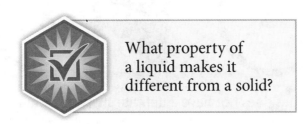

What property of a liquid makes it different from a solid?

91

Gases

The air in your bicycle tires is a gas. The helium in a balloon is also a gas. A **gas** has no definite volume or shape.

Like a liquid, a gas takes the shape of its container. The air in a tire takes the shape of the tire. If you pump air into a soccer ball, the air takes that shape. If you pump the same amount of air into a football, the air takes that shape.

Gases are different from solids and liquids. A gas expands, or stretches out. It takes the volume of its container. That means that it fills all the space inside of a closed container. A gas keeps expanding until something stops it. That something may be any kind of container or closed space. A tied balloon and a bicycle tire are examples of closed spaces.

A gas does not have a definite shape or volume.

You can use jars to compare how liquids and gases fill containers. When you pour water into a jar, all the water goes to the bottom. As long as you do not tip the jar, the water does not come out. When you allow air to fill a jar, the air does not all go to the bottom. Instead, the air fills the jar evenly. Without a lid on the jar, the air will expand and escape.

Solid	Liquid	Gas
Keeps its shape	Takes the shape of its container	Takes the shape of its container
Keeps its volume	Keeps its volume	Takes the volume of its container

What are the properties of a gas?

Changes in States

God wants people to use the things that He has provided in the world. One way we do that is by changing matter from one state to another. Think about the foods that you enjoy. Many have been frozen. When you freeze fruit juice to make an ice pop, the liquid juice becomes a solid frozen treat. Freezing also helps keep some foods from spoiling.

Sometimes states change without help from people. A piece of chocolate left in a hot car melts. The solid chocolate changes to liquid chocolate.

Solids and Liquids

Heating a solid causes it to melt and become a liquid. Solids melt at different temperatures. Chocolate melts at about 36°C (96.8°F), which is just a little lower than your body temperature. That is why chocolate melts on your hands or in your mouth. Ice melts at 0°C (32°F).

Ice cream melts quickly on a warm day.

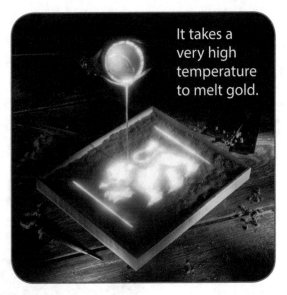

It takes a very high temperature to melt gold.

Some solids melt at very high temperatures. Solid gold will not become liquid unless it is heated to a temperature of over 1000 °C. That is over 1800 °F!

Cooling a liquid can cause it to become a solid again. A candy maker melts a block of chocolate and pours it into molds. As the liquid chocolate cools, it becomes a solid again. When the molds are taken off, the solid chocolate has taken the shape of the mold.

Candy can be heated and cooled to form fun shapes.

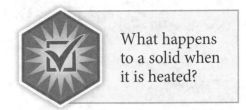

What happens to a solid when it is heated?

Liquids and Gases

Solids can change to liquids, and liquids can change to solids. Liquids can also change to gases. Liquids become gases when they are heated.

You have seen this happen when water boils in a pot or teakettle. The boiling water bubbles. Steam rises from the water. The steam is a gas called water vapor. As the water vapor spreads out in the room, it seems to disappear, but it is still there.

When water is boiled, it changes to a gas.

Water vapor forms from boiling water, but it also forms as the sun warms bodies of water. The sun's heat causes the water in lakes, ponds, and even mud puddles to change to water vapor. When a liquid changes to a gas, the process is called **evaporation**. The water that evaporates stays in the air for a while.

The sun causes water in a puddle to evaporate.

When a gas changes to a liquid, the process is called **condensation**. This can happen with water vapor in the air. When the water vapor cools, it condenses and can form clouds and rain. You can also see water vapor condense when you pour a cold drink into a glass on a hot day. Little drops of water form on the outside of the glass. The cold drink cools the glass and the air around it. The water vapor in the air condenses, or changes from a gas to a liquid.

Water vapor in the air condenses on the outside of a cool glass.

What is the process called when a gas changes to a liquid?

States of Water

Any type of matter can change to another state, but most do not change easily. We usually think of each kind of matter as being in the state we usually see it. Iron is a solid. Gasoline is a liquid. Oxygen is a gas.

However, water is different. Water can easily change from one state to another. We see water most often in its liquid state, but ice, frost, and snow are solid forms of water. You cannot see water vapor in the air, but it is water as a gas.

The Celsius temperature scale is based on the changing states of water. At 0 °C water freezes and changes to a solid. At 100 °C water boils and changes to a gas.

Most types of matter contract, or get smaller, as they freeze. Water is one of the few kinds of matter that does the opposite. Water expands when it freezes and changes from a liquid to a solid. Frozen water, or ice, takes up more room than liquid water does.

Try It Yourself

Pour some water into a tall, clear plastic cup. Place the cup on a level surface and mark the level of the liquid. Put the cup in a freezer. Leave it there until the liquid becomes solid. Compare the level of the solid with the mark on the cup.

 How is frozen water different from most other kinds of frozen matter?

Physical and Chemical Changes

Matter can change in different ways. It can change from one state to another. Some of its physical properties, such as color and shape, can change. Matter can also combine with other kinds of matter to form new substances. All changes to matter are either physical changes or chemical changes. Learning how to control these changes is one way to please God with our work.

Physical Changes

A **physical change** is a change in matter that does not form a new substance. If you have a cake to share with friends, you cut it into pieces. The cake's size and shape changed, but it did not turn into something new. If you put the pieces together, they would all have the same mass as the whole cake did.

Physical changes also happen when matter changes states. Ice cream straight from a freezer has a definite shape. It is a solid. When it melts, it changes to a liquid. The melted ice cream takes the shape of the bowl or container it is in. The ice cream has had a physical change, but it is still ice cream.

Physical changes can also happen when matter is mixed together. A **mixture** is two or more kinds of matter that are combined. A smoothie might have bananas, strawberries, and yogurt in it. It is a mixture.

The fruit and yogurt have had physical changes.

To make a smoothie, you might cut the fruit into smaller pieces. Cutting the fruit does not change the type of matter. A banana is still a banana. A strawberry is still a strawberry. The fruit has had a physical change. The pieces are smaller.

The fruit and yogurt are placed in the blender. Everything is chopped and mixed to form a thick liquid. The fruits are not easy to see, but you can still taste both fruits and the yogurt. Blending the ingredients together does not make a new kind of matter.

What is a physical change?

Chemical Changes

A **chemical change** is a change in matter that forms a new substance. Sometimes when two or more kinds of matter are combined they form a new kind of matter. The different kinds of matter lose their own properties and take on new ones.

For example, think about the properties of a raw egg. It is a sticky, clear liquid with a thick yellow liquid center. However, these properties change when an egg is placed in boiling water. The clear part becomes a white, rubbery solid and the yellow becomes a crumbly solid. The heat caused chemical changes to occur in the matter that makes up the egg. The egg changed and can never be liquid again.

Another chemical change happens when iron rusts. Nails, garden tools, and other objects containing iron rust when they get wet. Water contains oxygen. The oxygen in the water mixes with the iron. When oxygen and iron combine, they form a new substance called rust.

Chemical changes cause railroad spikes to rust.

Serving with Matter

Matter is all around us. Our food, heat, shelter, and clothing are all different types of matter or products of it. Matter is very changeable, and God made it that way for our good. Sometimes we change matter from one state to another. We may cause physical or chemical changes. We can change matter to meet our needs. We can also use it to help others.

God wants us to use matter to serve Him and other people. For example, cooking food is one common way we change matter every day. Cooking food well pleases God. It also gives us opportunities to serve others.

What is a chemical change?

6

Sound

Birds sing. Leaves rustle. Insects buzz. These are just a few outdoor sounds you might hear. Some sounds are quiet while others can be very loud. The sounds in our world are a gift from God.

God gave us sounds to help us observe our world. Sounds can tell us about the things around us and warn us of danger. Other sounds are simply for us to enjoy. Understanding how sound works will help us glorify God.

Sound

Vibrations

Sound is a form of energy that you can hear. Each sound is caused by a moving object that is vibrating. A **vibration** is a rapid back-and-forth movement. You cannot see sound, but you may be able to see and feel the vibrations.

A tuning fork is a device used by musicians. When the tuning fork is struck, it vibrates and produces a sound. You can feel the tuning fork's vibrations. You can see the vibrations if you place the tuning fork in water. The vibrations stop if you touch the tuning fork. The sound from the tuning fork also stops.

A tuning fork vibrates to produce a musical tone.

What is sound?

Making Vibrations

You can cause an object to vibrate by blowing on it, hitting it, plucking it, or rubbing it. Musicians use these actions to produce musical sounds. A trumpeter blows into a trumpet. The blowing causes the air inside the trumpet to vibrate. The top of a drum vibrates when it is hit. The strings of a guitar vibrate when they are plucked. A violinist rubs a bow across the strings of a violin to make them vibrate.

Plucking

Rubbing

Hitting

108

The sounds of your voice are also caused by vibrations. When you speak or sing, the air you breathe out makes your vocal cords vibrate. Place your fingers on the front of your neck. Now hum or say a word to feel the vibrations of your vocal cords.

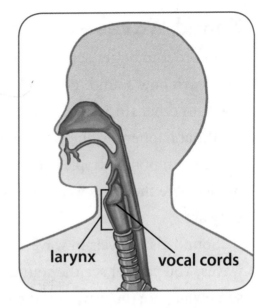

larynx   vocal cords

Psalm 150 tells us that sound can be used to worship God. Verse 6 says "Let every thing that hath breath praise the Lord." Some people can play an instrument and make music to glorify God. Christians can use their voices to praise Him.

Singing is one way we can use our voices to praise God.

What are four ways an object can vibrate?

Sound Waves

In order to better serve others with sound, you should first learn how sound moves. You also should learn how it reacts to other things.

What happens to the water when you drop a stone into a calm pond? Ripples, or waves, spread out from the place where the stone went into the water. The waves move outward.

Sound also travels in waves. A vibration causes sound waves. You cannot see the sound waves, but they act somewhat like the waves on the pond. The sound waves move outward from their source in all directions.

Because sound travels in all directions, the source of a sound does not need to be facing you for you to hear the sound. You can hear sounds beside, behind, and in front of you. You can also hear sounds above and below you.

Sound waves travel in all directions.

Sound and Matter

Sounds that travel through the air may also travel through other forms of matter. You can sit in a room with the doors and windows closed. But you still might hear sounds from outside or from the next room. The sounds travel through the air and then through the solid wall, door, or window.

Sound waves travel at different speeds through solids, liquids, and gases. Sound waves travel faster through liquids than through gases, like air. They travel the fastest through solids.

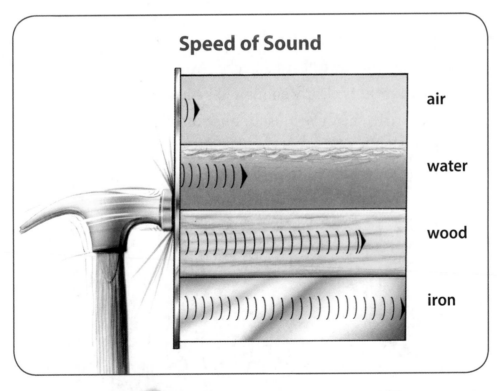

Speed of Sound

air

water

wood

iron

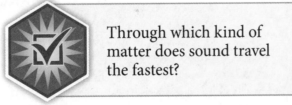

Through which kind of matter does sound travel the fastest?

Reflected Sounds

Sound waves travel outward from a source. They keep moving outward until something blocks their path.

When a sound wave hits an object, the object reflects the sound wave. **Reflect** means to bounce the sound wave off an object. Large, hard, smooth surfaces reflect sound waves better than other surfaces do. A large building or room might have these surfaces.

Sound reflects well in a canyon.

Canyon walls also have large, smooth surfaces.

Perhaps you have heard an echo. An **echo** is a sound wave that reflects clearly enough to be heard again. To reflect clearly, the wave must bounce off a large, smooth surface. That is why you hear echoes best when you are surrounded by hills, cliffs, or large buildings.

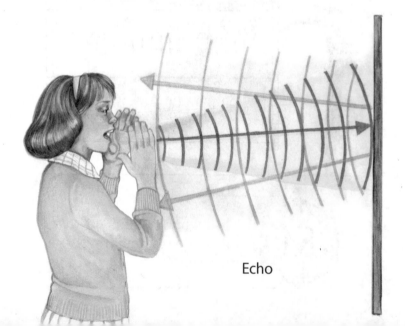

Echo

Absorbed Sounds

Sometimes sound waves are not reflected. When sound waves hit an object, the object may absorb the sound waves. **Absorb** means to take in the sound wave. Rough or soft surfaces absorb sound. Uneven surfaces also absorb sound.

Rooms that have hard, smooth surfaces can be very noisy. The walls, ceiling, and floor are all places that may reflect sound. Echoes are easily created in rooms like these.

Materials that absorb sound can be used to make a room quieter. Rough, uneven materials can help keep sounds from being reflected. Carpet, fabric, and ceiling tiles are materials used to absorb some of the sounds in a room.

What kinds of surfaces absorb sound?

Some materials absorb sound.

Characteristics of Sound

Pitch

Pitch is how high or low a sound is. Every sound has a pitch. Pitch depends on how fast the source of the sound is vibrating. A big bass has a low pitch. It has long strings, and they vibrate slowly. A small violin has a high pitch. The strings are shorter and vibrate faster.

A string player changes the pitch by moving the position of his fingers on the strings. When he makes the strings shorter, the instrument plays a higher pitch.

Volume

Volume is how loud or soft a sound is. When you shout to a friend across a ball field, you make a loud sound. When you whisper a secret to your friend, you make a soft sound. Volume depends on how much force is used to make an object vibrate. When a stronger force is used, the vibration makes a louder sound. A weaker force makes a softer sound.

Fantastic Facts

A mosquito beats its wings 300 to 600 times a second. The fast vibration of its wings causes the high buzzing sound you hear.

Loud

Soft

Sound waves spread out as they move farther away from the source of their vibrations. The vibrations become weaker. The sound becomes quieter.

Quality

Quality is what makes a sound different from all other sounds. Quality helps us identify people's voices. It also helps us hear the differences between the sounds of different instruments. Even when a clarinet and a flute play the same note, they sound different.

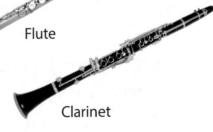

Flute

Clarinet

What is the difference between the pitch, volume, and quality of a sound?

Musical Jars

The pitch of an instrument is related to the length of the vibrating part. Long strings make low sounds. Short strings make high sounds. Some instruments, such as trumpets, control the amount of air that vibrates. This gives those instruments a high or low pitch.

In this activity you will find out how the amount of vibrating air affects pitch.

Process Skills
- Predicting
- Measuring

Problem

How does the amount of air in a jar affect its pitch?

Materials
2 glass jars, 400 mL
300 mL water
metric measuring cups
pencil
Activity Manual

Procedure

1. Complete the hypothesis in your Activity Manual.

2. Label one glass jar *A* and the other *B*.

3. Measure 50 mL of water. Pour the water into jar A.

4. Measure 100 mL of water. Pour the water into jar B.

5. Gently tap the top of each jar with a pencil. Listen carefully to the pitch of the sound.

6. Decide which jar has the higher pitch. Record your observation.

7. Measure 150 mL of water.

8. Pour that water into jar A. Jar A should now have 200 mL of water.

9. Tap the top of the jars again. Listen to the sounds.

10. Record your observation.

Conclusions

- How does the amount of vibrating air affect the pitch?
- How could you change the pitch of the sound?

Follow-up

- Repeat the activity but use larger glass jars.
- Fill eight glass jars with different amounts of water to make a musical scale.

The Ear and Hearing

Looking at the amazing design of the ear should cause you to glorify God as your Creator. The ears collect sound waves and send messages to the brain. This allows us to hear. The sound waves travel through the three main parts of the ear: the outer ear, the middle ear, and the inner ear.

The Outer Ear

When you think of your ear, you likely think of the part you can see on the side of your head. This is the outer ear. It includes the ear flap and the ear canal. The ear flap is the outside part of your ear that you can bend and pull. It protects the middle ear and collects sound waves.

The ear canal goes from the ear flap to the eardrum. It is shaped like a slightly curved tunnel. It is about 26 millimeters (1 in.) long. Sound waves travel through the ear canal to the eardrum. The sound waves cause the eardrum to vibrate.

Fantastic Facts

The stirrup is the smallest bone in the body. It is only about as tall as this letter *l*.

The Parts of the Ear

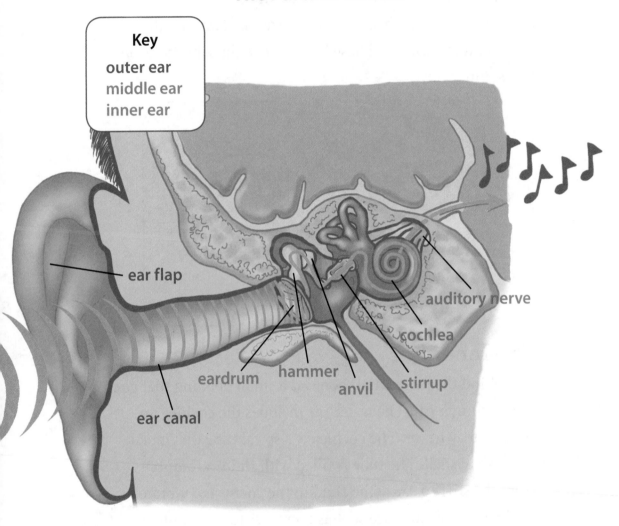

Key

outer ear
middle ear
inner ear

ear flap

auditory nerve

cochlea

eardrum   hammer

anvil   stirrup

ear canal

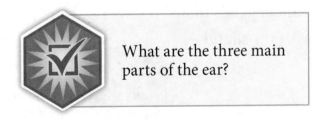

What are the three main parts of the ear?

The Middle Ear

The eardrum is a thin, tightly stretched membrane. As it vibrates, it causes three tiny bones in the middle ear to vibrate also. These three ear bones are the hammer, the anvil, and the stirrup. These bones move the vibrations on to the inner ear.

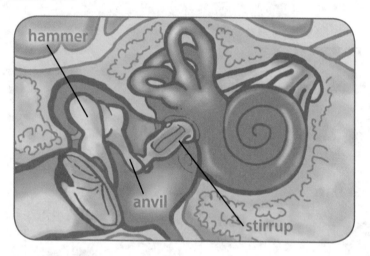

The Inner Ear

Behind the three small bones is a small opening that goes into the inner ear. The inner ear includes the cochlea and the auditory nerve. The cochlea is a spiral tube that looks like a snail shell. The tube is filled with fluid. Vibrations from the stirrup cause the fluid in the cochlea to vibrate.

These vibrations are sent as messages to the auditory nerve. The auditory nerve sends the messages to the brain. The brain understands these messages as sound. Your brain tells you what the sound is.

Which part of your body tells you what sound you are hearing?

All Ears

Most of the time we think about the outside parts of our ears. How big are they? Are they clean? But God put the most important parts of our ears inside our heads.

In this exploration you will build a model of the ear. It will help you learn how God's detailed design of the ear works.

What to Do

1. Get a stiff piece of cardboard or foam board. Use a pencil to draw a diagram of the ear. Use the diagram on page 119 as a guide.

2. Your model should be more than just a drawing of the ear. You will need to choose materials to represent some of the parts for your model. For example, you might choose to use part of a balloon for the eardrum.

3. Assemble your model. Be sure the pieces will not fall off your board. Label the ear flap, ear canal, eardrum, hammer, anvil, stirrup, cochlea, and auditory nerve.

4. Explain your model to others.

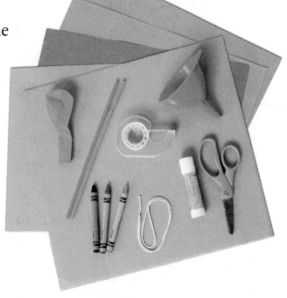

121

Uses of Sounds

Some sounds are pleasing to us. Most people enjoy listening to good music. We like to hear the voices of our friends and family.

Other sounds are harmful. Loud, harsh sounds can damage our ears. That is why people who work with loud machines should wear ear protection.

We use sound to communicate with each other. We hear the sounds others make, and we make sounds for others to hear. The words we say are very important. The Bible tells us that our speech should please God. Psalm 19:14 says, "Let the words of my mouth . . . be acceptable in thy sight, O Lord."

Speech is not the only way to communicate. Other sounds can communicate as well. A ringing alarm clock tells you it is time to get up. A stove timer buzzes when it is time to take something out of the oven. A siren on a police car, a fire truck, or an ambulance warns drivers to move out of the way.

Health and Safety

Sticking things in your ears can be unsafe. Some people like to stick cotton swabs in their ears to clean them. But if not done very carefully, it is easy to run the swab too far down the ear canal. Then the swab may make a hole in the ear drum. This would be painful!

You do not need to stick things in your ears. The lining of the ear canal makes wax. The wax picks up dead skin and other unwanted materials. Gradually the wax moves to the ear flap. Washing the outer flap with a washcloth usually keeps the ear clean. If the ear canal becomes clogged, a doctor should be seen.

In Bible times the sound of trumpets was often used to communicate information. The priests blew trumpets to tell the people to gather in one place. Trumpets were often used in the worship services at the temple as well. In times of war, trumpets were used to send men into battle.

God wants you to use what you have learned about sound and your ears to glorify Him (1 Corinthians 6:19–20). You can do that when you use sound to serve other people. You can serve people by protecting them from harmful sounds. You can also serve people by playing beautiful music or speaking kind words to them. You can use sound to worship God (Hebrews 13:15).

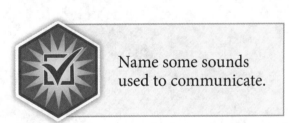

Name some sounds used to communicate.

7 Energy in Motion

As Kendra and her family arrive at the fair, the merry-go-round music welcomes them. Kendra is drawn to a booth by the smell of buttery popcorn. She munches the popcorn and sips lemonade as she watches her dad win several games. He pulls tickets from his pocket to pay for three darts. Taking careful aim, he hits the target with each throw. Kendra excitedly adds a pink bear to her armload of prizes.

Think about what Kendra was doing at the fair. She moved herself and other objects. Her feet moved as she walked. Her hands moved as she carried the popcorn and prizes. Her mouth and tongue moved as she ate.

Force

Kendra's movements were pushes and pulls. A **force** is a push or pull. Kendra used forces to move her hands and chew her food. You use a force to kick a ball. You also use force to turn a jump rope. Objects cannot move unless a force causes them to move.

Force also affects objects that are already moving. Force causes objects to go faster, slow down, or change direction. Think about a merry-go-round on a playground. Using force, you can make the merry-go-round go faster, go slower, or change its direction.

When you kick a soccer ball, you put a force on the ball. The ball goes in the same direction as the force. An object will move in the same direction as the force that moves it.

You may pass the ball to someone else on your team. Your teammate kicks the ball in another direction. When the direction of the force changes, the direction of the ball changes.

You swing a jump rope around in a circle for your friends to jump over. The force of your swing keeps the rope turning until another force stops it.

What causes objects to move?

127

Invisible Forces

When you kick a ball, you can easily see how the force from your foot causes the ball to move. But your kick is not the only force affecting the ball. There are other forces at work as well.

Even if no one stops the ball, at some point it will stop rolling. One force, called friction, causes the ball to roll more slowly and gradually stop. **Friction** is a force that slows or stops motion. As the ball rolls, friction occurs between the ball and the ground.

If you kick a ball into the air, it does not keep going up forever. It falls back to the ground. Another invisible force,

Friction causes a sled to slow and stop.

called gravity, is what pulls the ball down. **Gravity** is the force that pulls objects toward the center of the earth.

When you weigh an object, you are measuring the pull of gravity. **Weight** is the measure of the force of gravity on an object. Scientists use a scale to measure weight. Weight and mass are not the same. Remember that mass is the amount of material that an object has.

If you have ever played with a magnet, you have seen another invisible force at work. The force of a magnet is called **magnetism**. A magnet does not have to touch an object to pull or push it. Think of using a magnet to pick up a paper clip. You might hold the magnet over the paper clip. Suddenly the magnetic force pulls the paper clip up to the magnet.

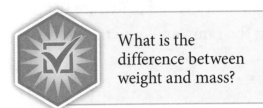
What is the difference between weight and mass?

Gravity causes the water in a fountain to fall back to the earth.

Magnetism pulls paper clips toward a magnet.

129

Friction Fun

Though we do not think about it, friction greatly affects our lives. Depending on what we are doing, we may need more friction or less friction. A baseball player does not want to slide and fall when he is trying to catch a ball. Shoes with cleats provide more friction and help keep him from slipping. Skiers rub wax on the bottom of their skis. The wax decreases the friction and helps the skis glide quickly on the snow.

In this activity you will test some surfaces to find out which one has the most friction.

Process Skills
- Observing
- Measuring

Problem

Which surface has the most friction?

Procedure

1. Complete the hypothesis in your Activity Manual.

2. Lay the towel on the floor. Smooth out the wrinkles. Lay the notebook (your ramp) on one end of the towel so that it slopes toward the towel.

3. Hold the golf ball at the top of the ramp. Release the ball and let it roll down the ramp and onto the towel.

Materials
3-ring notebook, 1 in.
golf ball
centimeter ruler
large towel
pan of sand
carpet
Activity Manual

4. Measure the distance from the lower edge of the notebook to the end of the ball. Record the distance.

5. Repeat with the sand and carpet.

Conclusions

- Did the ball roll the same distance on each surface?

- How can you tell which surface has the most friction?

- How is knowing about the friction of these surfaces helpful?

Follow-up

- Repeat the activity using other surfaces or steeper ramps.

Motion

In a baseball game, the pitcher throws the ball toward home plate. The position of the ball changes from the pitcher's hand to the air. The pitcher uses a force to move the ball. The force puts the ball into motion. **Motion** is a change of position.

You can describe the motion of an object in three ways. You can describe the direction the object travels, the distance it travels, and the speed it travels.

When a baseball is hit, its motion changes. The ball's direction changes from moving toward the bat to moving away from the bat. When hit, a baseball can travel in many directions. It might go left over third base or straight toward first base. It might even bounce up behind the batter.

The baseball can travel different distances. It might travel far into the outfield. Or it may go only a few meters in front of home plate. If you measure from where the ball was hit to where it stopped, you can know the distance it traveled.

The baseball can also move at different speeds. If the ball slowly rolls to the first baseman, he can easily pick it up. But if the ball quickly whizzes into the outfield, a player may not be fast enough to catch it.

Motion can be described by how fast an object travels.

Motion can be described by how far an object travels.

Motion can be described by what direction an object travels.

What are three ways to describe the motion of an object?

Work

Suppose you were told to read five pages in your book. You read the pages and put down the book. You might think that understanding the pages was hard work. A scientist, however, would say that understanding is not work.

Scientists say **work** is done when a force moves something. Turning the pages of a book is work because you are moving something. Even moving your eyes across the pages is work.

But understanding the text is not work. You are not moving anything.

If you carry some books across the room, you are doing work. If you only hold the books, you are not doing work. Nothing is moving.

Sometimes other forces do work. If you drop the books, you do not apply a force, but work is still done. The force of gravity causes the books to move.

When is work done?

135

People can do work. You work when you move yourself or an object. Some animals work by carrying or pulling things.

People and animals are not the only ones who do work, though. Wind and moving water can also do work. Wind works when it moves turbines, flags, or leaves. Flowing water moves logs, rocks, boats, and water wheels.

Machines do a lot of work. Cars, trucks, tractors, and airplanes move people and things every day. They are complex machines. They are made of smaller machines that work together called simple machines. Some simple machines are levers, wheel and axles, and inclined planes.

These machines make work easier. But they still need forces to cause them to run. People provide the force for some machines, but the forces of most machines come from engines. Engines help make the work easier for us.

 How are machines helpful?

Energy

You use energy every day. When you get out of bed, play on the playground, or even open a book, you use energy. Remember that **energy** is what is needed to cause change and to do work.

Kinds of Energy

There are many kinds of energy. Sound and light are two kinds of energy. Light from the sun provides the energy needed for photosynthesis.

Electrical energy is another kind. We use it to light our homes, charge phones and computers, and run appliances. Some homes use it for cooking and heating.

Most machines use mechanical energy. Mechanical energy is the energy caused by an object's motion or position. When you ride your bicycle you move the pedals. The motion is mechanical energy. Coasting down a hill on a bicycle is also mechanical energy. You do not provide the energy. The position of the bike at the top of the hill allows you to go down the hill.

Some objects have stored energy. Stored energy can be used at a later time to do work. A battery has stored energy. You probably have a toy, camera, or other device that uses batteries. Without the batteries, the device does not do the work that it was made to do.

Chemical energy comes from burning fuels. Gasoline is a fuel some cars burn to provide the energy needed for their engines to run. For our bodies to work, we burn the energy stored in the food we eat.

Gasoline and food have stored energy that is burned.

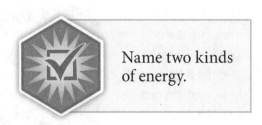

Name two kinds of energy.

Changes to Energy

Energy can change from one form to another. A plant uses light energy for photosynthesis. The light energy is stored by the plant as chemical energy.

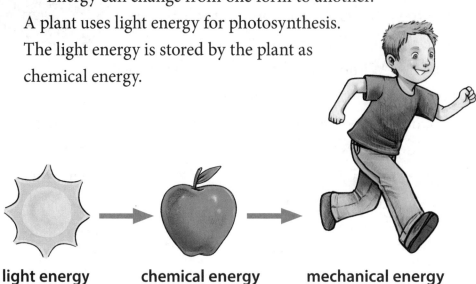

light energy   **chemical energy**   **mechanical energy**

A person eats the plant as food. The person then uses the chemical energy from the food to produce mechanical energy.

Science and the Bible

In Bible times, there were no flashlights. Instead, people carried small lamps for light. The lamps used olive oil for fuel. A piece of cloth or twisted string was put in the oil and lit. The flame produced light. The oil was the stored energy needed for the light. Just as a lamp gives light in the darkness, the Word of God shows us how to live in a world full of sin. Psalm 119:105 says, "Thy word is a lamp unto my feet, and a light unto my path."

Energy in a Flashlight

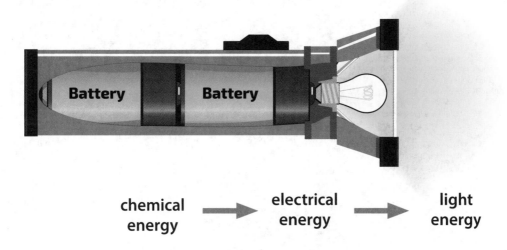

chemical energy → electrical energy → light energy

In a flashlight the stored energy in the batteries changes to electrical energy. The electrical energy heats the wire in the light bulb. Heat makes the wire glow, and you can see the light energy.

The world is full of forces, motion, and energy. We need to understand each in order to work wisely in God's world. Learning about His world will also give us the knowledge we need to serve other people.

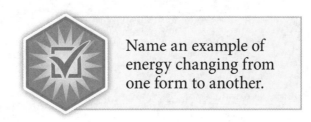

Name an example of energy changing from one form to another.

8

Soil, Rocks, and Minerals

What characteristics of minerals make them useful?

The Bible tells us that when God created the world, He separated the land from the water. The land is a wonderful gift from God. It provides many of the things we need to live. But the land today is different from what God created.

After Adam's sin, God changed many things on the earth. Then the Flood during the time of Noah covered the whole earth. The moving water changed mountains, valleys, and rocks. Plants grew again in the dirt that settled on the earth's surface.

Soil

Another name for dirt is soil. **Soil** is made of loose rock and bits of decaying plant and animal material. Many living things depend on the soil. Some animals live in the soil. Most plants need soil to grow. They can grow in loose soil or in the cracks of rocks. Both animals and people need plants for food.

Parts of Soil

If you pick up a handful of soil, you might see tiny pieces of rock in it. You will see other things as well. Soil is made of small bits of broken rock, humus, air, and water.

In the autumn, leaves fall from the trees. They become brown and dry. After a while they crumble into small pieces. The leaves seem to disappear, but they do not.

Over time the remains of the leaves become part of the humus in the soil. **Humus** is the remains of living things that have died and decayed. When plants and animals **decay**, they break apart or rot. Plants and animals decay after they die. After a while they become part of the soil.

Soil contains water and air as well as humus. Water is stored in the soil. There are also tiny spaces of air in the soil. To grow well, plants need both water and air.

Though plants need certain things to survive, not all plants need the same amounts of humus, water, and air. God has made the world with many types of soil so that different kinds of plants can grow.

 What is soil made of?

Layers of Soil

Soil forms in layers. Most of the time only the top layer is seen.

Topsoil is the layer that contains the most humus. Plants grow in this layer.

Subsoil has larger pieces of rock and contains no humus.

Bedrock is large, unbroken rock that lies under the subsoil.

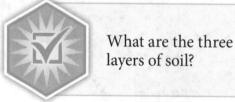

What are the three layers of soil?

Weathering

God designed the surface of our earth so that it is always changing. Rocks, even huge ones, are slowly broken into smaller pieces. These little pieces become part of the soil.

What causes rocks to break apart? Water, ice, wind, and plants can cause rocks to break apart. The breaking down of rocks into smaller pieces is called **weathering**.

Water and Wind

Flowing water weathers rocks. The water in a stream moves over and around the rocks. The water slowly wears away the rocks and makes them rounded and smooth. Rocks are also carried by the water. As the stream tumbles the rocks, the water wears away any sharp edges and carries away the bits.

Wind weathers rocks in somewhat the same way. The wind blows sand against rocks. The sand rubs the surfaces of the rocks. This continual rubbing eventually wears away bits of the rocks and makes them rounded and smooth.

Rocks weathered by water are rounded and smooth.

Ice and Plants

Flowing water and wind weather rocks by breaking off small bits. Ice and plants can also weather rocks. When water flows into the cracks of a rock and freezes, it becomes ice. The ice takes up more space than the flowing water did. The ice pushes the rock apart and breaks it into pieces.

Plants can also weather rocks. Over time even a tiny plant can break a strong rock. A seed can fall into a small crack in a rock. As a plant grows from the seed and gets bigger, it pushes with great force. It makes the crack wider and wider. The plant can eventually break the rock into pieces.

A growing plant can break apart rocks.

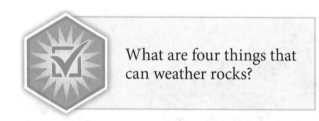

What are four things that can weather rocks?

148

Rocks

Perhaps you have dug up rocks in a garden or walked on large rocks in a stream. **Rocks** are hard pieces of the earth's surface. They have many sizes and shapes. Some are small and can easily be picked up. Others are larger and heavier than you can lift. A rock might be as big as a car or even a tall building. Some rocks are even bigger!

Though rocks come in many shapes and sizes, scientists classify them by how they are formed. The three groups are igneous, sedimentary, and metamorphic.

Igneous Rock

Igneous rock forms when melted rock cools. The melted rock comes from deep in the earth. There the rock is a very hot liquid.

A **volcano** is an opening in the earth that allows melted rock to come to the surface. Sometimes the melted rock may erupt, or come out quickly.

Volcano

Obsidian

Granite

The melted rock cools and hardens. Some melted rock cools quickly. It forms rocks that are smooth. Obsidian is a smooth igneous rock. It is so smooth that it looks like glass.

Granite is a common igneous rock. It forms when melted rock cools slowly. This rock is often speckled. It may have shiny crystal spots. Granite has a rough surface instead of a smooth surface. Some mountains are made of granite.

Science and History

Mount Rushmore is a famous granite mountain in South Dakota. Huge faces of four United States presidents have been carved in the side of this mountain.

What is igneous rock formed from?

Sedimentary Rock

Water and wind weather and move pieces of rock. The pieces that drop and fall to the bottom of the water are called sediment. The water presses down on the sediment. **Sedimentary rock** forms when layers of sediment are pressed together and harden. Because it is made of layers, sedimentary rock often has a striped look.

There are many different kinds of sedimentary rock. One kind is limestone. It forms from the shells and bones of sea animals. The shells and bones break apart after the animals die. When pressed together, the bits of shell and bone form limestone.

Limestone

Sandstone is a rock that is made when layers of sand get pressed together. Shale forms from layers of mud.

Sandstone

Fossils

Most fossils are found in sedimentary rock. A **fossil** is any remaining part of a living thing that died long ago. Fossils form when living things are buried quickly. The softest parts usually rot away first. The harder parts can sometimes be seen as fossils. A mark made by a living thing can also become a fossil. A mark can be a footprint, track, or burrow.

Most fossils formed during the Flood. The waters would have moved large amounts of sediment. This sediment settled into layers as the waters dried up.

Fossils of dinosaur footprints

Flood

The Bible tells us that God judged the earth with a great Flood. The waters of the Flood caused the soil and rocks to wear away. Large amounts of sediment formed in a short time. The sediment buried living things that were not on the ark. This included trees and other plants. The fossils seen today are evidence of this worldwide Flood.

Fossil of fish

Metamorphic Rock

The third kind of rock is metamorphic rock. The word *metamorphic* comes from the same word as *metamorphosis*. It means "to change." **Metamorphic rock** forms when igneous or sedimentary rocks are changed by great heat and pressure.

Limestone is a soft sedimentary rock. But after it is placed under heat and pressure, it becomes marble. Artists often use marble because of its beauty and hardness.

Marble statue

Shale can change into a rock called slate. Slate can be split into thin sheets. Landscapers use it for some walkways and yard decorations. It is also used as a material for roofs.

Granite can change into a rock called gneiss. Gneiss is strong and often used as a building material.

Rocks are always changing. Big rocks break into smaller rocks. Melted rock changes to solid rock. One kind of rock becomes another. These changes are called the rock cycle.

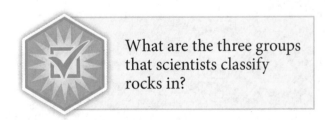

What are the three groups that scientists classify rocks in?

Minerals

Pirates sometimes had treasures of gold and silver. Their treasure was sparkly and shiny. Gold and silver are valuable treasures, but not all treasure sparkles and shines.

The rocks around us have many valuable treasures. Rocks are made of one or more minerals. **Minerals** are solid materials in nature that were never alive. The earth's minerals are a great treasure to us.

Uses of Minerals

Learning about the uses of minerals can help you honor God. You can use a knowledge of minerals to show love to other people. This knowledge can also help you manage the earth as God commanded us to do.

We use minerals in many ways. You probably have eaten some minerals today. Many breakfast cereals contain iron. Iron is a mineral that your body needs to work properly. Calcium is another mineral you need. Milk is a good source of calcium.

Some minerals are hard to find or hard to get. Because of this, they are called precious metals. Gold and silver are two precious metals. Other minerals are cut and polished to reflect light. These minerals are called gems. Precious metals and gems are often used in jewelry.

Gold

Other minerals are easier to find. We say they are common minerals. Halite, graphite, and quartz are some common minerals. We get salt from the mineral halite. The "lead" in our pencils is not really lead at all. It is really a mix of clay and the mineral graphite. Quartz is probably the most common of all the minerals. Most sand is made of tiny bits of quartz. It is an important mineral used to make glass. Quartz is also used in computers and cell phones.

Graphite

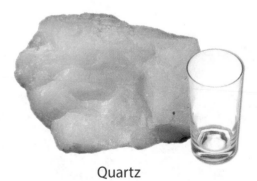

Quartz

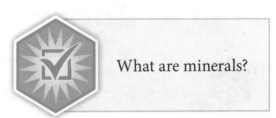

What are minerals?

Characteristics of Minerals

Minerals are not all alike. Some are hard, and some are soft. Scientists can test how hard or soft a mineral is. This is one way they can identify the mineral. A scientist named Friedrich Mohs studied some minerals and put them in order from softest to hardest. His arrangement formed a scale. Other minerals can be compared to the scale that Mohs made.

A scratch test may be done to find out how hard a mineral is. A harder mineral can scratch a softer one. The hardness of a mineral is shown by what it can or cannot scratch.

Talc is a very soft mineral. It is used to make a soft powder. Almost every other mineral can scratch talc. Diamonds are very hard. They can cut, or scratch, all other minerals. Diamonds are used in jewelry. But they are also used in drills and other tools that cut hard things.

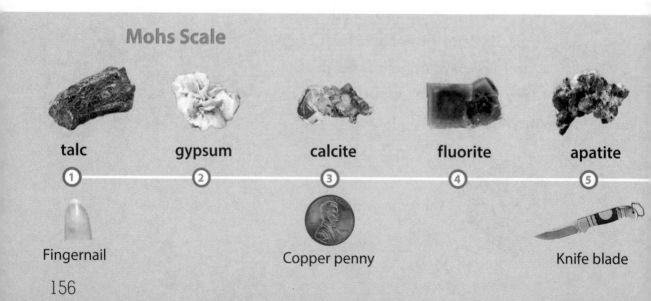

Mohs Scale

talc	gypsum	calcite	fluorite	apatite
1	2	3	4	5

Fingernail

Copper penny

Knife blade

Most minerals form crystals. Each mineral has its own crystal shape. Scientists can use the shape of a crystal to help them know what mineral it is.

Minerals are different colors, but the colors of some minerals look alike. Scientists may use a streak test to help them identify a mineral. They rub the mineral on a light-colored tile. The color of the mark on the tile helps them know what mineral it is.

Gold and pyrite look alike. They are both yellow, but a streak test can be used to tell them apart. Gold leaves a yellowish streak. Pyrite leaves a green streak.

Salt crystals look like little boxes.

The dark streak shows that this is pyrite, not gold.

What are two mineral characteristics that scientists can use to help tell minerals apart?

| orthoclase | quartz | topaz | corundum | diamond |
| 6 | 7 | 8 | 9 | 10 |

Glass mirror

157

Hard or Soft

Some minerals are soft. They can be scratched easily. Other minerals are more difficult to scratch.

In this activity you will test the hardness of several minerals.

Problem

Which minerals can be scratched with each tool?

Procedure

1. Complete the hypothesis for each mineral.

2. Scratch the copper with your fingernail. Check whether your fingernail left a scratch on the mineral. A scratch will not be able to be rubbed off.

3. Record the result.

4. Scratch the copper with the penny. Check whether the penny left a scratch on the mineral.

5. Record the result.

Materials
penny
steel nail
copper
gypsum
quartz
zinc
Activity Manual

6. Scratch the copper with the nail. Check whether the nail left a scratch on the mineral.

7. Record the result.

8. Repeat the procedure for each mineral.

Conclusions

- Which minerals can be scratched with your fingernail?

- Which mineral is the hardest?

- How is knowing about the hardness of minerals useful?

Follow-up

- Make your own hardness scale. Arrange your minerals from softest to hardest.

9 Weather

Wind blows. Rain falls. Lightning flashes. Thunder booms! Often we think of these events when we think of weather. But weather is also clear skies, pleasant breezes, warm days, and cool nights.

The activities you decide to do usually depend on what type of weather you're having. On a warm, clear day you probably spend time outside. Your family may even cook outside. During stormy weather you stay indoors. If the weather is extremely harsh, you may even need to travel to a safer location.

Weather is the condition of the air at a certain time and place. The weather when you wake up can be different from the weather when you eat lunch. Your town's weather is different from weather across the country. We study the weather to obey God in managing the earth and serving other people.

All our weather takes place in the atmosphere. The **atmosphere** is the layer of gases that surrounds the earth. We call these gases *air*. The atmosphere is pulled toward the earth by gravity. This gives air weight as it presses on the earth. This pressing is called *air pressure*. Changes in air pressure can affect the weather.

The atmosphere is very important to us. God designed it to protect the earth like a blanket. It helps keep the temperatures on the earth from being too hot or too cold for people, plants, and animals to live.

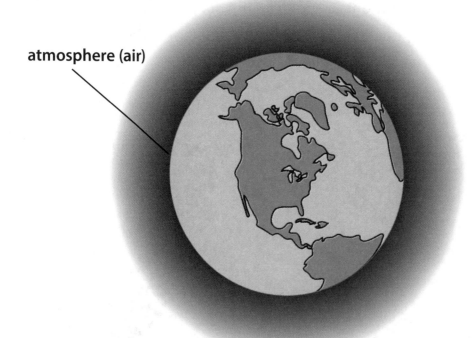

atmosphere (air)

Studying Weather

Checking the weather when you wake up helps you know what to wear that day. But to plan future activities, you may want to know the weather ahead of time. You may need to know what the weather will be like tomorrow or next week.

Weather Forecasts

Only God knows the future, but people can make predictions about what might happen. They study past events to find patterns. They use those patterns and present conditions to make predictions. These predictions help people plan how they work and live their lives.

A **meteorologist** is a person who studies the weather. He uses weather tools to measure and record weather information, or data. He compares the current data with past weather patterns. This helps him predict the kind of weather that is probably coming. A prediction of future weather is called a **weather forecast**.

Meteorologists get some of their data from weather satellites. Weather satellites are sent high into the atmosphere. From there they can gather temperatures, take pictures of the surface of the earth, and provide other useful information.

What does a meteorologist do?

A meteorologist uses a weather map to show weather data.

Some meteorologists record data and predictions on weather maps. These maps may show the temperatures for cities and towns. Color is often used on a weather map to show large areas with a similar temperature. Meteorologists use these maps to share weather information with others.

Color and symbols may also be used on a weather map to show the air pressure for large areas of the country. They also show where rain or snow is falling.

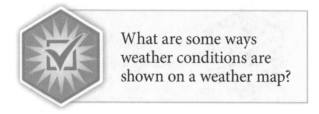

What are some ways weather conditions are shown on a weather map?

Measuring Weather

The weather affects many things we do. Measuring weather can help you plan and be safe. You wear a coat when it is cold and thinner clothing when it is warm. You might carry an umbrella if it is going to rain. You may not be able to have an outdoor event because of stormy weather. Meteorologists measure different characteristics of weather, and you can too.

Precipitation

One characteristic of weather that is easy to observe and measure is precipitation. **Precipitation** is water that falls from the sky to the ground. Rain, snow, sleet, and hail are all forms of precipitation. Precipitation is part of a cycle that moves water from the earth to the sky and back to the earth again. This movement of water is called the **water cycle**.

The Water Cycle

For the water cycle to occur, water must get into the air. Remember that water is a type of matter that easily changes states. When water changes from a liquid to a gas, this part of the water cycle is called *evaporation*. The gas that forms is called water vapor.

The warm water vapor rises in the atmosphere. Air temperature is cooler the higher it is above the earth's surface. The cooler air cools the water vapor.

Cooled water vapor changes to a liquid. This part of the water cycle is called *condensation*. The condensed water vapor forms clouds. Clouds grow as more and more water vapor condenses.

Water droplets form in the clouds. The droplets of water vapor attach to each other to form raindrops. When the drops become heavy, they fall to the ground as *precipitation*.

Water falls from the sky. It soaks into the ground or falls into a body of water. God placed exactly the right amount of water on the earth for people, animals, and plants to use. As water goes through the water cycle, it is used again and again.

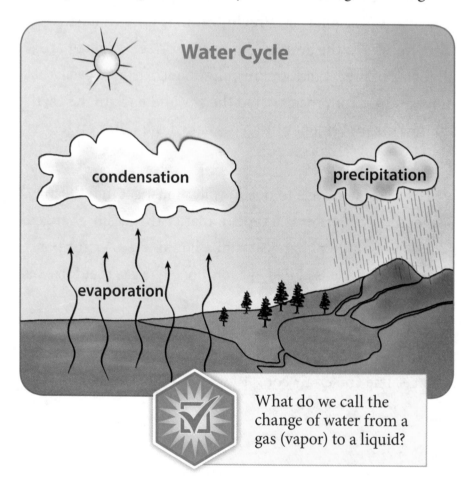

Water Cycle

condensation

precipitation

evaporation

What do we call the change of water from a gas (vapor) to a liquid?

Clouds

A cloud is a collection of very tiny water droplets or ice crystals. The droplets and crystals are so small and light that they can float in the air. Different kinds of clouds give us clues about the weather.

Stratus clouds

Stratus clouds are a wide, thin layer of clouds. They are low clouds that look like a blanket over the earth. Stratus clouds often cause gray skies but do not bring heavy rain.

Fog is a cloud that forms close to the ground. Fog forms when warm air blows over cold air near the ground. The water vapor in the warm air cools close to the ground and condenses.

Fog

Cumulus clouds

Cumulus clouds are fluffy, cottonlike clouds. They usually mean that the weather is fair, but these clouds can grow large and tall and form thunderclouds. The dark gray thunderclouds can bring stormy weather. The storms can have strong winds and heavy rain.

Cirrus clouds

Cirrus clouds are high, thin, wispy clouds. They often mean that a change in the weather is coming. Some cirrus clouds look like the scales on a fish. A cirrus cloud that appears thin and curly is sometimes called a mare's tail because it looks like the tail of a horse.

What is a cloud?

Rain, Sleet, and Snow

Rain is a liquid. It can fall only if the air temperature is above freezing. Rain falls on the ground and in the ocean and other bodies of water. It provides water for all living things. Even though rain is a natural process, the Bible tells us that God is responsible for it. Matthew 5:45 says that God sends the rain even on people who do not deserve this grace.

Rain

Rain gauge

Scientists use a tool called a **rain gauge** to measure the amount of rain that falls. Each day they record the rainfall data. To find out what the normal rainfall for an area is, they collect measurements for a long time. They use the data to look for patterns. The patterns show the usual amount of rainfall for a day. This information can be helpful to people, such as farmers, who rely on rain to do their work.

What is a rain gauge used for?

169

Places such as tropical rainforests receive a lot of rain. Other places, such as deserts, get very little rain. Sometimes an area does not receive as much precipitation as it needs. When this happens, the lack of enough precipitation is called a **drought**. A drought can affect the people, plants, and animals that live there.

When parts of the air are below freezing, precipitation may fall as a form of ice. Snow, sleet, and hail form when water freezes before it reaches the ground. Snow and sleet occur in cold weather. Hail sometimes forms in thunderstorm clouds.

Snow

Fantastic Facts

Measuring precipitation can be tricky. An inch of snow is not the same as an inch of rain. A scientist uses a snow gauge to measure how much snow fell. To compare the amount of snow to rainfall, you will need to measure melted snow in a rain gauge.

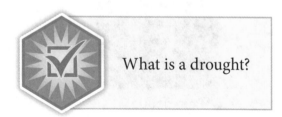

What is a drought?

Temperature

A characteristic of weather that we often ask about is "What is the temperature?" The temperature is the measure of how hot or cold something is. When we measure the weather's temperature, we are measuring how hot or cold the air is.

A thermometer is used to measure temperature. There are different kinds of thermometers. Some thermometers have degree markings. Many thermometers used for weather are digital. They show the temperature on a display.

Thermometer with degree markings

Digital thermometer

What is temperature?

Wind

Wind is another characteristic of weather. Though we cannot see the wind, we can see what it does. A gentle breeze causes tree branches to sway back and forth. A strong wind bends trees and breaks branches.

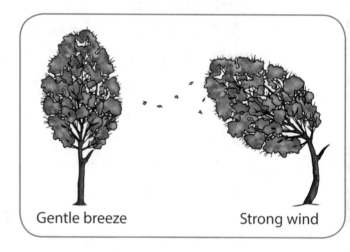

Gentle breeze   Strong wind

Wind is moving air. Changes in temperature cause air to move. The sun makes the earth's surface warm. This causes air closer to the ground to be warmer than air that is higher. Warmer air rises. Cooler air falls. As warmer air rises, cooler air moves toward the earth to replace it. This movement of air causes wind.

Some large wind patterns cause wind to blow all the time in certain directions. One large wind pattern causes the trade winds. These winds always blow from Europe to the Americas. Trade winds were used by sailing ships as they came to the New World.

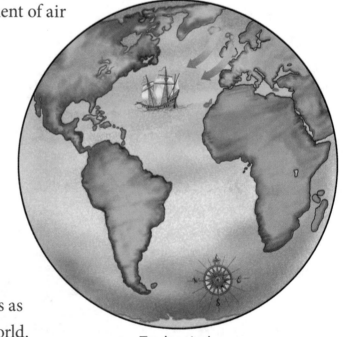

Trade winds

One of the oldest weather tools is a weather vane. A **weather vane** is a tool that shows which direction the wind is blowing. It is also called a wind vane. The arrow on a weather vane points to the direction the wind is coming from. Most weather vanes have letters that stand for the directions: *N* for north, *S* for south, *E* for east, and *W* for west. When wind blows from the north, the weather vane points to the *N*.

Weather vane

The direction of the wind might help us know something about the wind. Winds from the north are usually cold. Winds from the south are usually warm.

We might also want to know how hard the wind is blowing. This is a wind's speed. An **anemometer** is a weather tool that measures wind speed.

Anemometer

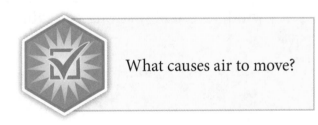
What causes air to move?

Weather Watcher

Meteorologists use many tools to study and predict the weather. You can use tools to study the weather too.

In this activity you will observe, measure, and record information about the weather. Then you can use your data to make predictions.

Purpose

Observe and record the weather.

Procedure

1. Glue the cloud cards from your Activity Manual onto a piece of card stock.

2. Cut out the cards. Punch a hole in each card at the dot.

3. Attach the cards with the brass fastener. You will use the cards as you observe the clouds.

4. Observe the weather on the morning of the first day, and record your data on a *Weather Record* page. Measure and record the temperature. Record any type of precipitation. Identify any clouds that you see. If there is any wind, record how strong you think it is.

Materials
card stock
glue
hole punch
brass fastener
thermometer
Activity Manual

5. Observe the weather again that afternoon and record your data. Repeat both times the next day.

6. Repeat for as many days as your teacher tells you to.

Conclusions

- Did any temperature, cloud type, or kind of wind seem to occur more often before a change of weather?

- What tools and observations can you use to predict the weather for tomorrow?

Follow-up

- Use other weather tools to collect additional data.

Severe Weather

Sometimes a meteorologist predicts severe weather. Severe weather includes strong thunderstorms, tornadoes, hurricanes, and blizzards. These kinds of weather can cause damage to homes and land. They can even be dangerous to people. Predicting severe weather is very important.

Strong **thunderstorms** are the kind of severe weather we have most often. They usually occur in warm weather. A strong thunderstorm has a lot of lightning. The lightning causes the thunder that gives the storm its name. A strong thunderstorm also has heavy rain and strong winds. It can even produce hail.

Health and Safety

Before severe weather happens, you need to know how to be safe. You can also show love to others by helping them be safe. Talk with your family about what to do if severe weather occurs and encourage them to make a plan. Your plan should include where to go. The best place to go is inside. If your area has a frequent type of severe weather, some homes or towns may have shelters designed for protection. Your plan should also include making an emergency kit. Include supplies such as bottled water, blankets, canned food, flashlights, a battery-powered radio, extra batteries, and emergency phone numbers.

Lightning

A thunderstorm can produce another kind of severe weather called a tornado. A **tornado** is a funnel-shaped cloud of swirling winds that reaches the ground. Usually a tornado is only a few hundred meters (yards) wide, but its winds are strong. They cause great damage to buildings that they hit.

Tornado

Another kind of severe weather is a hurricane. A **hurricane** has strong, swirling winds and produces heavy rain. A hurricane can be hundreds of kilometers (miles) wide. It covers a much larger area than a tornado does. Hurricanes form over warm ocean waters. They mostly affect places near the ocean.

Hurricane

Blizzards are snowstorms with strong winds. In a blizzard the snow blows very hard. It can be hard to see in a blizzard, and it is easy to get lost. The blowing snow and freezing temperatures make it unsafe to be outside.

Blizzard

Why is severe weather dangerous?

10

The Solar System

How did God design Earth for human life?

Look at the sky on a clear night and you will see thousands of stars. The Bible tells us that "in the beginning God created the heaven and the earth" (Genesis 1:1). We live on Earth, and we can say that the heaven is everything beyond our atmosphere.

Earth is just a tiny piece in what scientists call the universe. You see parts of the universe every time you look at the sky.

The Solar System

God placed the sun, planets, and other objects in the sky. The sun and the objects that revolve around it are called the **solar system**. The sun is a star. Some of the objects that move around it are called planets.

God designed the parts of the solar system to move in patterns. One pattern is called a revolution. A **revolution** is the motion of one object around another. Earth and the other planets revolve around the sun. One complete revolution of Earth or another planet around the sun is called a year.

A **planet** is a ball of rock or gas that revolves around a star. A total of eight planets revolve around the sun. These planets are Mercury, Venus, Earth, Mars, Jupiter, Saturn, Uranus, and Neptune. All the planets move around the sun in the same direction but on different paths called orbits.

Each day the sun appears to rise in the east. Then it appears to move across the sky and set in the west. This pattern happens because Earth spins. We call one spin a **rotation**. One rotation of Earth or another planet is called a day.

Neptune

Uranus

Mars

Mercury   Sun

Venus

Jupiter

Earth

Saturn

 What is a solar system?

Solar Mobile

If you were out in space, you would be amazed at how bright the planets and stars are. Space probes and other space equipment have taken pictures of the planets so that we can see what they look like.

Process Skills
- Classifying
- Communicating

In this activity you will make a mobile that models the order of the planets as they orbit the sun.

Purpose

Make a model of the solar system.

Materials
Solar Mobile Crossbars page
scissors
hole punch
14 pieces of string
Activity Manual

Procedure

1. Cut out the pictures of the sun and planets. Punch a hole in each.

2. Write the name and an interesting fact about the planet on the back of each picture.

3. Tie one string to each hole in the planets and two strings to the hole in the sun.

4. Cut out the Solar Mobile Crossbars pieces. Cut a slit at the center of each on the solid line. Punch a hole at each circle on both pieces.

5. Slide the slits of both pieces together so that the bars form an X.

6. Tie one string to each of the four holes at the top center of the *X*. Tie the other ends of the strings together to form a loop.

7. Tie each string on the sun to a hole marked *S* on the crossbars.

8. Arrange the planets in the order they orbit the sun. Tie the first planet to hole *1* of the crossbars. Tie the other planets to their correct places.

9. Hold or hang your mobile by the center loop.

Conclusions

- What does your mobile model?
- Describe some characteristics of the solar system that are not shown by this model.

Follow-up

- Make a model that shows how the planets compare in size.

The Sun and Other Stars

A **star** is an object in the sky that produces its own light. Our sun, like other stars, is a ball of burning gas. Its energy gives the light and heat that are necessary for life on Earth.

The sun is the largest object in our solar system. It looks bigger than any other star. This is because it is much closer to Earth than any other star. But compared with other stars in the universe, the sun is a medium-sized star.

The sun is very important for Earth. It is Earth's main source of energy. The sun gives light during the day. Plants use its energy for photosynthesis. The sun affects our weather as it heats air and causes the air to move. People can use the sun's energy for heat and power.

At night you can usually see many dots of light in the sky. A few of the planets appear as tiny dots of light. But most of the dots of light you see are stars.

What is the main source of energy for the earth?

Observing Stars and Planets

Throughout history, shapes of animals, people, and other objects have been seen in the stars. Many of these patterns in the sky are called **constellations**. Constellations are similar to dot-to-dot pictures. You may have seen the Big Dipper. Its pattern is part of a larger constellation.

People have been studying the stars since Bible times. Scientists who study the stars and planets are called **astronomers**. For a long time, people thought that on clear nights the stars that they saw were the only stars in the universe. Then in 1610, an astronomer named Galileo used a telescope for the first time to look at the night sky. He saw stars that no one had seen before.

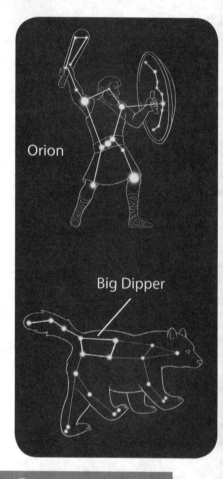

Orion

Big Dipper

• Meet the Scientist •   Lyman Spitzer Jr.

In 1946 Lyman Spitzer Jr. suggested putting a telescope in space. He thought a telescope above the earth's atmosphere would get better images. In 1990 the Hubble Space Telescope was launched into space. Spitzer had worked on it for more than 15 years. He stayed active in astronomy until his death in 1997. In 2003 a new space telescope was launched. It is called the Spitzer Space Telescope in his honor.

Telescopes are still used today. A **telescope** is a tool used to see objects that are far away. We can use it to study objects in space. Most telescopes are long tubes with curved pieces of glass and mirrors inside. The glass and mirrors cause faraway objects to appear closer. Astronomers use telescopes to learn many things about the planets and stars. Computers record data from telescopes. The data helps astronomers learn about the universe.

Telescope

What does an astronomer do?

Inner Planets

The four planets that are closest to the sun are called rocky planets. These planets are more like Earth than the outer planets are. But Earth is special. It is the only planet that has life on it.

Mercury: Closest to the Sun

Mercury is the smallest planet and the one closest to the sun. It is only a little larger than our moon. Sometimes Mercury can be seen just after sunset. It appears as a bright object in the sky, but it is so close to the sun that it is often hard to see.

Because Mercury is closest to the sun, its path around the sun is the shortest. This means that Mercury takes less time than any other planet to orbit the sun.

Though Mercury orbits quickly, it rotates slowly. This causes it to have great temperature changes. The side that faces the sun is very hot. The side facing away from the sun is very cold. The temperature on this side falls far below freezing.

Mercury

Mercury

Venus

Venus: Earth's Twin

Venus is the second planet from the sun. Clouds surround the planet. The clouds keep the planet very hot. Venus is the hottest planet in our solar system.

Venus is sometimes called Earth's twin. It is just a little smaller than Earth, and its surface has some features like Earth's. Scientists have sent spacecraft to the surface of Venus. These space probes have sent back pictures. The pictures show that Venus has plains, volcanoes, mountains, and valleys. But Venus has no water. The clouds are not made of water but of acid.

The clouds around Venus reflect the sun's light. This makes Venus look like a very bright star in the sky. People sometimes call it the morning star or evening star since it is best seen just before sunrise and just after sunset.

Venus

What causes Venus to be the hottest planet?

Earth: Our Home

Earth is the third planet from the sun. It is the only planet with both an atmosphere and liquid water that allow life. God perfectly designed Earth for us to live on.

Earth is 150,000,000 km (93,000,000 mi) from the sun. God placed Earth exactly the right distance from the sun. If it were closer to the sun, it would be too hot for anything to live. If it were farther away, it would be too cold.

Earth rotates once every 24 hours, so one day on Earth is 24 hours. The speed of rotation helps keep the temperatures from being too hot or cold. Earth orbits the sun every $365\frac{1}{4}$ days. We call one orbit a year.

Earth has one moon. It takes about 29 days for the moon to revolve around Earth.

Earth

Moon

Earth

Mars

Mars: The Red Planet

Mars is the fourth planet from the sun. It is about half the size of Earth. Mars is one of the brightest objects in the night sky. The planet's surface is covered with red dust. Because of its reddish color, it is known as the red planet.

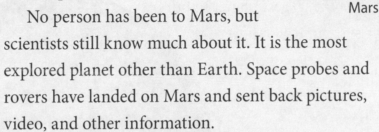

Mars

No person has been to Mars, but scientists still know much about it. It is the most explored planet other than Earth. Space probes and rovers have landed on Mars and sent back pictures, video, and other information.

Mars has two tiny moons named Phobos and Deimos. It also has the highest mountain of any planet in our solar system called Olympus Mons.

What characteristics of Earth allow life to be able to exist on it?

Outer Planets

The four outer planets have surfaces that are made of gas. Scientists call these planets gas giants because they are so large. They are also farther apart than the inner planets. The distance between two of the gas giants is greater than the distance from the sun to Mars.

Jupiter: The Largest Planet

Jupiter is the fifth planet from the sun. It is the largest planet in our solar system. If Earth were the size of a pea, Jupiter would be the size of a baseball.

Jupiter also spins faster than any other planet. Jupiter takes only about 10 hours to rotate, so a day on Jupiter lasts for only 10 hours.

Jupiter

Jupiter is covered with colorful clouds of gas. It has a giant red spot that scientists believe is a storm. Jupiter has more than 63 moons. The four largest are Io, Europa, Ganymede, and Callisto. Each of these moons is bigger than the planet Mercury.

Jupiter's red spot

Io

Europa

Ganymede

Callisto

Which planet is the largest?

Jupiter

Saturn: The Ringed Planet

Saturn is the second-largest planet. It is almost as large as Jupiter. The distance from the sun to Jupiter is about the same distance as from Jupiter to Saturn.

Saturn is best known for its rings. It has thousands of rings made of ice and rocks. Each ring travels in its own orbit around the planet. Some pieces of the rings are as small as dust, but others are as big as buildings!

Saturn has at least 62 moons. The largest one is called Titan. In old Greek stories, the Titans were giants. The moon Titan is a giant as well. It is larger than the planets Mars and Mercury combined.

Titan

Saturn

What is Saturn best known for?

Saturn

Uranus: The Sideways Planet

Uranus is a pale blue-green color. Its color comes from the gases in its atmosphere.

Uranus rotates in a way no other planet does. Other planets are tilted slightly away from the sun, so the sun shines mostly on their equators. Uranus spins on its side so that the sun shines on its poles.

Uranus has at least 13 rings and 27 moons.

Neptune: Farthest from the Sun

Neptune is known as a blue planet. It is the farthest planet from the sun. Neptune is a very cold planet covered with gas. The wind on the surface of Neptune sometimes blows over 1600 km (994 mi) per hour.

Neptune has several faint rings and 13 moons. Triton is Neptune's largest moon. It is one of the coldest objects in space.

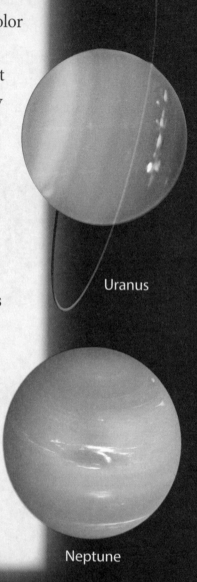

Uranus

Neptune

Asteroids and Dwarf Planets

Asteroid

Asteroids are small rocky objects in space that orbit the sun. They are not round like planets but are different shapes and sizes. Some are hundreds of miles across. Others are as tiny as pebbles. Most asteroids are found in an area between Mars and Jupiter called an asteroid belt.

A dwarf planet is the size of a large asteroid but round like a planet. Ceres is the largest object in the asteroid belt between Mars and Jupiter. Because of its size and shape, it is called a dwarf planet.

Pluto and Eris are also dwarf planets. Pluto was once called a planet, but it was classified as a dwarf planet in 2006. Eris is the largest dwarf planet. It is the farthest object scientists have seen to orbit the sun.

Pluto

No matter where we look in the universe, we are amazed at God's creation. The greatness of the universe shows the greatness of God.

What is different about the way Uranus rotates?

Uranus

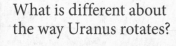

Neptune

For thousands of years, people did not know what plants and animals were made of. Scientists could only observe characteristics of them. They could observe a plant's stems, leaves, and flowers or an animal's fur, eyes, and even its heart. But they could not study the tiny parts that make up each of these.

Then a tool was invented that allowed scientists to see the parts of living things that they could not see before.

199

Cells

Observing Cells

One of the main tools scientists use to observe the tiny parts of living things is the microscope. A **microscope** is a tool used to see things that are very small.

About 350 years ago, an English scientist named Robert Hooke looked at a thin slice of cork under a microscope. Cork is a type of plant. He drew what the cork looked like up close. He wrote about what he observed.

Robert Hooke wrote about "little boxes" in his report. He thought these boxes looked like rooms or chambers. He called these little boxes cells. The word *cell* comes from a Latin word meaning "chamber."

Many scientists began to use microscopes to help them observe and study living things. When they placed pieces of living material, such as a leaf, under a microscope, they could see tiny structures for the first time. Imagine how exciting that was! Over time scientists observed that all living things are made of cells.

Today people in many jobs continue to use microscopes. Microscopes help doctors fight diseases. They help scientists know how to make unclean water safe for explorers and missionaries to drink. You can use a microscope to observe the tiny parts of God's creation around you. Perhaps one day you will use a microscope to solve a problem and help others.

Microscopes help scientists and students study cells and other tiny things.

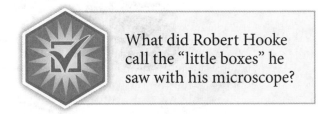

What did Robert Hooke call the "little boxes" he saw with his microscope?

Kinds of Cells

A **cell** is the smallest living part of any living thing. Most cells can be seen only under a microscope.

Cells come in many shapes. Some, such as the cork observed by Robert Hooke, look like little boxes. Others look like rods, circles, coils, or even blobs of jelly.

Cells also come in many sizes. Some cells are so small that if 50,000 of them were lined up, the row would be only a little more than two centimeters long. Some cells are much larger. The yolk of an egg is one cell. The largest single cell is the yolk of an ostrich egg.

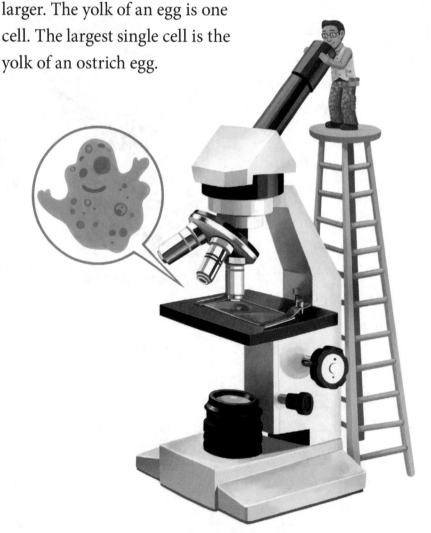

Plants and animals are made up of many cells. The size of a living thing is related to the number of cells it has. An elephant and a huge redwood tree have millions of cells.

Some living things are made up of only one cell. A microscope can help you see single-celled creatures more clearly. An amoeba is a single-celled creature. It is about half the size of the period at the end of a sentence. It looks like a blob of jelly and lives in water or moist soil.

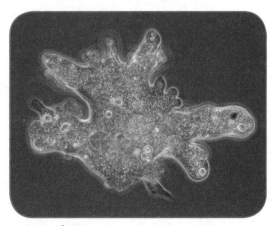
Amoeba

Paramecium

Another single-celled creature is a paramecium. It is shaped like a flattened football. Large parameciums may be seen with a magnifying glass. They are about the length of a period.

What is the smallest living part of any living thing?

Parts of Cells

Whether big or small, all cells have the same main parts. God designed each part to do its own job for the cell.

Nucleus

The **nucleus** of a cell is its control center. It regulates the activities of the cell. The nucleus looks like a large, dark area in the cell.

Cytoplasm

Surrounding the nucleus is a jellylike fluid as well as structures that help the cell live and grow. Together these are known as **cytoplasm**. Without the cytoplasm, the cell would not work properly.

Animal Cell

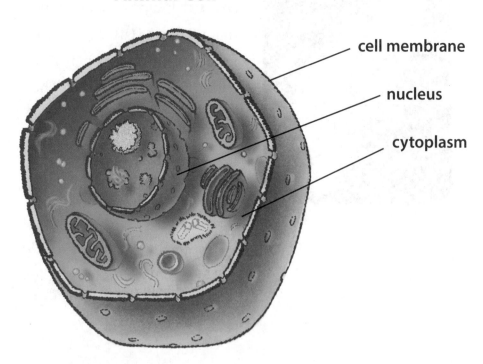

cell membrane

nucleus

cytoplasm

Plant Cell

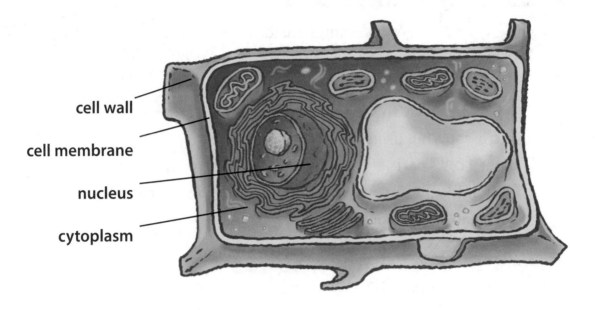

cell wall

cell membrane

nucleus

cytoplasm

Membranes and Walls

A cell has a thin covering that holds it together called a **cell membrane**. Both plant and animal cells have cell membranes.

In addition to a cell membrane, a plant cell also has a cell wall. A **cell wall** is a stiff layer on the outside of the cell membrane. The cell wall gives the plant shape and support.

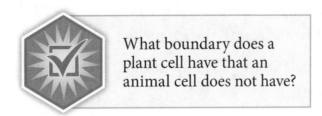

What boundary does a plant cell have that an animal cell does not have?

Edible Cell

ACTIVITY

When things are too small for us to see without an instrument to help us, it is useful to have a model. To see a cell, we need a microscope, but using a model helps us learn about a cell's parts.

In this activity you will make a model of an animal cell. Then you can eat your "cell"!

Process Skills
- Making a model
- Defining operationally

Purpose

Model an animal cell.

Procedure

1. Place the rolled fruit strip around the inside of the cup. The fruit strip should touch the bottom of the cup all the way around.

2. Mix the hot water and gelatin powder in a bowl. Stir until the powder is dissolved.

3. Add $\frac{1}{2}$ cup of ice cubes to the gelatin mixture. Stir until the ice melts.

4. Pour gelatin into the cup until it reaches the top of the fruit strip.

Materials
clear plastic cup, 9 oz
rolled fruit strip
measuring cups
1 cup hot water
gelatin powder
spoon
2 bowls
ice cubes
towel
round gumball
Activity Manual

5. Fill the other bowl with ice. Place the gelatin cup in the bowl of ice. Cover the bowl with a towel.

6. Let the gelatin sit until it is firm and not a liquid. Remove the cup from the ice bowl. Push the gumball into the gelatin.

7. Draw and color a diagram of your cell and label the parts.

8. Display your model and diagram. Then eat your "cell."

Conclusions

- Identify what each part of the model represents.
- List ways that your model is different from a real cell.

Follow-up

- Add another food item to change your model of an animal cell into a plant cell model.

Tissues

A cell has the characteristics of a living thing. It needs food. It grows. It uses energy. It reproduces.

Sometimes a cell works alone. Single-celled creatures are examples of this. In most living things, though, groups of cells work together. A **tissue** is a group of cells all doing the same kind of work.

There are two kinds of tissues that a plant uses to make and move food—xylem and phloem. Xylem moves water from the roots to the leaves for photosynthesis. After the plant makes food, phloem moves the food to other parts of the plant.

God gave people special kinds of tissues too. Epithelial, connective, muscle, and nerve tissues are the four main kinds of tissues in the human body. Each type has an important job.

Epithelial tissue is smooth tissue. Its job is to provide covering and protection. The surface of your skin is this kind of tissue. Epithelial tissue also lines the insides of your mouth, throat, and parts of your lungs.

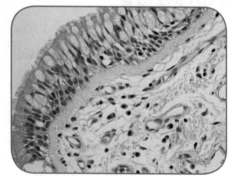

Epithelial tissue

Connective tissue holds parts of your body together. Bones and fat are connective tissues. Blood is also a special kind of connective tissue. Your body has more connective tissue than any other kind.

Connective tissue

Muscle tissue allows your body to move. You can see and feel some of your muscles as they work. Other muscles, such as the ones that help you digest your food or cause your heart to beat, you cannot see. Whether they can be observed or not, all your muscles are very important.

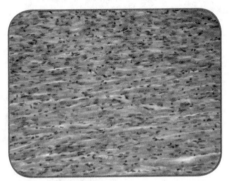

Muscle tissue

Nerve tissue carries messages between your brain and your body. The messages tell your body what is happening and what to do. They allow you to respond to the things around you. Nerve tissue has billions of tiny connecting fibers. These fibers "talk" to each other by passing signals back and forth.

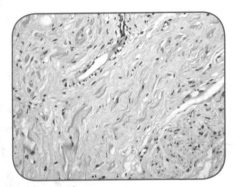

Nerve tissue

Name the four main kinds of tissues found in your body.

Organs

A group of tissues working together to do a job is called an **organ**. Organs are the major parts of the body. One organ may use several different kinds of tissue. A good example of an organ is the eye. The outside of the eye is epithelial tissue. A layer of connective tissue gives the eye flexibility. Muscle tissue focuses and moves the eye. The nerve tissue sends messages to the brain to tell what is seen. Each tissue in the eye has its own job, but the tissues also work together. When they all do their jobs, the eye can do its job.

Upper-Body Organs

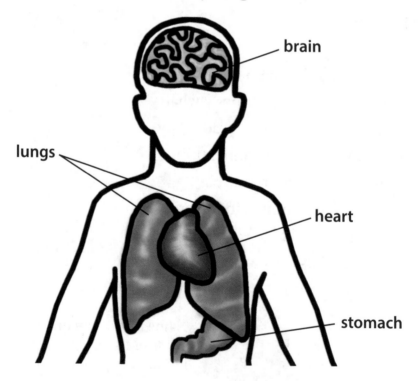

brain

lungs

heart

stomach

God gave your organs important jobs. Your eyes let you see. Your lungs allow you to breathe. Your heart pumps blood to your body. Your stomach helps you digest food. Your brain is the control center for your body. These are just a few of your many organs.

Systems

A group of organs working together makes a **system**. One system in your body is the digestive system. The stomach is part of this system, but other organs are as well. The tongue, esophagus, liver, and small and large intestines work together with the stomach to digest your food.

Cells make up tissues. Tissues form organs. Organs work together to form systems.

cell ➡ tissue ➡ organ ➡ system

Each part of the body has its own job as it works together with the other parts. You and your parents need to understand how the parts of your body work to be able to keep you healthy. Doctors need to understand how the body works so that they can give you proper care when your body is not well.

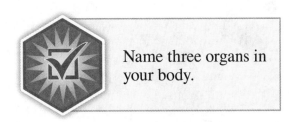

Name three organs in your body.

12

Skin

Have you ever taken a close look at your skin? The first thing you may notice is its color. God gave skin many wonderful shades. You may have dark skin or light skin. You may have freckles or be sunburned. If you look closely, you may see that your skin is not all the same color.

Feel the palm and back of your hand. They probably feel different. Not all of your skin feels the same. The skin on some parts of your body is thin and smooth. Your eyelids have smooth skin. But other places, like your elbows or knees, may have rough skin.

213

Skin does more than cover your body. It folds and stretches as you move. Your elbows and knees bend many times during a day. Each time they do, the skin at those places moves and stretches.

As you grow, your skin grows with you. When it gets hurt or torn, it can even heal itself.

God made your skin to cover your body. It protects your muscles, bones, and organs. Imagine what you would look like without it!

Layers of Skin

Every organ in your body has a job to do. Remember that an organ is made of many cells and tissues working together. Your skin is the largest organ in your body. Though it has many parts, it has just two layers. The **epidermis** is the top layer of the skin. Under the epidermis is the second layer called the **dermis**.

Even though you cannot see anything happening, your skin is hard at work. New skin cells are always being made in the lowest part of the epidermis. As the new cells move to the surface, they push older cells ahead of them. After a while the old, dead skin cells at the surface of the epidermis fall off.

Most of the skin you see is the dead cells waiting to fall off. You do many things that help remove them. Washing your skin or even changing your clothes removes some of the dead cells.

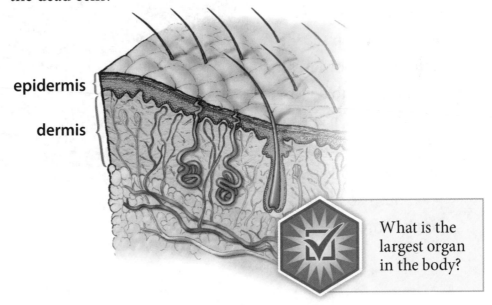

epidermis {

dermis {

What is the largest organ in the body?

The Epidermis

God made skin as a marvelous protection for your body. Although the epidermis is very thin, it works like a strong shield. It helps keep harmful things out of your body. Dirt and germs cannot pass through the skin. If these things could get through, you would get sick much more often.

The epidermis also keeps in things that your body needs. One important thing your body needs is water. Water keeps your body from drying out. It helps keep your body's organs working properly and keeps your blood flowing.

Water also helps keep your body at the right temperature. When you get warm, sweat comes out on your skin to help you cool down. Because sweat is mostly water, you need to replace the water your body loses. The best way to do this is by drinking plenty of water. A cold drink of water not only tastes good but also helps keep you healthy.

Drinking plenty of water is important for your health.

The sun causes your skin to make more melanin.

The epidermis also contains a substance called melanin. **Melanin** is the coloring in your skin. When you are in the sun, your body makes extra melanin to help protect your skin from damage. The more melanin you have, the darker your skin. Using sunscreen can also help protect your skin.

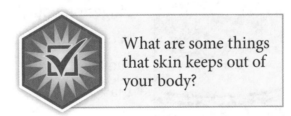

What are some things that skin keeps out of your body?

Fingerprints

The epidermis has many lines and grooves in it. An interesting part of your epidermis is your fingertips. If you look closely at them, you can see dozens of curved ridges.

These ridges are also found on the palms of your hands and the bottoms of your feet. These parts of your body never grow hair. The ridges on your skin are formed in the deepest layers of the skin. The ridges were formed even before you were born. They will be the same your whole life.

The ridges on your fingers are useful for the tasks that you do every day. They provide the friction you need to help pick things up. They also help keep objects from slipping out of your grasp. Without the ridges on your skin, it would be hard for you to pick up something smooth like a glass.

Think of trying to hold on to a glass when your hands are wet. The water on your hands fills in the ridges on your fingers and reduces the friction. This makes it harder to grip the glass.

The ridges on your fingers help you grip things.

The prints made by the ridges on your fingertips are called **fingerprints**. Every person in the world has an individual set of fingerprints. Even identical twins have different prints. When you were born, a copy of your footprint or handprint may have been made. The print is a record that can identify who you are.

Fingerprints have many uses. Police use them to help identify criminals. Schools and some businesses use fingerprints to identify who is working for them. In some places, fingerprints are used like a key. A machine scans a person's finger. If the print matches the machine's records, the person is allowed to pass through a door or use special equipment.

What are fingerprints?

Patterns on My Skin

No one else has the same fingerprints as you. However, there are three main fingerprint patterns. Some fingerprints have arches. Others have loops. Still others have whorls.

Process Skills
- Classifying
- Observing

In this activity you will record your fingerprints and compare them to the patterns. Which pattern best matches your fingerprints?

Purpose

Identify and compare fingerprint patterns.

Procedure

Materials
washable ink pad
hand sanitizer
paper towels
magnifying glass
Activity Manual

1. Complete the first two rows of your fingerprint card.

2. Gently roll your right thumb across the ink pad at a steady speed. Find the spot on the card for your right thumb. Press down lightly, rolling your thumb again.

3. Repeat with each finger on your right hand. Clean your hand and repeat with your left hand.

4. Find the square marked *Left Four Fingers*. Ink your left four fingers at once and press them in the square at the same time. Clean your fingers. Repeat with your right hand.

5. Ink your thumbs and put your thumbprints in the spaces between the fingerprint groups. Clean your thumbs.

6. Compare your fingerprints with the patterns in your Activity Manual. Use the magnifying glass to help you see the details. Decide which pattern best matches your prints. Write the type of pattern near each print.

7. Then compare your prints with those of other people.

Conclusions

- Which pattern best matches your fingerprints?
- Are your fingerprints similar to anyone else's?
- How do you think identifying people by fingerprints is helpful to police?

Follow-up

- Make a graph showing how many people doing this activity have each fingerprint pattern.

The Dermis

The dermis is much thicker than the epidermis. It has a different job to do for your body. It contains the nerves, blood vessels, sweat glands, and oil glands.

Nerves

Nerves are a small but important part of the dermis. The nerves allow you to feel things. **Nerves** are the tiny pathways that carry messages between the brain and other parts of the body. Some nerves tell you how things feel. Some tell you when something hurts. Others tell you whether you are hot or cold.

The dermis all over your body has nerves. But some areas have more nerves than others. You use your fingers and hands to touch things. God designed the skin on your fingers and hands to have many nerves. Places such as your back and your earlobes have fewer nerves.

God gave you nerves in your skin to protect you. They help you prevent injury. For example, without nerves you could not feel whether something is hot. Your nerves cause you to feel pain so that you can avoid getting badly burned.

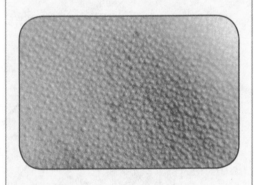

What do the nerves allow you to do?

Blood Vessels

The **blood vessels** are the thin tubes that carry the blood. Blood vessels have two very important jobs. They carry oxygen and nutrients to all parts of your body, including the skin. In the skin, the blood vessels are in the dermis. There are no blood vessels in the epidermis. This is why when you scratch your skin it does not easily bleed.

Your blood vessels also help keep your body at a constant temperature. The blood vessels in the dermis do this by getting wider or narrower. When you get hot, the blood deep inside your body gets warmer. When this happens, the blood vessels automatically become wider. The wider vessels bring more blood than usual to your skin. When the blood

Layers of Skin

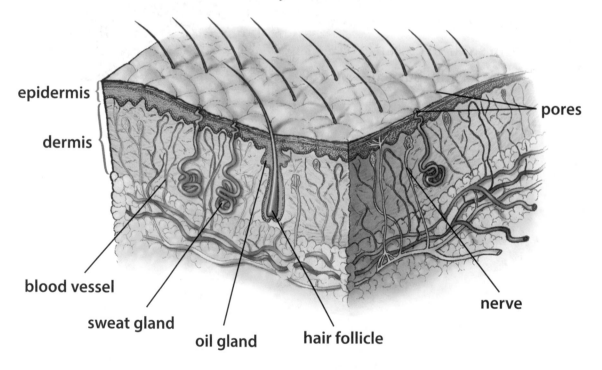

epidermis

dermis

pores

blood vessel

sweat gland

oil gland

hair follicle

nerve

comes close to the surface of your skin, the heat is released to your surroundings. When you get cold, the blood vessels become narrower. This holds most of the blood deeper inside your body to keep the heat in.

Sweat Glands

When you run or exercise, your body gets hot. Your skin feels damp. The drops of liquid on the surface of your skin are called sweat. Your sweat is another way that God gave your body to cool down. Your skin has special structures called **sweat glands** that make the sweat and move it to the skin's surface. There the body releases the sweat from tiny openings called **pores**. The sweat is mostly water, so it evaporates quickly and cools the surface of your skin.

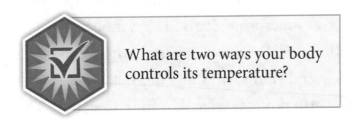

What are two ways your body controls its temperature?

Oil Glands

Most of your body has hair. Hair is made up of dead cells. It does not hurt to cut hair, but it does hurt to pull out a strand of hair. Each strand of hair starts in a hair follicle in the dermis. If you pull out a hair, you feel pain from the nerves around the hair follicle.

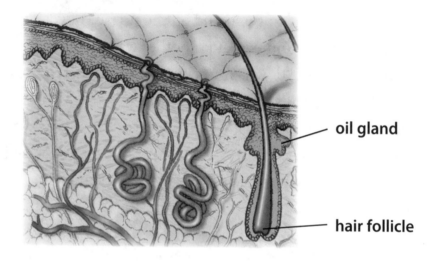

oil gland

hair follicle

Near the base of each hair is an oil gland. **Oil glands** release oil, which helps protect your body. Oil keeps your skin soft and waterproof. It also keeps moisture inside your skin. Without oil, the water in your body would come out too quickly and your skin would dry out.

The oil also protects your skin from infection. The oil and hair work together to trap dirt on the skin until it can be washed off. That is why it is important to keep your skin and hair clean.

How does oil protect the body?

Under My Skin

You can see only the epidermis layer of your skin. But most of the important parts of your skin are in the dermis. In this exploration you will make a model that shows all the parts of the skin.

What to Do

1. Get a piece of cardboard or posterboard. With a pencil, sketch a large diagram of the skin. Use the diagram on page 224 as an example.

2. Use two colors of modeling clay, one for each layer of skin. Press the clay down firmly so it sticks to the board.

3. Use ribbon or colored yarn to show blood vessels, sweat glands, oil glands, and hair.

4. Label the parts of your model.

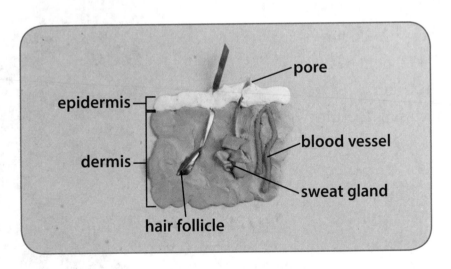

Skin Care

You were made in God's image. This means that you are important. You also have a special job from God. You are supposed to take care of His world. This includes your body. Your care begins with your skin, the largest organ your body has.

Keeping clean helps your skin stay healthy. It also helps to keep you from getting sick. The oil on your skin can cause dirt and germs to get trapped on the skin. Use soap, water, and a clean washcloth to remove the dirty oil as well as any dead cells.

Your hair and nails also trap dirty oil and germs. Washing your hair and fingernails regularly helps remove the oil and germs. Your nails should be cut or filed, but they should not be bitten. Biting your nails puts the dirt trapped under them into your mouth.

Sunlight is good for you, but too much sun can burn your skin. You should be careful to protect your skin from too much sun. Clothing covers some of your skin. Sunscreen can protect your exposed skin.

Sunscreen helps protect your skin from getting burned by the sun.

You can also protect your skin by being careful around sharp objects. A cut in your skin requires special care. If not treated properly, it can allow dirt and other harmful things to enter your body.

If you get a cut, clean it with soap and water to remove any dirt. You may need to put medicine on it. It is also a good idea to cover a cut with a bandage. Covering the cut helps keep dirt out.

Cuts should be checked by an adult. Some cuts may require a visit to a doctor. Proper care of a cut is important because it helps the cut to heal quickly.

We often do not think about our skin unless it gets hurt. But it is always working to keep us safe and healthy. God, the Creator, designed each part of the body just right. Psalm 139:14 says, "I will praise thee; for I am fearfully and wonderfully made."

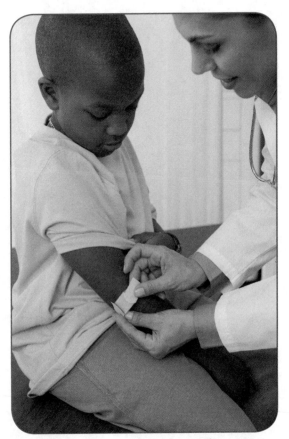

Bandaging a cut helps keep dirt out.

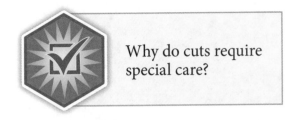

Why do cuts require special care?

Glossary

A

absorb—To take in a sound wave.

amphibian—A cold-blooded vertebrate that lives part of its life in water and part of its life on land.

anemometer—A weather tool that measures wind speed.

astronomer—A person who studies the stars and planets.

atmosphere—The layer of gases that surrounds the earth.

B

balance—A tool scientists use to measure mass.

bedrock—The layer of large, unbroken rock under the subsoil.

bird—A warm-blooded vertebrate that has feathers and wings.

blizzard—A snowstorm with strong winds.

blood vessel—The thin tube that carries the blood.

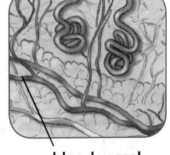

blood vessel

C

camouflage—The color or pattern that allows something to blend in with its surroundings.

carbon dioxide—A gas in the air that a plant needs for photosynthesis.

carnivore—A consumer that eats only other animals.

cell—The smallest living part of any living thing.

cell membrane—A thin covering that holds the cell together.

cell wall—A stiff layer on the outside of the cell membrane that gives the plant shape and support.

characteristic—A special feature of something.

chemical change—A change in matter that forms a new substance.

chlorophyll—Where the green coloring of a plant comes from.

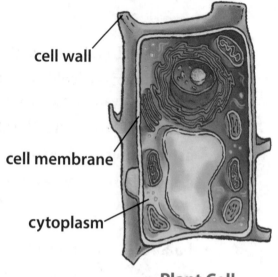

cell wall

cell membrane

cytoplasm

Plant Cell

chloroplasts—The tiny parts of a plant's leaf that help the plant make food.

cold-blooded—An animal that has a body temperature that changes depending on its surroundings.

community—All the living things in one area.

condensation—The process by which a gas changes to a liquid.

constellation—A group of stars that forms a pattern or picture in the sky.

consumer—A living thing that gets its energy by eating other living things as food.

Creation—The six-day event described in Genesis 1 when God made all things very good.

cytoplasm—A jellylike fluid that surrounds the nucleus of a cell. It helps the cell live and grow.

D

decay—To break apart or rot.

decomposer—A living thing that helps break down dead things and wastes.

dermis—The second layer of skin under the epidermis.

drought—A period of time with very little precipitation.

E

echo—A sound wave that reflects clearly enough to be heard again.

ecosystem—All the living and nonliving things in one area.

energy—What is needed to cause change or to do work.

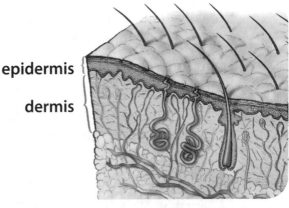

epidermis

dermis

Layers of Skin

environment—The nonliving things that surround a living thing.

epidermis—The top layer of skin.

evaporation—The process by which a liquid changes to a gas.

F

Fall—The event described in Genesis 3 when the first man sinned and brought death into the world.

fingerprint—The print made by the ridges on a fingertip.

fish—A cold-blooded vertebrate that lives in the water and has gills, fins, and scales.

Flood—The event described in Genesis 6–9 when God caused the entire earth to be covered with water.

food chain—The movement of energy from one living thing to another living thing.

food web—Several food chains linked together.

force—A push or pull.

fossil—The remains of a living thing that died long ago.

friction—A force that slows or stops motion.

fruit—The part of the plant that contains the plant's seeds.

Tomato Plant

G

gas—The state of matter that has no definite volume or shape.

graduated container—A tool scientists use to measure volume.

gram (g)—A commonly used metric unit of mass measurement.

gravity—A force that pulls objects toward the center of the earth.

H

habitat—The place where a living thing has the food, water, and shelter that it needs to live.

herbivore—A consumer that eats only plants.

humus—The part of the soil formed from the remains of living things that have died and decayed.

hurricane—A storm of strong, swirling winds and heavy rain that forms over warm ocean waters.

I

igneous rock—The type of rock formed when melted rock cools.

instinct—The basic knowledge and skills that an animal is born with.

invertebrate—An animal without a backbone.

L

leaf—The part of the plant where food is made.

learned behavior—Something that an animal learns to do.

liquid—The state of matter that has a definite volume but not a definite shape.

liter (L)—The standard metric unit of measurement for volume.

M

magnetism—The pushing or pulling force caused by a magnet.

mammal—A warm-blooded vertebrate that has hair or fur and feeds milk to its babies.

marine—Describes something that lives in salt water or the ocean.

marsupial—A mammal with a pouch.

mass—The amount of material that an object has.

Mammal

matter—Anything that has mass and takes up space.

melanin—The coloring in the skin.

metamorphic rock—The type of rock formed when igneous or sedimentary rocks are changed by great heat and pressure.

metamorphosis—The process of an animal changing form as it grows.

meteorologist—A person who studies the weather.

meter (m)—The standard metric unit of measurement that scientists use to measure length and distance.

Matter

microscope—A tool used to see things that are very small.

mineral—A solid material in nature that was never alive.

mixture—When two or more kinds of matter are mixed together.

motion—A change of position.

N

nerve—A tiny pathway that carries messages between the brain and other parts of the body.

nucleus—The control center of a cell that regulates the cell's activities.

nutrient—A substance that helps plants and animals live and grow.

O

oil gland—A gland found at the base of each hair in the skin that releases oil to protect the body.

omnivore—A consumer that eats both plants and animals.

orbit—The path a planet takes around the sun.

organ—A group of tissues working together to do a job.

P

photosynthesis—A process that plants use to make food.

physical change—A change in matter that does not form a new substance.

physical property—Anything about an object that can be observed with our senses.

pitch—How high or low a sound is.

Photosynthesis

planet—A ball of rock or gas that revolves around a star.

population—All the living things of one kind that live in one area.

pore—A tiny opening on the skin where the body releases sweat.

precipitation—The water that falls from the sky to the ground.

predator—Any animal that hunts and eats other animals.

prey—An animal that a predator hunts.

producer—A living thing that makes its own food and gets its energy directly from the sun.

Q

quality—The characteristic of sound that makes one sound different from all other sounds.

R

rain gauge—A tool used to measure rainfall.

reflect—To bounce a sound wave off an object.

reptile—A cold-blooded animal with tough, dry, scaly skin.

revolution—The motion of one object around another object.

rock—A hard piece of the earth's surface.

rocky planets—The four planets that are closest to the sun.

root—Absorbs water and nutrients from the soil and holds the plant in place.

rotation—One spin of the earth or other planet.

Reptile

S

sedimentary rock—The type of rock formed when layers of sediment are pressed together and harden.

soil—Loose rock and bits of decaying plant and animal material.

solar system—The sun and the objects that revolve around it.

solid—The state of matter that has a definite shape and volume.

sound—A form of energy that you can hear.

star—An object in the sky that produces its own light.

stem—The part of the plant that transports water and food to different parts of the plant.

stomata—The tiny openings on the underside of plant leaves.

stored energy—Energy that can be used at a later time to do work.

subsoil—The second layer of soil, which contains larger pieces of rock and less humus than topsoil.

sweat gland—A special structure in the skin that makes sweat and moves it to the skin's surface.

system—A group of organs working together.

T

telescope—A tool used to see objects that are far away.

thermometer—A tool used to measure temperature.

thunderstorm—Severe weather that usually occurs in warm weather and has lightning, thunder, heavy rain, and strong winds.

tissue—A group of cells all doing the same kind of work.

topsoil—The top layer of soil that contains the most humus. Plants grow in this layer.

tornado—A funnel-shaped cloud of swirling winds that reaches the ground.

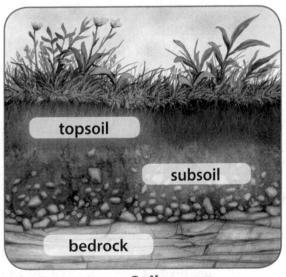

Soil

V

vertebrate—An animal with a backbone.

vibration—A rapid back-and-forth movement.

volcano—An opening in the earth that allows melted rock to come to the surface.

volume—**1.** The amount of space that an object takes up. **2.** How loud or soft a sound is.

W

warm-blooded—An animal that has a body temperature that stays about the same all the time.

water cycle—A cycle that moves water from the earth to the sky and back to the earth again.

weather—The condition of the air at a certain time and place.

weather forecast—A prediction of future weather.

Weather

weathering—The breaking down of rocks into smaller pieces.

weather vane—A tool that shows which direction the wind is blowing; also called a wind vane.

weight—The measure of the force of gravity on an object.

wind—Moving air.

work—Occurs when a force moves something.

worldview—A way of looking at or understanding the world around you.

Index

prey, 70–71, 72, 78–79

producer, 66–67, 70

Q

quality, 115

R

rain gauge, 169

reflect, 112, 113

reptile, 16–18, 19

    characteristics, 16

    ways to identify, 16–17

revolution, 180

rock, types of, 149–155

    igneous, 149–150

    metamorphic, 153

    sedimentary, 151–152

rocky planet, 188–191

root, 47, 50, 56

rotation, 183, 188

S

sedimentary rock, 151–152, 153

skin, 213–229

    care of, 228–229

    dermis, 215, 222–226

    epidermis, 216–219, 220–221

soil, 144–146, 152

solar system, 179–197

solid, 90, 94–95, 98, 100, 102

sound, 105–123

    characteristics, 114–115

    echo, 112–113

    pitch, 114, 116–117

    quality, 115

    volume, 114–115

star, 184–187

stem, 47, 50, 56

stomata, 50

stored energy, 139–141

subsoil, 148

sweat gland, 225

system, 211

T

telescope, 187

thermometer, 20–21, 22–23, 173

thunderstorm, 176–177

tissue, 208–209, 210–211

topsoil, 148

tornado, 177

V

vertebrate, 8–9, 10–11, 14, 16, 28, 32–33

vibration, 106–109, 110, 114, 120

Photo Credits

Key: (t) top; (c) center;
(b) bottom; (l) left; (r) right;
(bg) background; (fg) foreground;
(i) inset

Cover
front/back Craig Oesterling

Chapter 1
4 Thomas Kitchin & Victoria Hurst/First Light/Getty Images; **6** © iStockphoto.com/Peter ten Broecke; **7t** © iStockphoto.com/milosluz; **7c** © fotolia.com/Lijuan Guo; **7b** PhotoDisc, Inc.; **10** Vlada Z/Shutterstock.com; **12,13** © iStockphoto.com/IBorisoff; **14t** Brandon Alms/Bigstock.com; **14c** © iStockphoto.com/David Coder; **14b** © iStockphoto.com/Dieter Spears; **16** all PhotoDisc, Inc.; **17t** © Cosmos Blank/Photo Researchers, Inc.; **17b** PhotoDisc, Inc.; **18** © E. R. Degginger/Photo Researchers, Inc.; **20** © 2008 JupiterImages Corporation; **23** BJU Photo Services

Chapter 2
24 Jami Garrison/Shutterstock.com; **27** © iStockphoto.com/lissart; **28** PhotoDisc, Inc.; **29** Jerry J. Davis/Shutterstock.com; **30t** © iStockphoto.com/Kitch Bain; **30c** © iStockphoto.com/lightasafeather; **30b** Steve Byland/Bigstock.com; **32t** PhotoDisc, Inc.; **32c** © iStockphoto.com/WLDavies; **32b** © iStockphoto.com/Holger Mette; **33** © iStockphoto.com/GreyCarnation; **34tr** © iStockphoto.com/kurkul; **34l** Stockxpert/JupiterImages; **34br** © iStockphoto.com/pablographix; **35t** © iStockphoto.com/Gijs Bekenkamp; **35c** © 2008 JupiterImages Corporation; **35b** Minden Pictures / Superstock; **36t** © iStockphoto.com/Richard Schmidt-Zuper; **36b** © iStockphoto.com/ Peggy Easterly; **37t** © 2008 JupiterImages Corporation; **37b** © iStockphoto.com/Sandra Caldwell; **38** Design Pics / Superstock; **39t** thomasheen/Bigstock.com; **39b** © Carolyn A. McKeone/Photo Researchers, Inc.; **40t** Prin Pattawaro/123RF.com; **40b** Mint Images/AP Images; **43** BJU Photo Services

Chapter 3
44 smarnad/Bigstock.com; **46** PhotoDisc, Inc.; **49** Breck P. Kent; **49i** © iStockphoto.com/GoranStimac; **50** George Collins; **52** BJU Photo Services; **53** both Rita Mitchell; **55** BJU Photo Services; **56tr** © Fotolia/robynmac; **56cl** © 2008 JupiterImages Corporation; **56cb** © 2007 JupiterImages Corporation; **57tr** © 2008 JupiterImages Corporation; **57cr, br, l** PhotoDisc, Inc.; **58t** © JupiterImages Corporation; **58c** morganlstudios/Bigstock.com; **58b** © 2008 JupiterImages Corporation; **59** DOE/NREL, Warren Gretz

Chapter 4
60 Stock Connection / Superstock; **62** © iStockphoto.com/davidf; **63** © Noonie | Dreamstime.com; **66** filmfoto//Bigstock.com; **67t** © iStockphoto.com/ewastudio; **67c** © iStockphoto.com/Alasdair Thomson; **67b** Borislav/Kosijer/iStock/Thinkstock; **68t** © iStockphoto.com/Sawayasu Tsuji; **68b** © 2008 JupiterImages Corporation; **69tl** © iStockphoto.com/Oksana Perkins; **69tr** dzain/Bigstock.com; **69b** Skipper64/Bigstock.com; **71** James Warwick/The Image Bank/Getty Images; **74** © iStockphoto.com/Jose Gil; **75l** PHIL A DOTSON/Science Source/Getty Images; **75r** Steve and Dave Maslowski/Science Source/Getty Images; **76** Jeff Henry; **77** © iStockphoto.com/Andy_Astbury; **79** BJU Photo Services

Chapter 5
80 Rolf Hicker / All Canada Photos / Superstock ; **84, 85t** BJU Photo Services; **85b** Used with permission by Brecknell, a division of Avery Weigh-Tronix, LLC; **86t** Gjermund Alsos/123RF; **86b, 88, 89, 90, 91** both, **93** BJU Photo Services; **94** © sparkia - Fotolia.com; **95t** © Mark Sykes / Alamy; **95b** © iStockphoto.com/sumnersgraphicsinc; **96t** © 2008 JupiterImages Corporation; **96b** © iStockphoto.com/Claudio Arnese; **97** © iStock.com/Kelly Cline; **98** BJU Photo Services; **101** both BJU Photo Services; **102t** © iStockphoto.com/bluestocking; **102c** © iStockphoto.com/kolipik; **102b** Anne Kitzman - Fotolia.com; **103** alenkasm/Bigstock.com

Chapter 6
104 © Paul Springett 09 / Alamy; **107** BJU Photo Services; **108tr** Chris Alvanas/MediaBakery; **108tl** Wendyday © Fotolia; **108bl** Jose Luis Pelaez/Media Bakery; **108br** © TongRo Images / Alamy; **109** Edward Lara/Shutterstock.com; **112** © iStockphoto.com/Nick Schlax; **113** © iStockphoto.com/Tarzan9280; **115tl** © iStockphoto.com/GregorBister;